SHIFTING SPACES

Dedication

I would like to dedicate this book to my mum, *Helen Margaret Wright Ackers* (nee Ashcroft). Her own experience as a woman who moved, so many times, in support of my father's career, in the process negotiating her own career, her role as wife and mother of four children, and as a daughter herself, very much mirror those of the women we interviewed. I think, for her, the tensions of dislocated family networks, across continents, at a time when her children were very young and her mother quite ill, proved the hardest to bear. Nevertheless, she has grown in strength and has never ceased to support us all. The strength of her affection and sheer tenacity has provided me with the skills and courage to develop in my own roles as mother, partner and academic.

SHIFTING SPACES

Women, citizenship and migration within the European Union

Louise Ackers

First published in Great Britain in 1998 by

The Policy Press
University of Bristol
Rodney Lodge
Grange Road
Bristol BS8 4EA
UK

Tel   +44 (0)117 973 8797
Fax   +44 (0) 117 973 7308
e-mail tpp@bristol.ac.uk
http://www.bristol.ac.uk/Publications/TPP

© The Policy Press, 1998
British Library Cataloguing in Publication Data
A catalogue record for this book is available from the British Library

ISBN 1 86134 127 X

Louise Ackers is Deputy Director of the Centre for the Study of Law in Europe at the University of Leeds.

Front cover: Photograph supplied by kind permission of Mo Wilson, Format Photographers, London.
Cover design: Qube Design Associates, Bristol.

Printed and bound in Great Britain by Hobbs the Printers Ltd, Southampton.

Contents

Acknowledgements

The research reported upon in this book was funded by the Equal Opportunities Unit of the European Commission (DGV). I am most grateful for this support and I would like to thank, in particular, John Darcy, for his assistance with the project.

The University of Plymouth, as my employer at the time of the research, also provided financial assistance in the form of a grant to support the Swedish partnership and, more importantly in the research studentship provided for my linked PhD student, Jane Sweeting. Jane assisted in all aspects of the project and proved to be a great source of support throughout the project. She also organised and undertook all the London-based UK interviews, on which her thesis is based. Les Ebdon, Deputy Vice-Chancellor for Academic Affairs took a keen interest in the project and assisted with project financing. John Lewis, in his capacity of Head of Department at the time, was more than generous in providing pump-priming funding to enable the partnerships to be established; an investment which, I hope he will agree, paid off well. Rob Mawby gave me invaluable advice on the organisation and management of a cross-national project.

This project was undertaken in cooperation with academic partners in four countries. Without the support and commitment of these partners the project could not have been a success. I would like to acknowledge the contribution of Heloisa Perista, of the Centre for Studies in Social Intervention, Lisbon; Martha Blomqvist and Kristina Eriksson, of the Centre for Feminist Research, University of Uppsala; Mary Mulcahy and Lydia Sapouna of University College, Cork; and Julia Balaska, of the Mediterranean Centre for Women's Studies, Athens. Simona Beretta also assisted with interviewing in the UK.

My particular thanks go to those partners in non-English-speaking countries for the considerable amount of effort put into translating the interviews.

Jane Sweeting and Heloisa Perista have both contributed to chapters in this book[1].

Professor Jim Kemeny has maintained an interest in the project over the last three years and proved a constant source of friendship and support which I miss very much since his return to Sweden. I am grateful to Jim Kemeny, Paul Skidmore and Jo Shaw for taking the time to read and comment on draft chapters.

Finally, I would like to thank my partner, Eric and our three boys, Matthew, James and Gavin for looking after me and maintaining a balance in my life; for welcoming my research partners into our home, as friends; and understanding my absences during the course of the research.

Note on the title *Shifting spaces*

The concept of 'shifting spaces' has been used in the title for this book for a number of reasons. Firstly and most directly, it refers to the notion of mobility over space; of women moving around within the European Union. In addition to the geography of migration, however, it also represents the interconnection of different sorts of 'space': of mobility within and across different social and legal spaces. Moreover the concept of space need not be temporally defined but can extend to study spaces over a period of time suggesting the different spaces women inhabit as their lives unfold.

In yet another context, the reference to shifting spaces reminds us of our commitment to interdisciplinarity and the idea of moving within and between intellectual spaces in order to better understand the phenomena of intra-Community mobility and its impact on the lives of women who migrate.

---

[1] Jane Sweeting prepared the first draft of Chapter Five and Heloisa Perista, the first draft of Chapter Six.

ONE

Introduction

This book considers the impact of the European Union (EU) on the citizenship experience of EU migrant women (that is, EU nationals moving *within* the Community). It focuses on this group of women for two reasons: firstly, because these women constitute an important, and under-researched, group in their own right and secondly, because the study of this group provides a litmus test for the future development of citizenship in Social Europe. It is in its capacity as guardian of the rights of internal migrants that the EU behaves most like a modern welfare state. Once a national of an EU Member State leaves his or her country of nationality to reside in another Member State, the EU assumes important social responsibilities shaping their experience of citizenship.

Over the past three years I have frequently been called to task by feminist academics, anti-racist and community activists for squandering precious research resources on already-privileged, white, European women; an accusation most forcefully and aggressively made during a conference presentation at the Fourth International Feminist Research Conference in Coimbra[1]. My response has been to question the underlying assumption that EU migrant women are equally 'privileged', particularly given the history of European migrations on the one hand, and the variation in women's backgrounds in terms of social class, family status and also migration destinations on the other. Furthermore, I have argued for the need to focus on this group of women, who theoretically share a broad universality of status with EU men, in order to demonstrate the gendered nature and experience of European citizenship. I make no apology for the focus on this group of women but neither would I wish to prioritise their interests over and above other migrant or non-migrant women. I hope that the ends will justify the means, not only in terms of throwing light on the lives of this group of women, as women in their own right, but further, that we shall learn something of relevance to all women whether or not they have migrated.

---

[1] July 1997.

'Citizenship of the Union'

It might be argued that limited legal competency in the social field has largely restricted the role of the EU to one of safeguarding the interests of paid workers. This is certainly true of most areas of EU social policy. In terms of its equal opportunities strategy, the European Commission (and the Equal Opportunities Unit in particular) has endeavoured to step beyond a narrowly defined 'public' world of work and extend Community competence into the 'private' world of domestic responsibilities and familial roles in recognition of the fact that women's positions in the labour market cannot be improved by measures which focus exclusively on equal pay and equal treatment in employment. This concern to reconcile women's positions in the labour market with their role in caring for dependants has been reflected in the development of initiatives on childcare, atypical work and parental leave. The resolution on sexual harassment similarly demonstrates a commitment to go beyond a narrow interpretation of the single market. The fact that the majority of these initiatives have either taken the form of non-binding measures (such as the recommendation on childcare) or have failed to get beyond the Council of Ministers, remaining in 'draft' stage for over a decade (such as the proposed Directive on atypical work) does not reflect the commitment of the Commission or the wider Community as such. The lack of progress on equal opportunities is due to a combination of the weak legal base for social policy in general and a lack of political consensus across Member States[2]. The requirement for unanimity in voting procedures in particular has meant that individual Member States (notably the UK) have been able to effectively block initiatives in this area. Despite the lack of legislative progress the Equal Opportunities Action Programmes and their proposals for legislative action suggest a commitment to a strategy which locates women's employment position within the broader context of gender inequality.

While measures to improve the status of women in the labour market,

---

[2] This situation *may* change in the near future as measures are taken under the Social Policy Protocol and the UK 'opt-out' reversed. The equal opportunities provisions have also been strengthened under the Amsterdam Treaty with a new Article on non-discrimination. The phrasing suggests a broader approach and possible support for forms of positive discrimination, "the Community shall aim to eliminate inequalities, and to promote equality, between men and women" (Article 6A, Treaty of Amsterdam).

together with measures aimed at labour market integration (such as training programmes, for example) may prove politically and legally acceptable, these in many ways serve to reinforce the relationship between social status and employment status, according primacy to paid work as the basis of social contribution and a trigger to independent entitlement, further marginalising those women who remain outside the labour market. Wider issues of family policy, it seems, fall within the exclusive preserve of Member States and equal opportunities become little more than a form of labour market regulation aimed primarily at the pursuit of procedural equality in the workplace. This would certainly seem to be the approach taken by the European Court of Justice (ECJ) in a case involving a father's claim for paternity leave under the Equal Treatment Directive[3]. The Court found that it was not in contravention of the Directive to restrict such leave to women on the grounds that: "the Directive is not designed to settle questions concerned with the organisation of the family, or to alter the division of responsibility between parents"[4]. As far as the equal opportunities laws are concerned, it seems that the impact of the EU is largely restricted to the regulation of public dependency and the protection of paid workers.

Nevertheless, academic interest in the role of the EU in relation to gender equality has until recently typically focused on those aspects of intervention explicitly concerned with the promotion of equal opportunities – notably equal pay, equal treatment and the Equal Opportunities Action Programmes[5]. While the role of the EU in these areas is of considerable significance to women, it is also important to consider the implications of the evolution of EU law in general for gender equality. A focus on 'gender law' as opposed to 'gendered law' may, inadvertently, serve to marginalise the debate on gender equality and detract concern from the evolution of more fundamental rights determining the future nature of European citizenship. It may also lead to generalisations about the impact of EU law which fit uneasily within a broader understanding of its influence. Analysis of the role of the EU in the

---

[3] Council Directive 76/207 (OJ 1976 L39/40).

[4] *Hofmann v Barmer Ersalzkasse,* Case 184/83 [1984] ECR 3047 para 25.

[5] Pillinger, J. (1992) *Feminising the market. Women's pay and employment in the European Community,* London: Macmillan. Prechal, S. and Burrows, N. (1990) *Gender discrimination law of the European Communities,* Aldershot: Dartmouth. McRudden, C. (ed) (1987) *Women, employment and European equality law,* London: Eclipse Publications.

promotion of equal opportunities, for example, has lead one author to speak optimistically of 'state feminism' and conclude that, "national law is ... considerably more marked by patriarchal traits than Community law. The EC can hardly be said to have entered into an alliance with patriarchy"[6].

While feminist concern has focused on developments in social rights arising from the equal opportunities legislation, developments have been taking place in other areas of EU law, with more profound implications for citizenship and social rights. The ECJ has interpreted the free movement provisions broadly thus elevating the principle of free movement of persons into one of the fundamental rights of Community law[7]. Indeed, the extension of a framework of social rights under these provisions has been said to mark a trend towards the realisation of an overall European citizenship[8]. Here the principle of subsidiarity restricting EU incursion into areas of social assistance and family policy has been waived as a more holistic approach to citizenship developed. The evolution of citizenship rights under the free movement provisions thus provides a basis for comparing EU citizenship with that in Member States. In this sense it serves as an indicator of how 'Social Europe' might develop in the future[9].

The free movement provisions do not provide a common floor of social rights for all EU citizens but essentially constitute a prohibition on discrimination on grounds of nationality[10]. The precise nature of the social rights on offer to a Community migrant will therefore depend upon the country of immigration. In certain circumstances, however, these rights may be quite substantial. Whatever the limitations on the rights available, they nevertheless constitute a valuable, if imperfect, social benefit. It is the issue of *eligibility* or *entitlement* to that benefit that is of

---

[6] Ruth Nielsen (1981) cited in Pillinger, supra, note 5.

[7] Nielsen, R. and Szyszczak, E. (1993) *The social dimension of the European community*, Copenhagen: Handelshojskolens Forlag. Ackers, H.L. (1994) 'Women, citizenship and EC law: the gender implications of the free movement provisions', *Journal of Social Welfare and Family Law*, vol 16, no 4, pp 391-406. Scheiwe, K. (1994) 'EC law's unequal treatment of the family:the case law of the European Court of Justice on rules prohibiting discrimination on grounds of sex and nationality', *Social and Legal Studies*, vol 3, no 2, pp 243-65.

[8] Nielsen and Szyszczak (1993, p 55), supra note 7.

[9] These issues are explored in Chapter Two.

[10] Between EU citizens; there is no general prohibition against racial discrimination involving third country migrants.

---

concern here and whether this may result in a gendering of Community citizenship. Policies reinforcing the importance of occupational status as the basis of independent social entitlement (and marriage as the basis of derived entitlement) raise the issues of access to and definition of 'employment' as a key concern for women. This, coupled with the general shifting emphasis, across all Member States, on informal, largely unpaid, care provided primarily by women has clear implications for women's labour force participation and as a consequence, their access to social rights[11]. Janet Finch expresses her concern that the impact of the EC will "lead to pressure for strengthening the welfare benefits associated with being employed ... [which] is certainly bad news for women"[12].

The extent to which the nature of an evolving European citizenship based on employment status disadvantages women depends both on developments in national welfare systems and how the Community interprets its role. A narrow interpretation of employment status which fails to take account of the complex nature of women's relationship with paid work and the structured nature of women's domestic obligations is ultimately set to damage women's interests. Jane Pillinger's analysis of Community social policy came to the conclusion that, despite apparent gender-neutrality, "Patriarchal policy-making was clearly evident, as the objectives of securing a common market failed to recognise sexual divisions in the labour market and the disadvantaged position of women in society"[13]. Of equal importance is the failure to acknowledge the sexual division of caring labour outside the formal labour market.

Where academic concern has focused on migration, in an EU context, the problem of defining membership (inclusivity and exclusivity) has dominated discussion about citizenship, fuelled on the one hand by concerns about social dumping and welfare tourism and, on the other, by genuine concerns about racism and xenophobia in 'Fortress Europe'. Here,

---

[11] Cochrane, A. and Clarke, J. (1993) *Comparing welfare states*, London: Sage. Glasner, A. (1992) 'Gender and Europe: cultural and structural impediments to change', in J. Bailey (ed) *Social Europe*, London: Longman Sociology. Lewis, J. (1992) 'Gender and the development of welfare regimes', *Journal of European Social Policy*, vol 2, no 3, pp 159-73.

[12] Finch, J. (1990) Guest Editorial: 'Women, equal opportunities and welfare in the European Community: some questions and issues', in L. Hantrais, M. O'Brien and S. Mangen (eds) *Women, equal opportunities and welfare*, Cross National Research Papers, Birmingham: Aston University, pp 1-6.

[13] Pillinger (1992, p 80) supra, note 5.

the agenda has been dominated by concerns about the immigration of third country nationals and the citizenship status of those third country nationals legally resident within the EU[14]. In a recent paper to a conference on mobility within the EU, Ann Singleton[15], speaking in her capacity as 'Expert Statistician' to the Eurostat Migration Team in Luxembourg, outlined the current agenda, in terms of migration research, as follows:

> **Political debate on international migration in the United Kingdom and in the member states of the European Union is increasingly dominated by concerns both over numbers of documented migrants and over the supposed numbers of undocumented migrants. This was particularly evident during the years which led up to the signing of the Maastricht Treaty and a series of inter-governmental agreements on the control of immigration and asylum, a period spanning the late 1980s and early 1990s. More recently, discussion has focused on the success or failure of these measures and on monitoring and demonstrating their effectiveness. It is now understood that the previously anticipated mass migrations have not occurred and the focus has now turned to specific categories of migrants, defined as 'illegals', as 'asylum seekers' and as 'labour migrants' from non-EU countries.**

Relatively little interest has been shown either at the political level or indeed, in migration research, in intra-Community migration and the movement and status of nationals within the borders of the Union. Preoccupation with concerns about immigration from outside the EU and the status of persons within the Union who do not possess Community nationality, however important, has tended to reinforce the presumption of a duality of entitlement based on ownership of EU nationality creating the impression of a broad equality among those defined as EU citizens. The position of internal migrants is typically dismissed, in research and

---

[14] There has also been increasing concern about illegal immigrants, asylum seekers and refugees given the events of recent years.

[15] Paper to the Immigration Law Practitioners' Association and the Centre of European Law, King's College London Conference, 'The legal framework and social consequences of free movement of persons in the European Union', 27-28 November 1997.

academic debate, on the presumption of relative privilege, broad cultural homogeneity (within the Union) and broad equality of citizenship status[16]. As such it obscures the complexity and gendered nature of EU citizenship. In practice, social entitlement does not derive from simple membership of the Union, as is often inferred, but from more complex notions of social contribution. In this sense, as we shall see, all citizens are not equal.

Furthermore, the lack of interest in internal migration has left us with a somewhat limited body of migration theory with which to begin to understand intra-Community mobility[17]. The limitations of mainstream migration theory, in terms of explaining the mobility of women and understanding its impact on social entitlement and citizenship (in an EU context) has lead to an attempt, in this research, to 'link' migration theory with work in the area of feminist comparative social policy. The migration literature, in common with the development of theory around the concept of 'welfare regimes', has centred around presumptions about employment trajectories and family relationships. To see the 'link' one only has to compare Taylor-Gooby's work on welfare state regimes and citizenship with Lichter's work on migration trajectories. Taylor-Gooby stresses the importance of inequalities in wages and employment prospects in explanations of the 'gender imbalance in care' stating that such labour market inequalities, "make it a rational household strategy for men to devote more energy to waged work, where they can get a higher rate of return"[18]. Lichter, on the other hand, concludes his evaluation of the impact of migration on married women in a similar vein arguing that, "migration would appear to be rational from the standpoint of the family as a whole ... many women willingly sacrifice their careers provided that migration improves the economic well-being of the family"[19].

In response to the limitations of recent attempts, at comparative level, to compare welfare systems, particularly their failure to consider the unpaid work undertaken by women, Jane Lewis has developed an alternative

---

[16] An important exception to this can be found in Hervey, T.K. (1995) 'Migrant workers and their families in the European Union: the pervasive market ideology of Community law', in J. Shaw and G. Gilmore (eds) *New legal dynamics of European Union*, Oxford: Clarendon Press, pp 91-111.

[17] Issues developed in Chapter Five.

[18] Taylor-Gooby, P. (1991) 'Welfare state regimes and welfare citizenship', *Journal of European Social Policy*, vol 1, no 2, pp 93-105 at p 101.

[19] Lichter, D. (1983) 'Socio-economic returns to migration among married women', *Social Forces*, vol 62, no 2, pp 487-503 at p 488.

framework which stresses the universal dominance of a male breadwinner family model which, she argues, cuts across established typologies of welfare regimes:

Modern welfare regimes have all subscribed to some degree to the idea of a male breadwinner model – the strength or weakness of [that] model serves as an indicator of the way in which women have been treated in social security systems, of the level of social service provision particularly in regard to childcare; and of the nature of married women's position in the labour market.[20]

According to Lewis, then, the domestic welfare systems of most European countries are all based, to a greater or lesser extent, on the notion of a male breadwinning family model. In other words, the distribution of social resources, within the mixed economy of welfare, is organised around certain assumptions about family structure and gender relations which ascribe primacy to the role of the male partner in securing access to social goods. To some extent this reflects 'rational household decision making' to the extent that men have generally secured more privileged labour market status (better pay and more secure posts) but also ideologically-driven beliefs about women's roles within the family as wives, mothers and carers.

Given the emphasis, within this model, on the male wage as the key to both his individual social status and the derived entitlement of his wife and children, effectively institutionalising dependency with the nuclear family, its impact on migration theory is hardly surprising. Indeed, the male breadwinning model of family relations underpins explanations of migration behaviour both in terms of the process of migration (who moves where) and the rationale behind migration. Arguably the explanatory potential of this model is even more powerful in a migration context when the principle motivation behind virtually all 'voluntary' (that is, not forced) migrations is deemed to be one of economic maximisation. Migrant households may thus represent households who are prepared to take their commitment to career progression and employment status that bit further. Furthermore, the isolation of migrant wives, as a result of the dislocation of family ties and the focused pursuit of economic advantage,

---

[20] Lewis, J. (1992) 'Gender and the development of welfare regimes', *Journal of European Social Policy*, vol 2, no 3, pp 159-73.

on the part of the principle wage-earner, potentially reinforces their role as primary, unpaid carers.

The male breadwinning family, as the basis of social organisation (and the distribution of social resources) thus conveniently translates into explanations of migration behaviour; migration is primarily economically and male-determined with an initial phase of male pioneer migration followed by a phase of passive family reunion migration as wives and children join the economically-established male breadwinner. A further implicit assumption underlying this notion of the migrant family, possibly with racist undertones, concerns the issue of inter-marriage. Literature on international migration rarely, if ever, considers the degree and implications of mixed-nationality partnerships; the presumption is that migrants 'marry their own kind' and move with them to the host state[21].

Such 'common sense' presumptions, rendered credible and respectable by mainstream migration theory, have doubtless informed policy-making structures within the European Union, committed to securing labour mobility within the Single Market. The extension of competency in the social sphere, for migrant workers, is largely based upon the desire to 'facilitate mobility' and progressively erode barriers to migration (in an EU context). As long as migration is conceptualised in essentially gendered terms, the barriers identified, and the solutions developed, will also be gendered.

Evaluation of the theories and ideas referred to above has resulted in the identification of two key research objectives, to be developed through the empirical work:

- to examine the influence of this model of social organisation and migration behaviour on policy making at EU level (and the extent to which these presumptions about migrant families are enshrined in systems of social entitlement);
- to empirically test its relevance in the context of intra-Community migration.

---

[21] This underlying, implicit, assumption reminds us of the influence of socio-biology on the phenomena referred to as 'the New Racism' in 1980s Britain and the close relationship between racism, eugenics and the control of female sexuality and fertility (see Rose, S. and Rose, H. [1986] 'Less than human nature: biology and the new right', *Race and Class*, XXVII, vol 3, pp 47-66; Gordon, P. and Klug, F. [1986] *New Right, new racism*, London: Searchlight Publications; Barker, M. [1982] *The new racism*, London: Junction Books).

Comparative method: developing a feminist approach

In addition to these substantive concerns, a key objective of this research has been to develop and evaluate an approach to feminist comparative research. Julia O'Connor notes the limitations in feminist enquiry when she states that, "there is an absence of gender analysis in almost all comparative research while most studies that focus on gender are not comparative"[22]. Moreover, when feminist researchers have undertaken research at comparative level they have tended to replicate the 'model-building' methodologies and policy-evaluation approaches of mainstream comparativists. The heavy reliance on official statistics and public expenditure data in this kind of work, in places softened by attempts to include elements of policy description, has limited explanatory potential and tells us little about how women actually experience citizenship.

Working within tight resource constraints, this project has attempted to return to a combination of quantitative and qualitative techniques. In talking about 'feminist comparative method' I am not therefore referring to a distinctive method as such, exclusive to feminist research, but a synthesis and evolution of approaches, in keeping with principles of feminist research practice, which seek to expose the conditions shaping the lives of women and women's experiences. The substantive focus of the research (on gender) is less relevant here than the approach; indeed the strategy developed in this project is currently being developed in three projects concerned with women researchers, children and elderly people[23].

It is important not to connect feminist enquiry with any particular research method but to select a method appropriate to the case in question. There is no reason why every feminist comparativist should engage in qualitative research – or indeed empirical work. The nature of their

---

[22] O'Connor, J.S. (1993) 'Gender class and citizenship in the comparative analysis of welfare states: theoretical and methodological issues', *British Journal of Sociology*, vol 44, no 3, September, pp 501-19 at p 501. A point also made in Bussemaker, J. and van Kersbergen, K. (1994) 'Gender and welfare states: some theoretical reflections', in D. Sainsbury (ed) *Gendering welfare states*, London: Sage, p 15.

[23] The author is currently directing three projects on aspects of intra-Community mobility. The first is an evaluation of the impact of the European Commission's 'Training and mobility of researchers' programme on women researchers. The other projects include one on 'Children, citizenship and migration in the EU' (funded by the European Commission and the Nuffield Foundation) and one on 'Retirement, migration in the EU' (funded by the Wellcome Trust).

approach should depend upon the locus of enquiry and the claims they wish to make on the basis of their work. If, however, we wish to say something about such things as the impact of policy on citizenship experience or identity then we need to exercise extreme caution, humility and reflexivity. This type of work demands an approach to theorisation which is grounded in the everyday lives of women; lives which are, in many ways, so different to those of feminist academics. In that sense we should not purport to speak on behalf of the other women, but to use research as a means of representing their voices and concerns. It is difficult to effect this without undertaking some form of empirical enquiry. Having gathered our 'data' we should resist the attraction of excessive interpretation and abstraction and accept what we find at face value. I am not proposing a return to empiricism here, nor indeed to the dishonesty of many 'inductive' approaches when theoretical ideas have permeated the entire research process. Rather than filtering responses through academic lenses and forcing them into categories we should seek to understand and evaluate them in a contextually-relevant manner and then permit them to challenge pre-existing concepts and ideas; working at the interface of theorisation and social 'reality'. The development of theory then takes place neither 'top-down' nor 'bottom-up' but somewhere in the fusion of ideas and research experience, 'in the middle'. We are neither simply testing theoretical constructs 'in the field'[24] nor pretending that we can enter into people's lives without any preconceptions (or vested interests).

This approach to research demands a certain openness and courage; a willingness to reappraise, not only our academic ideas, but the values and justifications around which we have constructed our own roles as mothers, partners, friends, employers, employees and citizens in the widest sense. It is neither possible nor, I would suggest, desirable to talk extensively and frankly with women about their children, partners or parents without reflecting upon and evaluating their perspectives in the context of our own relationships.

This project has sought information at a variety of levels. On the one hand it has endeavoured to document dimensions of 'policy-input', often neglected in social science analysis (that is, the role of Courts in policy evolution) and so important to formal citizenship status, through a detailed

---

[24] In this context, the notion of being 'in the field' seems highly problematic; it implies removing oneself to somewhere foreign; to a space we do not, as researchers, inhabit. As feminist researchers we should endeavour to situate ourselves within the research context; it is difficult to imagine any research context in which there is not a certain degree of empathy – or sharing of experience.

evaluation of the legislation and its interpretation in the case law of the European Court of Justice. In the process of establishing the formal legal status of migrant women, it has tried to understand, and expose, the 'gendered' preconceptions and assumptions that have informed policy development and to juxtapose these with 'hard statistical evidence' (migration statistics). This presents no particular challenge to feminist methodology, and the 'facts' themselves have no explanatory potential; they just stop us short and force us to reconsider. The more challenging aspect of the research design has been the qualitative dimension, given the geography and scale of the project and the complications of language. The difficulties of understanding and working with cultural diversity, an argument often cited as a reason to avoid comparative work, is so much a feature of migration research, whatever the scale or scope, that the comparative nature of the project made little difference; we were interviewing migrant women from up to 15 different countries in each of the Member States. Indeed, in that sense having women from five Member States represented in the project team actually helped us to understand our own findings at national level. An understanding of the national context and, in particular, the national migration histories, was, however, very important; we rejected an administratively easier 'safari' approach of posting research assistants to different research locations and opted instead for a team of partnerships, run as far as possible on a democratic basis, to plan and execute the research.

More detailed discussion of the research strategy is contained in Chapter Three. I would like, however, to say something here about the research process in terms of our relationships as women researchers. Designing feminist research is not simply about the relationships between researchers and the 'subject' of their study but also about the quality of our relationships with each other as students, project managers, partners, research assistants and typists. An important motivation behind this research was to demonstrate the possibility of creating positive working relationships in what is an increasingly competitive and alienating academic environment. Moreover, that investment in the fostering of a principled and supportive working environment does not only generate genuine friendships but also pays dividends in the quality of work produced.

The explosion in comparative research in recent years has created new forms of exploitation; large teams are typically hierarchically organised and managed with the majority of partners operating simply as 'data gatherers' under the instruction of a privileged inner-circle of project managers, often located in Northern or Western Europe.

———

In this project the partners from five different countries (and together representing as many disciplines), together with my doctoral student and various research assistants, have worked together, for the most part, in an atmosphere of mutual respect, through all phases of the research. The fact that I have taken principle responsibility for the production of this book does not reflect exclusive control of the research output but the constraints of colleagues' workloads, research priorities, and the lack of funding specifically to buy time to write[25].

Feminist commitment to the dismantling of unnecessary hierarchy and structures of control and exclusion has lead to the kind of questioning of relationships between researchers and the subjects of research and between theory and practice referred to above and leads naturally into a critique of disciplines – or at least of disciplinary myopia. My own formal academic background, both as a student myself and as a teacher and researcher, spans geography, sociology, social policy and law. Migration research, in common with gender studies, represents an area of study which demands interdisciplinarity both in terms of concepts and methods. To begin to understand why people move and the impact this movement has on them, as individuals and families, but also on receiving communities, requires a broad interdisciplinary approach. The barriers referred to above did not develop fortuitously, however, but as a means of preserving and creating forms of elitism and control. Failing to respect this delineation thus exposes us to certain forms of risk in an academic environment which pays lip-service to interdisciplinarity, while prizing and rewarding specialism above all else. Interdisciplinary work therefore demands confidence and conviction to overcome the fear of being judged too harshly by specialists reading or listening to our work: 'Is my law good enough to represent to a group of lawyers?', 'Am I using the correct language to impress an audience of sociologists?'. This perhaps explains the development of an interdisciplinary forum of a socio-legal or feminist nature providing opportunities for us to present the breadth of our work and celebrate the diversity of our approaches. In the clamour for recognition of the value and validity of our work (and to attract future funding), however, we must guard against the tendency to erect new boundaries, create new disciplines and new forms of exclusivity, effectively replicating that which we sought

---

[25] It also reflects the development of the Nud*ist software at the time of the project which made it impossible to 'share' data analysis. This problem is now potentially resolved and more concerted attempts will be made in the current projects to involve the wider team in data analysis and dissemination.

to dismantle. It is with this caveat in mind that I locate this research within the broad, interdisciplinary field of socio-legal studies.

The box below contains an outline of the project proposal and objectives as originally presented for funding to the European Commission.

Women, citizenship and European Community law: the gender implications of the free movement provisions [European Commission, DGV reference: SOC-94-101784-05A03]

Project objectives

To undertake research into the gender implications of the free movement provisions and the nature of an evolving European citizenship. This will involve work at three different levels:

1.1 The legal framework: the free movement provisions and social rights

Background legal research on the evolution of Community law in this area assessing the development of legislation and the case law both in terms of the material and personal scope of the rights available and the Court of Justice's interpretation of its role.

1.2 Identifying patterns of labour migration at European Community level

Analysis of secondary data to identify the degree of labour mobility between Member States, assessing patterns and identifying the nature of the movement from labour exporting states to labour importing states with a breakdown by gender.

1.3 In-depth empirical work in selected Member States in collaboration with partner academics

This aspect of the research will involve the selection of a number of Member States for further, in-depth research including both quantitative and qualitative analysis. Criteria for selection of Member States will be informed by research on comparative social policy[26]. The qualitative research will involve the identification of migrant women (as workers, the spouses of migrant workers or return migrants) for in-depth interviews. The interviews will assess the range of factors affecting women's decisions to migrate and the impact of migration on them.

1.4 Comparative method

The research seeks to counter the tendency in comparative research to "follow the primrose path of doing what was easiest to do on the basis of information gathered by others"[27]. It seeks to combine quantitative analysis of the position of migrant women with qualitative information on the impact of the European Union on women's lives. As such it also raises important methodological questions about the nature of comparative research on gender-related issues[28].

The sheer quantity of qualitative data collected in the course of this research has made it impossible to report on all aspects of the work; some selectivity has necessarily taken place. As a consequence some important and interesting areas are not covered in this book. This includes material on the impact of migration on the children of migrant workers, on women's identity and also aspects of social integration. The first of these has informed and is currently being carried forward into a more focused study of children[29]. Evaluation of the issue of identity is similarly in progress[30].

The book is structured in the following way: Chapter Two outlines and discusses the 'theoretical framework' shaping the project – or at least some of the ideas and concepts that have informed the research and influenced its direction. Chapter Three then considers approaches to comparative enquiry, primarily in the social sciences, and the limitations of secondary analysis and policy-evaluation, as tools for an understanding of citizenship. Following a more general discussion, this chapter moves on to outline the methodological basis of the research. The discussion around citizenship leads into a more detailed analysis of the concept of 'citizenship of the Union' and the evolution of social entitlement under the free movement of persons provisions in Chapter Four. Chapter Five

---

[26] Cochrane, A. and Clarke, J. (1993) *Comparing welfare states*, London: Sage. Dominelli, L. (1991) *Women across continents: Feminist comparative social policy*, Hemel Hempstead: Harvester Wheatsheaf. Esping-Andersen, G. (1990) *The three worlds of welfare capitalism*, Oxford: Polity Press. Ginsburg, N. (1993) *States of welfare division*, London: Sage. Langan, M. and Ostner, I. (1991) 'Gender and welfare: towards a comparative perspective', in G. Room (ed) *Towards a European welfare state*, Bristol: SAUS Publications. Leibfried, S. (1991) *Towards a European welfare state?*, Zes-Arbeitspapier No 3, Bremen: Universität Bremen Zentrum für Sozialpolitik. Lewis, J. (1992) 'Gender and the development of welfare regimes', *Journal of European Social Policy*, vol 2, no 3, pp 159-73. Taylor-Gooby, P. (1991) 'Welfare state regimes and citizenship', *Journal of European Social Policy*, vol 1, no 2, pp 93-105.

[27] Cochrane and Clarke (1993, p 8) supra, note 26.

[28] Hakim, H. (1991) 'Cross national comparative research on the EC: the EC Labour Force surveys', *Work, Employment and Society*, vol 5, no 1, pp 101-17. Roberts, H. (1986) *Doing feminist research*, London: Routledge. Harding, S. (1987) *Feminism and methodology*, Buckingham: Open University Press.

[29] Supra, note 23.

[30] Spear, L. (1997) 'Dimensions of difference within circles of influence', Paper to the 3rd European Feminist Research Conference, Coimbra, Portugal, July 1997.

---

turns to examine some of the literature on international migration and to assess its relevance to an understanding of the gender dimension, in the context of intra-Community migration. While acknowledging the limitations of migration statistics, this chapter uses data from the European Labour Force Survey, together with interview findings, to challenge the myth of a predominantly male-determined and male-dominated migration. Chapters Six, Seven and Eight then consider, in depth, the qualitative findings focusing on the impact of migration on employment trajectories (Chapter Six); migrant women's experiences of living in different welfare systems (Chapter Seven); and the impact of migration on caring networks and obligations (Chapter Eight). I have tried to achieve a balance, in these three chapters, when reporting on the interviews[31], providing in some instances more detailed case studies to preserve the context of women's lives, while in other places, pulling together a range of experiences and perspectives to evidence examples of diversity and commonality. Powerful arguments can be made in favour of the collection of qualitative material; doing justice to the interviewees in presentational terms is less straightforward!

---

[31] *The reporting of qualitative findings.* Given the constraints of time and money we decided not to attempt to translate every word of the interviews. In some cases the transcript will thus summarise a point or factual detail where full translation was not deemed necessary. In such cases, or when interviewers made observations about the interview, the text is not in italics but contained within square brackets. The document numbers in the footnotes refer to the interview reference: a prefix of 0 refers to interviews undertaken in the UK, 2 to those in Sweden, 3 to Portugal, 4 to Greece and 5 to Ireland. Six interviews took place in Italy and are prefixed by the number 6.

TWO

Citizenship and dependency in comparative analysis

Introduction

This chapter examines a range of work around the study of citizenship, mainly in comparative social policy analysis, and focusing particularly on the 'social' dimension, in order to identify the relevance of existing concepts for the analysis of the citizenship status and experience of this group of European Union (EU) migrant women. Before turning to the literature itself, it raises some questions about the role and nature of theorising in academic work. It then turns to examine some of the concepts used as the basis for evaluating citizenship in comparative work including feminist critiques of mainstream approaches and alternative proposals. Finally, it suggests an approach which defines citizenship more broadly in terms of personal autonomy as a more holistic and meaningful basis for the examination of migrant women's experiences.

The role of feminist theory

An important function of this chapter is to establish the 'analytical' framework within which the research took place and, in keeping with the 'academic mode of production', to situate it within relevant theoretical work. The purpose of this component of research is to evaluate the relevance and explanatory potential of existing work and to enable us to build constructively upon the work of others; the ultimate objective is not to construct the most elegant structure, using the most sophisticated language, through the destruction of the ideas of others, but rather to build a useful interplay between ideas and experience with the ultimate aim of informing social change. This method of presenting research, however, implies a simple chronological process moving from theory through empirical investigation to final analysis and eventual refinement of theory. It is important at this stage to question this form of presentation on a number of grounds. Firstly, in terms of written form, it suggests a deductive approach with the development of theory preceding the generation of hypotheses and the collection of data. Furthermore, it presumes that the theoretical argument is undertaken in a separate 'ivory-tower' phase in the research process. To some extent this is an accurate representation as the development of research proposals and strategies does not take place in a vacuum but rather requires the articulation of ideas. These ideas develop from engagement in the work of other academics and from personal interest and experience. On the basis of these ideas – or theories – we can then begin to formulate research questions. In practice, however, the initial ideas shape only a tentative framework for the research and theoretical development occurs throughout the research process in constant interplay with experience (both as a researcher within a wider research team and also in our relationships with the 'subjects' of our research) and through exposure to new academic material. To that extent this chapter is both a beginning and an end; it does not attempt to present the theoretical argument prior to the collection of empirical data, subsequently refined in a concluding chapter which attempts to synthesise the contribution of the latter to the former, but rather to raise some ideas which have informed and continue to inform the research. In that sense I would reiterate my support for the development of an alternative approach to research evident in the Youth Development Trust's call for "the abolition of finished structures"[1].

In addition to the problem of producing a written text suggesting a model of research practice which is far more linear, uncomplicated, managed and 'logical' than experience merits, I would like to raise some general concerns about the role of theory in feminist scholarship. Prue Chamberlayne identifies an increasing gap between feminist theoretical work on family and gender issues and the existence of good, primary, cross-national research into the dynamics of the informal sector[2]. The tensions between feminist epistemology and the development of

---

[1] Youth Development Trust (1976) 'Alternative research', Occasional Paper No 4. Point referred to in my doctoral thesis (unpublished), 'Racism and political marginalisation in the metropolis: the relationship between black people and the Labour Party in London', London School of Economics (1985).

[2] Chamberlayne, P. and King, A. (1996) 'Biographical approaches in comparative work: the "cultures of care" project', in L. Hantrais and S. Mangen (eds) *Cross-national research methods*, London: Pinter, p 95.

comparative research partially responsible for this chasm are discussed in more detail in Chapter Three. The concern here is rather to examine the role and effect of abstract or 'grand' theory in feminist strategy. While acknowledging the important 'synthesising' contribution of feminist philosophy, the dangers in certain forms of feminist theorising are considered by Liz Stanley:

> **The focus has turned to the relationship between analytical categories 'women', 'patriarchy', 'capitalism', 'race' and 'class' among them. However, the inconvenient fact that much human behaviour cannot be described let alone understood in unexplicated categorical terms is largely ignored, or rather 'resolved' by treating people's experiences as faulty versions of the theoretician's categories. This is theory with a capital T, one produced by theorists who are supposed experts on the relationship between categories and thus on the 'real meaning' of social experience and behaviour. Here 'academic feminism' becomes the legitimation of a new form of expertise, that of feminist theoreticians over 'mere women'. Whether as an intended or unintended consequence, feminist social scientists working with such assumptions necessarily position themselves as experts on and over other women's experiences.[3]**

The point is not that feminist academics should be denied the space in which to develop theoretical ideas (in common with their male peers), nor indeed that they should all be involved in 'empirical' research, but rather that the nature of theory-building should be reflexive, grounded in their own experience (and that of other women) and be accessible to women. It should not be used as a means of developing hierarchies of knowledge and specialism which simply disempower women. These arguments are developed further by Stanley and Wise in their second version of *Breaking out*. Here they criticise the role of abstract feminist theorising which, they suggest, replicates the conventions adopted in non-feminist theories about what constitutes 'knowledge', the search for mono-causation and a generally 'masculinist world view' which over-simplifies and stereotypes everyday experience. Referring specifically to Marxist-feminist writing, Stanley and Wise question not only the high level of

---

[3] Stanley, L. (1990) *Feminist praxis*, London: Routledge, p 24.

abstraction and lack of connection with reality in this type of work, but also the opaqueness of the language used[4] suggesting that most writing, "is so jargon-ridden, mystificatory and elitist in its content and expression that it is difficult to believe that it is produced by feminists at all ... The language of theory exerts a conceptual imperialism over experience"[5].

This tendency, fostered by masculinist structures of hierarchy and control within academia, to compare theoretical construct with theoretical construct and model against model rather than testing their relevance to contemporary social realities, has unfortunately, if understandably, been replicated by feminist academics. To take one example from a relevant area, in an important discussion around the question, 'Is citizenship gendered?' Sylvia Walby criticises the tendency of citizenship theory to conflate the concepts of 'family' and 'individual', in the process 'erasing' women. Walby explains the problem, and the required response, in the following way:

> **So what can be the relationship between the private realm of the family and citizenship? Is the family intrinsically an obstacle to the inclusion of all people as citizens? Or can it be accommodated, or, even embraced? The answer to this depends upon the theorisation of the family, in particular the relationship between gender inequality and the family. This depends on the theorisation of women's interests.[6]**

These are without doubt interesting and important questions. My point is, however, that they call not so much for elaborate theorisation but for more detailed and careful research to explore and understand relationships between men, women and children within families. In the process, we will undoubtedly develop new ideas and explanations grounded in our interpretations of women's experiences of citizenship.

Stanley and Wise promote radical feminist approaches on the grounds

---

[4] The language and presumptions behind Stanley and Wise's own work, however, seriously limit its accessibility to a relatively small group of relatively experienced academic feminist sociologists.

[5] Stanley, L. and Wise, S. (1993) *Breaking out again. Feminist ontology and epistemology*, London: Routledge, pp 54-5 and p 162.

[6] Walby, S. (1994) 'Is citizenship gendered?', *Sociology*, vol 28, no 2, pp 379-95 at p 389. For a more detailed discussion see Walby, S. (1997) *Gender transformations*, London: Routledge.

that they support a quite different relationship between theory and practice; a relationship in which theory is, "pragmatic, practical and everyday. It should be a set of understandings or conceptual frameworks which are directly related to, and derive from, particular facets of everyday relationships, experiences and behaviours"[7]. In this way some radical feminist approaches reject the 'grand theory' view of the world as one determined by structures and categories in preference to an approach which requires consideration of the role of individuals, and groups of individuals, as active participants in the process of social change on a variety of levels. This stance reflects not only a different view about the impact of social structures on individuals but also a different perspective on the nature and mechanism of social change. While not rejecting the principal of campaigns at the level of 'high' politics for wider systemic change, radical feminism locates the political within both the public and the personal spheres of women's lives. Change may occur at the level of attitudes, understanding and behaviour within domestic relations with partners, children and through relationships with other women. Furthermore, 'political' change may be taking place at the level of the local state, through the setting up of self-help and voluntary organisations and through the lobbying of local political structures[8].

The best way of examining and understanding the 'system' is thus through an examination of its effects on relationships and experiences in women's everyday lives (including our own as researchers), on the meaning attributed to structures of constraint, the negotiation of those and the impact of that process on the structures themselves, over time. Stanley and Wise advocate an interpretation of theory which, "recognises that we are all of us 'theoreticians' because we all of us use our values and beliefs to interpret and so construct the social world"[9]. As feminist researchers, we are seeking to examine not only the 'facts' of women's existence and experience, but also the ways in which women theorise about their social

---

[7] Stanley and Wise (1993, p 57), supra, note 5.

[8] For examples of this, see Rose, D. (1993) 'Local childcare strategies in Montreal, Quebec: the mediations of state policies, class and ethnicity in the life-courses of families with young children', in C. Katz and J. Monk (eds) *Full circles: Geographies of women over the life course*, London: Routledge, pp 188-208. These points are also developed in the second half of Chapter Seven, which considers the experiences of migrant women living in Ireland.

[9] Stanley and Wise (1993, p 64), supra, note 5.

---

world, and their responses to that, in the light of our own work and experience.

The process of demystifying the social research process brings with it serious risks for the feminist academic, however, in terms of her standing within a profession in which status is accorded to those able to construct the most elegant theories or massage the greatest quantities of statistical data. Academic women, in common with all women, are located within structures which both constrain them (through pressures to conform to dominant norms and meet relevant performance criteria) but also present them with opportunities and vest in them power which they may exercise in a variety of ways. While one could not reasonably expect feminist academics to eschew the benefits of financial and job security, status and recognition, arguably, the tacit acceptance of structures of hierarchy and the replication of forms of elitism cannot be said to concord with feminist practice.

The views expressed here reflect my own observations and concerns about the role of an evolving academic 'femocracy' or 'femigarchy' and the responsibilities of feminist academics in this context; it does not seek to undermine feminist theorising but rather to suggest a more conscious awareness of the power vested within us as academic women and the need to resist the temptation to replicate male academic structures and posturing. The contribution of 'theory' should be tested against its ability to identify relevant questions, provide explanatory frameworks and inform and facilitate social change through an interaction with the agents of change (from individual women themselves to policy-making structures on a variety of levels), not an end in itself. Ironically, the pursuit of explanations of power and inequality in society as a whole, may lead to the construction of a new, more pernicious, vehicle for the exercise of intellectual elitism, bounded by the construction of disciplines (and professionalism) and rendered exclusive through the skilful evolution of linguistic sophistication.

The concept of citizenship represents a prime example of an area of social science enquiry dominated by abstract theorising on the one hand and crude empiricism on the other. Theoretical debates around the concept have developed from an entirely masculinist foundation although the subject has attracted much attention in recent years by feminist academics keen to question the gendered assumptions underlying the various categories and approaches. Very little of this work has attempted to develop the interplay of theory and experience suggested above, particularly at comparative level. In the context of the previous discussion it would not be unreasonable to question the appropriateness of utilising such a concept as a framework for the evaluation of the experiences of European migrant women. Sylvia Walby raises a very similar point questioning, "whether 'citizenship' is so imbued with gender assumptions related to the public sphere and the nexus of the market and state that it is necessarily only a partial rather than a universalistic project"[10].

The 'choice' of citizenship in this project came not from some extensive philosophical debate, however, but reflected a concern to maximise the impact of the research and immediately engage in the policy-making process. My own interpretation of feminist research involves a commitment to action-research, defined in the broadest sense as research which seeks to bring about and influence social and political change. It could be argued that there is nothing distinctively feminist about this. We are, in practice, raising wider issues concerning the social responsibility of academic research and guarding against the abuse of power. Early in my own academic career, as a doctoral researcher, I was influenced by the work of Gideon Ben-Tovim and John Gabriel. In a paper focusing on the failure of sociology (and the 'sociology of race-relations') to respond in an effective way to the growth of racism in society, they question the contribution of academic disciplines and of social science research more generally arguing that, "The discipline [of Sociology] is only worth saving in so far as it is prepared to define its objectives in political and not academic terms"[11]. Tom Shakespeare, a researcher who is himself disabled, makes a similar assessment of two decades of research on children and disability, insisting that academic work must start from the voices of disabled people:

> **Almost none of [the research] was from the perspective of disabled children ... The idea that disabled people are the best experts on disability is a relatively new thing ... disabled people are all too familiar with sociologists colonising their experiences.**[12]

Perhaps the key contribution of feminism to this debate has been its re-definition of what constitutes 'politics' to embrace the personal lives of

---

[10] Walby (1994, p 379) supra, note 6.

[11] Ben-Tovim, G.S. and Gabriel, J. (1982) 'The sociology of race – time to change course?', in A. Ohri, B. Manning and P. Curno (eds) *Community work and racism*, London: Routledge and Kegan Paul, pp 60-74 at p 61.

[12] Quoted in, Ochert, A. (1997) 'Impaired by our limitations', *Times Higher Education Supplement*, 28 November, p 19.

women. In that sense simply engaging with formal political structures may fail to take us beyond predominantly male-determined public agendas and experiences to begin to identify and understand women's lives (and the complex inter-meshing of public and private that shapes their experiences and actions). Stanley and Wise similarly stress the importance of research which consciously seeks to inform policies and advance feminist strategy suggesting that, "the product of feminist research should be directly used by women in order to formulate policies and provisions necessary for feminist activities"[13]. These policies encompass anything from our working relationships with research assistants, students, colleagues and the subjects of our research to our input at the more formal level through active dissemination.

Citizenship, gender and intra-Community migration

The gender and migration project developed out of an interest in the free movement provisions as a key dimension of EU social policy – an area defined within the Treaty itself by reference to 'citizenship of the Union'. In that sense then, 'citizenship' is a legal concept defining membership. Indeed, concerns about the more legalistic dimensions of citizenship and nationality have dominated the debate around European integration and citizenship. The problems and implications of defining membership, and excluding certain groups, has precipitated genuine fears about the development of a 'Fortress Europe'. As such the agenda, in relation to freedom of movement and citizenship, has, quite understandably, been dominated by concerns over the status of third country migrants including those legally resident in the EU, refugees and asylum seekers. The unfortunate consequence of this agenda has been to reinforce the notion of a broad universality of status and experience among the membership (or the 'in-group'). Chapter Four clearly outlines the fact that the citizenship concept, as legally defined and interpreted in the law-making of the EU, does not confer a broad equality of status, however, but depends upon specific notions of social contribution and marital status.

The adoption, or inheritance, of 'citizenship' as a key dimension of the research framework thus reflects not so much a theoretical 'choice' but a pragmatic recognition of its usage within EU policy making and an attempt to understand and evaluate those processes from the perspectives of the individual women concerned. It effectively delineates a policy arena. While

---

[13] Stanley and Wise (1993, p 32) supra, note 5.

---

the research has not uncritically adopted this framework, it has, for reasons of expediency, chosen to 'stick with it' with the intention of maximising our input into both EU and national policy making. It enables policy makers to immediately engage with the subject matter in a way that alternative social science concepts (such as patriarchy or decommodification or distributive justice) would not. At the same time, in both the social policy and socio-legal literature, which formed the broad disciplinary base of my interest, the development of work at comparative level has generally been structured around the concept of citizenship. It thus situates the research within a relevant body of academic debate.

The following section draws on some of the literature around citizenship and social welfare focusing selectively on aspects of the debates of particular interest to this piece of research and which provide a context for the research findings. As such the chapter does not set out to present a detailed and comprehensive summary of the literature around citizenship but rather to develop some ideas which we can build on throughout the book[14].

Approaches to the citizenship concept

The concept of citizenship has been used to describe the relationship between the State and individuals and, connected with that, the relations between individuals within a given community. In that sense it provides a framework for the analysis of social relations, not only in abstract terms but also in terms of the distributional implications of certain forms (how social relations in a given context determine the allocation of key social goods and political resources) and ultimately the welfare of citizens. This concern about welfare and the role of the State in social redistribution, developed out of Marshall's attention to what he referred to as the 'social element' of citizenship. This he defined as encompassing, "the whole range from the right to a modicum of economic welfare and security to

---

[14] For this the reader must look elsewhere. See, for example, O'Connor, J. (1996) 'From women in the welfare state to gendering welfare state regimes', Trend Report, *Current Sociology*, vol 44, no 2; Lister, R. (1997) *Citizenship: Feminist perspectives*, London: Macmillan; Roche, M. (1992) *Rethinking citizenship*, London: Polity Press; Meehan, E. (1993) *Citizenship and the European Community*, London: Sage; Shaw, J. (1997) 'Citizenship of the Union: towards post-national membership?', Paper delivered to the Academy of European Law, Florence, July 1995.

the right to share to the full in the social heritage and to live the life of a civilised being according to the standards prevailing in the society"[15].

Citizenship, according to this definition, did not confer an immediate equality of entitlement but rather access to a point in a continuum, the definition of which would shift from a subsistence definition to a more relative definition over time as the 'civilising forces' of citizenship progressively modified the relationship between social class and social status. The social dimension of citizenship is thus very much concerned with notions of need, equality and access to material resources. In the context of this research on EU migrant women, we are not so much dealing with absolute or subsistence poverty but rather with dimensions of social and territorial justice and inequality; notions of need, welfare and social status (which form constituent elements of the citizenship concept) must therefore, to a large extent, be normative and relative[16]. As such they are not reducible to simple measurement or enumeration but infer a more complex relationship between individuals and their society; a relationship echoed in Peter Townsend's classic definition of relative poverty:

> **Individuals ... can be said to be living in poverty when they lack the resources to obtain the types of diet, participate in the activities and have the living conditions and amenities which are customary or at least widely encouraged or approved in the societies to which they belong.**[17]

A very similar definition of poverty is adopted by the EU in its second poverty programme which defines as poor those, "persons, families and groups of persons whose resources (material, cultural and social) are so limited as to exclude them from the minimum acceptable way of life in the Member States in which they live"[18]. This approach is interesting, in the context of integration, given that the reference point is that of the Member State and not the EU, as a whole; a fact that is evident in the

---

[15] Marshall, T.H. (1950) *Citizenship and social class*, Cambridge: Cambridge University Press, pp 10-11.

[16] This does not imply the eradication of forms of absolute poverty. Some of the women interviewed in the course of the research were indeed living in poverty, in some cases unable to secure their own accommodation and live with their families.

[17] Townsend, P. (1979) *Poverty in the UK*, Harmondsworth: Penguin.

[18] CEC (1989) 'The fight against poverty', *Social Europe*, 2/91.

---

development of entitlement under the free movement provisions (based on the principle of non-discrimination as opposed to harmonisation). The point here, however, is to emphasise the fact that, increasingly, the vocabulary of poverty is being replaced by terms such as marginalisation, 'dualisation' and 'social exclusion'. Linda Hantrais welcomes the acceptance, by the EU, of this broader definition, as recognition of the fact that, "poverty brings with it a sense of powerlessness and marginalisation, or exclusion, and engenders dependence"[19]. The use of the term 'dependence' here, as opposed to access to material resources, reflects an increasingly common concern to understand the impact of welfare policies and should not be confused with the narrower political concerns with 'welfare dependency' which have fuelled welfare retrenchment. In this context the concern with dependency is much broader than this limited focus on welfare dependency (and work as the key source of independence) and suggests that, for most people, dependency is spread across a range of systems of support within the mixed economy of welfare[20].

The notion of dependency as a fact of life for most citizens is made by Raymond Plant who suggests that, "dependency and vulnerability are endemic features of the human condition and the question then is how these dependencies are to be handled, whether through the state or more through private charity and voluntary sector provision"[21].

To illustrate this situation, Oppenheim juxtaposes a statement made by the Conservative Bow Group stressing the image of the credit-dependent middle-class family, "drawing no welfare benefits or dole, but mortgaged up to the eye balls" with the situation of a young single mother who, on failing to secure State assistance, turned to her family[22]. Dependency in these contexts may thus be on private sector institutions (which cover an increasing range of social 'risks'), on public or voluntary sector welfare provision or on informal systems of support (from both the immediate 'nuclear' and wider extended family). Furthermore, social insurance schemes designed to reduce one form of dependency (on paid work) may themselves encourage new forms of dependency

---

[19] Hantrais, L. (1996) *Social policy in the European Union*, London: Macmillan, p 157.

[20] A point made by Carey Oppenheim (1990) in *Poverty: The facts*, London: Child Poverty Action Group.

[21] Plant, R. (1990) 'The new right and social policy: a critique', *Social Policy Review 1989-90*, London: Longman; cited in Oppenheim (1990, p 12), supra, note 20.

[22] Cited in Oppenheim, supra, note 21.

(on the State or on male partners). As Oppenheim suggests, it may simply be that the 'focus' shifts.

This relationship between economic or material inequality, dependency and social and political participation is mirrored in the citizenship literature. While Marshall's evolutionary model[23] refers to distinct elements of citizenship, implying to some degree that one or more of these forms of 'status' may be achieved in isolation (for example, that political rights may be meaningfully exercised in the presence of abject poverty and social inequality), Elizabeth Meehan refers to the interlocking of social rights with other aspects of citizenship arguing that, "social, civil and political rights must form an indivisible triad for universal citizenship to be a reality"[24]. The interconnection of social and political rights proved to be quite central to the citizenship experience of many migrant women living in Ireland, as Chapter Seven indicates.

Reference to the notion of political rights, and participation as a key element of citizenship (or social status), immediately widens the debate from a concern with the distribution of social goods and the patterning of material inequality in any given community (as evidence of structures of constraint) to a wider consideration of citizens as actors or agents (exercising 'choices' or at least making decisions) the cumulative effect of which may, in turn, influence the nature of social distribution[25]. Evaluating citizenship thus requires more than a mapping of social inequality (and social provision) but an understanding of how social inequalities impinge on individuals as human agents, how they facilitate or constrain decision making; of how inequalities are 'lived' and acted upon. This shift, evident within both the poverty and citizenship literature, from a simple enumeration of resources and entitlement to notions of dependency and individual agency (as the exercise of power) opens the way for a much more holistic and meaningful evaluation of social relations and quality of life issues (including analyses of how the welfare state may, through its own actions, generate dependency). The methodological problems raised are, however, enormous.

---

[23] Marshall, T.H. (1950) *Citizenship and social class*, Cambridge: Cambridge University Press.

[24] Meehan, E. (1993) *Citizenship and the European Community*, London: Sage, p 101.

[25] For a full discussion of the importance of recognising citizenship as a process as opposed to simply a material status and the centrality of human agency to an understanding of citizenship see Lister, R. (1997) *Citizenship: Feminist perspectives*, London: Macmillan.

The citizenship concept itself is too 'slippery' (and distorted in popular usage) to provide a sound framework for rigorous comparative social policy analysis; researchers have thus developed various operational 'tools' to serve as the basis for comparison. Attempting to capture the relationship between material welfare, dependency and agency, Esping-Andersen developed the now, well-rehearsed, concept of decommodification as a key indicator of social citizenship providing a basis for the categorisation of welfare systems according to the extent to which they grant social rights independently of market position[26]. Rather than a measure of material equality, as such, decommodification constitutes a specific interpretation of dependency; it is not so much what one has, or is entitled to, but how that translates into different forms of dependency (or a restriction on the power to make decisions). This process of insulation from the labour market or 'decommodification' occurs, "when a service is rendered as a matter of right, and when a person can maintain a livelihood without reliance on the market"[27].

This does not imply, as it suggests, that a person has free choice over the decision of whether to undertake paid work, but rather measures the impact of predictable life-course events (such as sickness, injury, unemployment and retirement) on the ability to work. The right (to social services and benefits etc) derives not so much from citizenship status but from forms of social contribution (via paid work). The evolution of social rights with the development of the 'modern' welfare state ameliorated, to varying degrees, reliance on waged labour as the sole determinant of social status (or access to key social resources such as health care or income support). Citizenship – or decommodification – is thus a mark of a civilised society, which through the socialisation of healthcare, education and income support, protects its contributing citizens from the vagaries of the market. It is thus a form of social distribution operating in parallel with social class which modifies pre-existing patterns of social inequality. The status of citizens in different social systems is therefore open to evaluation according to the extent to which paid workers are cushioned, through socialised insurance schemes and the provision of State services, from a variety of forms of 'risk', all of which would otherwise require citizens to continue in waged labour in order to meet their social needs.

Despite acknowledgement of the usefulness of this work in developing

---

[26] Esping-Andersen, G. (1990) *The three worlds of welfare capitalism*, Oxford: Polity Press.

[27] Esping-Andersen (1990, p 22), supra, note 26.

a new approach to comparative social policy and highlighting some important issues about the position of women in the labour market (and of economic dependency), it has been widely criticised by feminists on the grounds that it theoretically privileges social class, equating economic autonomy with independence from waged labour[28] and fails to adequately account for the role of the family and the position of women in relation to social welfare.

The question of key concern here is whether this method of categorisation, according to the principle of insulation from labour market dependency, adequately reflects the gendered nature of welfare regimes[29]. Social class is only one system of inequality in society and to judge welfare systems solely in terms of their impact on social class is clearly inadequate for women. As Gillian Pascall notes: "While Marshall asserts the rights of citizenship, nowhere does he analyse the problematic relationship between citizenship and dependency in the family as he does between citizenship and social class"[30].

Dependency is far more complex than the previous analysis suggests, not only for women but for all persons, requiring an evaluation of the interaction of competing systems of inequality, oppression and opportunity and their evolution over time and space. From a feminist viewpoint then, we need to consider not only the impact of welfare systems on social class (and the relationship between paid work and welfare) but also the impact of patriarchy as a competing system of inequality creating additional forms of dependency (and power). This has lead to a focus on the ways in which modern capitalist societies have constructed a specific family form as a system of institutionalised dependency responsible for the allocation of gender roles. The family constitutes a system of welfare provision largely operating outside of the formal labour market based on relationships of 'mutual' obligation and 'compulsory altruism'[31]. This leads immediately to a critique of the decommodification concept on the grounds that men

---

[28] Point raised by Bussemaker, J. and van Kersbergen, K. (1994) 'Gender and welfare states: some theoretical reflections', in D. Sainsbury (ed) *Gendering welfare states*, London: Sage, p 9.

[29] These issues are discussed again in Chapter Three in the context of limitations in comparative method.

[30] Pascall, G. (1986) *Social policy: A feminist analysis*, London: Tavistock, p 6.

[31] Taylor-Gooby, P. (1991) 'Welfare state regimes and citizenship', *Journal of European Social Policy*, vol 1, no 2, pp 93-105.

---

and women are not the same but are in fact "gendered commodities"[32]. Feminists have been quick to point out that women are already operating in a 'decommodified' (or pre-commodified) sphere in the home. The implications of this form of decommodification, as a response to caring obligations are, however, quite different to those envisaged by Esping-Andersen. In practice, women may be simply shifting from one form of dependency to another – from 'public' labour market dependency to 'personal' dependency on a male breadwinner.

Mainstream theories have overlooked the fact that social resources are provided and needs met within a broader mixed economy of welfare within which informal care dominates welfare provision across all welfare systems[33]. Consideration of informal systems of care and support are thus crucial to understanding not only the dependency status of paid workers (which is very much mediated by their access to informal support) but also the status of women, the majority of whom have gained social entitlement by virtue, not of employment status, but through heterosexual marriage.

Recognition of the importance of this form of dependency upon male breadwinning partners, as the principal source of social entitlement for the majority of married and cohabiting women, has led to the development of new 'models' stressing the relationship between paid work, unpaid work and the State. Jane Lewis suggests that all modern welfare regimes subscribe to a greater or lesser degree to the idea of a male breadwinner model which, "cuts across established typologies of welfare regimes"[34] emphasising the gendered nature of the division of labour and its implications for social entitlement and citizenship. While acknowledging the strength of Lewis' approach Diane Sainsbury is critical of her final category (of 'weak' male breadwinner states) on the grounds that their characterisation, "indicates what a country's policies are not rather than what they are" and suggests, instead, their designation as 'individual models' to reflect the greater

---

[32] Langan, M. and Ostner, I. (1991) 'Gender and welfare: towards a comparative perspective', in G. Room (ed) *Towards a European welfare state*, Bristol: SAUS Publications, p 131. Lewis, J. (1992) 'Gender and the development of welfare regimes', *Journal of European Social Policy*, vol 2, no 3, pp 159-73 at p 160.

[33] Even in Norway, Kolberg (1991) estimates that public authorities deliver less than one fifth of the total volume of non-residential care, cited in Daly, M. (1994) 'Comparing welfare states: towards a gender friendly approach', in D. Sainsbury (ed) *Gendering welfare states*, London: Sage.

[34] Lewis (1992, p 162), supra, note 32.

degree of individualisation evident in Scandinavian societies[35]. A significant advantage of Lewis' approach, however, which may be lost in Sainsbury's proposal, is the emphasis on similarity and the notion of a continuum, reflecting degrees of difference, rather than divergence and polarity. The importance of this is magnified when we come to consider the relationship between formal policy and citizenship experience (or 'outcome')[36]. It is important that feminist analysis avoids the temptation, through categorisation, of over-simplification and determinism. Langan and Ostner's characterisation of the position of Scandinavian women as one of "*relative economic dependency*" supported by the State in contrast to the 'dependent' position of women in Anglo-Saxon and Conservative regimes[37] illustrates this problem. While there are important differences to be explored in terms of the impact of different social systems on women's experience of citizenship, this position of relative economic dependency effectively describes the position of the majority of women in Europe, to varying degrees, particularly if we take a wider 'life-course' approach. Increasing levels of female labour market participation and the concentration of women in 'atypical' work suggests some convergence in experience.

Women's roles as paid worker/informal carer lead them into a duality of experience in terms of dependency[38]. Women may be both commodified through their participation in the labour market (which may reflect increased independence) and decommodified, through their role as unpaid informal carers in the home, at once or consecutively. Indeed, for most women decommodification and commodification are processes which they experience intermittently or simultaneously throughout their life-course depending to a large extent on familial obligations and the extent and nature of social provision. Women may be, at once, bread winners with additional responsibility for ensuring the effective commodification of male workers (as wives tending the household), for social reproduction (as mothers responsible for the raising of families) and for the care of

---

[35] Sainsbury (1994) supra, note 33. See also more recent authored text: Sainsbury, D. (1996) *Gender, equality and welfare states*, Cambridge: Cambridge University Press.

[36] More detailed discussion of the concept of policy and policy evaluation is contained in Chapter Three.

[37] Langan and Ostner (1991, p 135), supra, note 32.

[38] The notion of dependency itself implies not only financial or economic dimensions but also social or moral obligations (to care or support) and the freedom to make decisions or exercise choices.

---

those 'non-producers' excluded from the labour market (as a result of sickness, disability or old age). It is the interaction of different forms of autonomy and dependency, as both commodified and decommodified, simultaneously and at different phases over the life-course, that conditions women's status and experience of citizenship: it is the impact of paid work on family roles and vice versa that creates the dynamic of pressures, conflict and opportunities which form the context of women's lives. While acknowledging the usefulness of Lewis' model, Daly suggests the need for modification to incorporate the reality of 'role combinations' more effectively on the basis that welfare states are more likely to encourage a combination of activities through the development of often contradictory and even ambivalent policies[39].

A very interesting example of the role of this blurring of boundaries between public and private and of the role of State welfare in moulding and reproducing gender relations lies in the development of schemes, across Europe, for the payment of informal care, effectively commodifying women as the primary source of caring labour[40]. The commodification of female caring labour is, of course, not a recent phenomenon with the bulk of paid caring, in both social and health services, performed by female workers. Indeed many of the 'advances' made in integrating women into Scandinavian labour markets have been achieved via programmes to socialise care through an extension of female employment by the State. In that sense, it could be argued that the decommodification of male workers, through the provision of State welfare has been achieved via the commodification of women who provide the services. In other words, the insulation from labour market dependency of many male (and female) workers has been achieved through the reliance on the paid labour of female care and service providers. What is new about more recently introduced systems of payment for informal care lies in the geography of caring (which takes place in the 'private' space of the carer, or person-cared-for's own home) and the conflation of economic 'contract' with kinship obligation. The extent to which such schemes constitute new sources of exploitation or a partial recognition of caring as 'work' is open to debate. The development of schemes of payment for informal care, even at highly exploitative levels of remuneration, nevertheless represent

---

[39] Daly, M. (1994) 'Comparing welfare states: towards a gender friendly approach', in D. Sainsbury (ed) *Gendering welfare states*, London: Sage, p 113.

[40] For more details of developments in schemes of payment for informal care see references in Chapter Eight, note 5.

an, albeit indirect, form of recognition of caring as a basis for social entitlement (via waged labour). However we choose to theorise these relationships, what matters in the end is how women in such situations interpret these policy developments and the effect they have on the range of choices open to them.

Feminist critiques raise concerns not only about the division of (unpaid) labour within the home and its effects on women's labour market activity, but also the mechanisms through which presumptions about such gender relations have shaped the formulation of 'public' welfare systems and of social entitlement. As such, systems of social entitlement may both 'liberate' women from dependency on male partners and reinforce that dependency. Elizabeth Wilson argues that assumptions about women and their roles are so deeply embedded within social policy planning at both a conscious and unconscious level that, "One way of looking at social policy would be to describe it as a set of structures created by men to shape the lives of women"[41]. While Wilson is referring here to UK domestic social policy a similar point could be made in relation to the development of family rights and entitlement under the free movement provisions. This work cautions us against treating the 'public' and the 'private' as distinct spheres; in practice there are not two competing, autonomous, spheres but rather sets of assumptions at the level of the 'private' which condition not only power relations within domestic family relations but also the distribution of resources by the welfare state. One consequence of this is reflected in the priority attached to certain forms of 'risk' in social insurance schemes; risks which Mary Daly refers to as 'male risks', without suggesting that these aspects of dependency and insurance are unimportant to women, but rather reflecting their dominance in public agendas:

> **Across welfare states contingencies typical of male lifestyles (such as retirement, industrial accidents, unemployment) were more readily incorporated into social programmes than those of women (widowhood, family caring and pregnancy). The bias, then, was towards de-commodifying male risks.**[42]

While welfare provision itself is not static, and important developments

---

[41] Wilson, E. (1983) 'Feminism and social policy', in M. Loney, D. Boswell and J. Clarke (eds) *Social policy and social welfare*, Buckingham: Open University Press.
[42] Daly, M. (1994) 'Comparing welfare states: towards a gender friendly approach', in D. Sainsbury (ed), p 113, supra, note 33.

have taken place incorporating caring (or at least mothering) as a social risk (through the introduction of maternity and parental leave[43] and nursery provision etc), mainstream theories have largely constructed their models around the former, highly gendered, agenda.

Diane Sainsbury[44] is critical of Lewis' model on the grounds that it emphasises only two bases of entitlement: primary individual entitlement as breadwinner (paid worker) or derived, secondary entitlement as the dependant of the breadwinner (typically as a wife). As such the model fails to examine the nature of social entitlement which accrues to women as mothers and carers. Although such benefits are typically low rate, means-tested and stigmatised (as in the case of payments to single mothers in the UK, for example) they nevertheless constitute an important source of entitlement for many divorced women and single parents insulating them from dependence on both paid work and reliance upon male partners. Bussemaker and van Kersbergen, for example, note that some 90% of social assistance benefits in The Netherlands are paid to women[45]. Ruth Lister similarly cautions against dismissing the value of such benefits, arguing that the real meaning of such forms of public dependency must be considered in the context of alternatives: for even dependency on means-tested income support, "with all its inadequacies and indignities" can be preferable to dependency on an individual man[46]. In an article aptly titled, 'Lone mothers on welfare in West Berlin: disadvantaged citizens or women avoiding patriarchy?', Madje and Neususs' research with lone mothers criticises simplistic correlations of dependence on welfare with marginalised status. Taking a life-course perspective they reveal an ambivalence in women's experience of citizenship:

> **... being 'on welfare' can be seen as a positive opportunity for certain groups of lone mothers at certain periods in their lives ... On the one hand they feel various constraints as a result of their dependence on welfare; on the other, however, they feel it**

---

[43] Although the UK has until recently bitterly resisted EU attempts to introduce a legal framework for parental leave.

[44] Sainsbury, D. (1994) 'Women's and men's social rights: gendering dimensions of welfare states', in D. Sainsbury (ed), pp 150-69, supra, note 33.

[45] Bussemaker, J. and van Kersbergen, K. (1994) 'Gender and welfare states: some theoretical reflections', in D. Sainsbury (ed), p 21, supra, note 33.

[46] Lister, R. (1990) 'Women, economic dependency and citizenship', *Journal of Social Policy*, vol 19, no 4, pp 445-69.

also enables them to lead a life-style they prefer. They are unwilling to marry or remain in marriages simply because of the presence of children. They are willing to take responsibility for childcare themselves and to abandon or cut back paid employment, at least for a period of time; but they refuse to depend upon a husband's maintenance. In this situation, the state becomes the more acceptable breadwinner.[47]

In criticising feminist work which emphasises the distinctiveness of forms of public and private dependency, we must also recognise the atemporal or static nature of analyses which focus attention on a very limited period in most women's lives when, in practice, women shift into and out of different forms of dependency over the life-course[48].

Dissatisfaction with decommodification as a tool for understanding the relationship between gender, welfare and citizenship (and with attempts at reformulation) has lead to the demand for new concepts. Bussemaker and van Kersbergen, referring to Orloff's proposal for a more generic measure of independence linked with notions of individualisation[49] suggest the need for a concept which captures the complex interplay of forces:

It is important to analyse independence as changing patterns of work and care, rights and needs between individuals, the state, the family and the market. This means that the concept has to deal not only with economic independence, although this is a very important part of it, but also with independence understood as the *possibility of making choices* and of insulation from emotional or psychological dependence. (author's emphasis)[50]

---

[47] Madje, E. and Neususs, C. (1994) 'Lone mothers on welfare in West Berlin: disadvantaged citizens or women avoiding patriarchy?', *Environment and Planning*, vol 26, pp 1419-33.

[48] The limitations of feminist work on caring which restrict analysis to consideration of 'mothering' – and the importance of life-course perspectives are – developed in Chapter Eight.

[49] Orloff, A.S. (1993) 'Gender and the social rights of citizenship: state policies and gender relations in comparative perspective', *American Sociological Review*, vol 58, no 3, pp 303-28.

[50] Bussemaker, J. and van Kersbergen, K. (1994) 'Gender and welfare states: some theoretical reflections', in D. Sainsbury (ed), p 24, supra, note 33.

Julia O'Connor similarly criticises the decommodification concept and its central concern with labour market participation. For women, she argues, any changes in productive relations are likely to be severely limited if they are not accompanied by changes in the conditions of reproduction. She proposes that the concept is supplemented by the concept of 'personal autonomy' or, "insulation from involuntary personal and/or public dependence (by the family and the state)"[51]. This does not imply the absence of interdependence where this is based on choice, equality and reciprocity. Indeed, in many cases, interdependence and the consensual sharing of responsibilities and resources, is the bedrock of autonomy. In that sense the term 'dependency' loses the negative connotations accepting that dependency is a fact of life for us all and it is through dependency that we exercise autonomy. It should not, therefore, be seen as synonymous with the pursuit of individualism. Involuntary interdependence (akin to Taylor-Gooby's use of the concept of compulsory altruism[52]) on the other hand implies unequal power relations and the absence of choice: "full interdependence is possible only when involuntary economic dependence is absent"[53]. We are dealing with fairly fine and shifting balances here which may easily tilt in either direction; in reality, relationships are somewhat less finely and rationally distinguished but evolve over time in response to changing circumstances. Nevertheless, the concept of personal autonomy provides us with a more effective means of assessing the impact of welfare systems on a variety of interrelated aspects of dependency on the labour market, male breadwinners and on the State. In addition to relations of 'dependency', the concept permits the recognition and evaluation of forms of interdependency and reciprocity, usually between women as members of wider kinship groups or simply as friends and neighbours, within the 'community, which, in practice, have a major, and, in some cases, the most significant impact on women's ability to exercise choice and independence. Perhaps one of the limitations of the male

---

[51] O'Connor, J.S. (1993) 'Gender class and citizenship in the comparative analysis of welfare states: theoretical and methodological issues', *British Journal of Sociology*, vol 44, no 3, September, pp 501-19 at p 511.

[52] A term first coined by H. Land and H. Rose (1985) 'Compulsory altruism for all or an altruistic society for all?', in P. Bean, J. Ferris and D. Whynes (eds) *In defence of welfare*, London: Tavistock.

[53] Lister (1990, p 446) supra, note 46 – or indeed, other forms of coercion which may include fear of physical or sexual abuse or social stigma.

breadwinning model, as it stands, lies in the primacy it appears to attach to nuclear family relations as the basis of informal care. As such citizenship, for women, is framed by the nexus of paid work, state welfare and male breadwinning partner. Langan and Ostner's designation of Mediterranean Rim countries as 'mother-daughter economies'[54] highlights the key role played by grandmothers effectively under-writing the labour market integration (and financial autonomy) of their daughters, through the provision of childcare[55]. While it may be legitimate to emphasise the role of grandmothers in the 'welfare societies' of Southern Europe, in practice, such relationships are common across Europe and may reflect not only the lack of public alternatives and the prohibitive cost of private provision (constraints) but also positive preferences for family care[56]. In addition to grandparents, we must also consider the role played by sisters, sister-in-laws, other family members and by other women, outside the bounds of kinship, in providing resources which together shape the 'resource framework' of women's lives. The importance of other women, as friends and neighbours, in providing services which enable women to combine their roles as mothers and paid workers – or simply to cope with the isolation of child-rearing in a post-migration context – is clearly evident in the life experiences of the migrant women interviewed in the course of this research. If we took just a minute to reflect upon our own experiences as women, sisters, mothers and daughters and our reliance upon infrastructures of paid and unpaid support, it should come as no surprise that, to many women, the contribution of the 'State' pales into insignificance in comparison with that of our friends and neighbours and generally, other women.

A crucial question here concerns women's experiences of these relationships as purchasers, consumers (or users) and providers of care. From the consumers' viewpoint the financial implications of different systems are key determinants of a woman's ability to use the service. Of equal concern, however, is the quality of care, its flexibility and the range of options available. Damaris Rose's unique analysis of childcare strategies

---

[54] Langan and Ostner (1991), supra, note 32.

[55] This relationship is itself a good example of reciprocity over the life-course as the daughters will inevitably be expected to care for their mothers when they themselves are in need of support; whether this can be defined as voluntary or not will depend on the relationship concerned and the range of 'options' available.

[56] Howard Meltzer's study (1994) *Day care services for children*, London: OPCS, evidences the important contribution of grandparents to childcare in the UK.

---

in Montreal illustrates some of the dilemmas women face in making decisions about childcare: on the one hand she exposes the rhetoric of 'choice' behind the transfer of State support away from direct provision and into tax relief while, on the other, drawing attention to the limitations of State provision and regulation which, "standardises and rigidifies" childcare services[57]. Furthermore, the 'benefits and tensions' of informal care referred to by Langan and Ostner (above) require examination from the viewpoint of those women concerned. Discussions over the implications of the concentration of women as paid service providers in Scandinavian countries have tended to obscure the commonality of women's predicament in this respect, (in the sense that most women who achieve economic independence do so through reliance on the labour of other women) and the importance of understanding the quality and nature of these relationships, many of which are highly exploitative.

A reduction in levels of dependency in any one of these areas (by, for example, the provision of services and policies to promote women's labour market integration as in Scandinavia) may not imply increased personal autonomy but simply a 'transfer' resulting in increased dependency elsewhere (on the State). This situation has been referred to as a shift from personal to public patriarchy reflecting, in part, the depressingly limited evidence of role-sharing or interdependence within domestic relationships[58]. Analysing these relationships in terms of their impact on personal autonomy provides the opportunity for a clearer understanding of women's experiences. The extent to which such transfers may be heralded as a means of empowerment (as the lesser of two evils) or viewed, alternatively, as Hobson's choice (out of the frying pan – into the fire) is then open to more critical analysis.

The previous discussion has emphasised the need to understand the relationship between formal citizenship status and outcome. Only by thoroughly examining the wider context of dependency which both shapes and is shaped by formal rights (and the articulation of public and private forms over time) can we begin to understand how formal status is understood and negotiated by women and translated into citizenship

---

[57] Rose, D. (1993) 'Local childcare strategies in Montreal, Quebec', in Katz and Monk (1993, p 191), supra, note 8. Similar arguments could be made in relation to domiciliary home care in the UK where increasing regulation and professionalisation often results in inflexible and unsatisfactory service, from the consumer's perspective.

[58] An issue developed further in Chapter Seven.

experience. Citizenship is evidently not an undifferentiated status but rests upon implicit notions of contribution (and of gender relations). A hierarchy of forms of social entitlement exists comprised of an elite grouping of citizens who gain individual entitlement by virtue of labour market contribution followed by a group of, mainly married women, who derive indirect entitlement by virtue of their relationship with a male breadwinner and finally, a residual stratum, mainly comprising single mothers and divorced women (among other economically marginalised 'citizens') whose claim to means-tested low level benefits is based on identifiable need. A significant proportion of the last group are typically claiming rights based upon caring as a form of social contribution although increasingly, in the UK at least, measures are being introduced to shift the dependency of single mothers from the State and onto fathers and the labour market. In practice, the citizenship status of women depends on the various claims they can make across this hierarchy over their life-course.

Important questions remain concerning feminist strategy and the most effective and appropriate vehicle for the enhancement of women's interests. The Scandinavian 'model' advocating full labour market integration via measures to socialise aspects of caring may take us a step nearer to realising citizenship on an equal footing with men. On the other hand, persistent inequalities in the division of labour within the home suggest that such a strategy may not only be dependent upon possible 'fragile' welfare state support but also result in the extension of a double burden for women and pressures on women's time. An equally important but often overlooked aspect of personal autonomy is that of the distribution of time. Increased levels of full-time paid work coupled with the unequal distribution of unpaid work in the home means that, in practice, many women end up doing a 'double shift' leaving them little, if any, time for themselves. Ruth Lister documents the growing problem of 'time poverty' facing women in the UK[59]. For women, she argues, the time budget may be just as crucial as the financial budget. Jane Lewis concludes her analysis of the relative position of women under Scandinavian or 'weak-breadwinner' regimes in a similar vein, "In material terms they [women] are the best off, but at the consequence of being particularly time poor"[60]. Concern here is not just with the unequal distribution of exhaustion (Ruth Lister reports a survey which found that 52% of women felt tired most of the time) but also with

---

[59] Lister (1990), supra, note 46.
[60] Lewis (1992, p 170), supra, note 32.

the implications of dual roles for the ability of women to physically and mentally participate in political activity – demonstrating the link between women's social and economic condition and the realisation of political citizenship: "Whether trapped in the home full-time or exhausted by the double shift, women's caring and domestic responsibilities in the private sphere make it very difficult for many of them to participate as citizens in the public sphere"[61].

It is unsurprising that support for a strategy of labour market integration (through the socialisation of care) as the principle means of equalising status has come from women in academia and politics, as this strategy reflects the priority this group of women place on economic autonomy and, deriving from that, political representation. Ruth Fincher refers to the distortion in resource distribution which has occurred in Australia as a result of the successful incursion of 'younger' middle-class women into positions of influence at senior government level in Australia over the past decade suggesting that one effect of the success of this 'femocracy', as a political strategy, has been to advance the interests of a particular group of women who share the interests and characteristics of the femocrats[62]. These might include, for example, a higher prioritisation of life-course related concerns of middle-class women, particularly of childcare concerns over and above issues concerning care for elderly relatives, for example, and programmes promoting equal employment opportunity. As this group of women age, the agenda will no doubt broaden to reflect the life-course concerns of older women. The close relationship between economic and political marginality (reflecting the dominant basis of political group formation), however, suggests that femocrats will continue to pursue a strategy of labour market integration as the basis of notions of social contribution and inclusive citizenship[63].

The implications of different forms of interdependency, between women, and the impact of the State on these relationships is of central concern to feminist debate. This leads to consideration of the relative advantages of labour market segregation and the concentration of women in services and public sector employment. In practice, women in different

---

[61] Lister (1990, p 457), supra, note 46.

[62] Fincher, R. (1993) 'Women, the state and the life-course in urban Australia', in Katz and Monk (1993), supra, note 8.

[63] The relationship between economic and marginality is discussed in more detail, in the context of the political marginalisation of black people in Britain, in my doctoral thesis, supra, note 1.

regimes share a common experience of constraint with the labour market, the State and private patriarchal control forming three parallel, but interconnected continua. A shift in one direction results not in a reduction in overall dependence but merely a transfer. Analysis of these subtle transfers and their impact on personal autonomy requires a new, more qualitative and collaborative, approach to feminist comparative research. Janice Monk and Cindi Katz's recent comparative study argues that one of the most important lessons of the life-course perspective, "is that women construct and can change their lives, even against the insistent structural constraints associated with capitalist and patriarchal social relations"[64].

There is a tendency in much of the literature to define citizenship in terms of formal status and to view women as passive victims of patriarchal legal and social structures. This to a large extent reflects and reinforces the limitations of comparative method. One of the key objectives of this research has been to incorporate, alongside an evaluation of formal structures, an understanding of their relationship to women's lives, accepting that, as Lister succinctly puts it, "People can be, at the same time, both the subordinate objects of hierarchical power relations and subjects who are agents in their own lives, capable of exercising power in the 'generative' sense of self-actualisation"[65].

The concept of choice in this type of research is problematic not least because it presumes a universality of interest and condition but also a static, linear and rational process. This project has thus not attempted to find out 'what women want' but rather to understand how individual women attribute meaning to structures and respond to evolving patterns of constraint; how they make sense of (or theorise about) their experiences and how, in their daily lives they exercise autonomy[66]. The following section turns to consider the relevance of some of the issues discussed

---

[64] Monk, J. and Katz, C. (1994) 'When in the world are women', in Katz and Monk (1993, p 22), supra, note 8.

[65] Lister, R. (1996) 'Citizenship, agency and rights: feminist perspectives', Paper to the DIOTIMA conference, 'The gendering of rights, power and citizenship', Athens, 9-10 February.

[66] A very interesting dimension of this can be seen in the interviews with women in Ireland and their negotiation of Irish domestic social policy (on reproductive and marital rights). More detailed discussion of this material is contained in Chapter Seven and also in, Ackers, H.L. (1996) 'Internal migration and the negotiation of citizenship; the struggle for reproductive determination in Ireland', *Journal of Social Welfare and Family Law*, vol 18, no 4, pp 413-28.

---

above for the lives of the women interviewed in the course of this research. As such it gives some indication of the type of material discussed in the qualitative findings.

Citizenship, dependency and autonomy in a migration context

Citizenship, at least in its social and political guise, has been operationalised, in comparative social policy, through the use of concepts of dependency. The previous section has argued that, in order to begin to understand women's experiences as citizens we must consider a complex of interrelated dependencies and interdependencies. Building on the work of O'Connor and Orloff's concepts of individualisation and autonomy this project seeks to evaluate the migration process from the point of women's experience. The utilisation of a life-history approach permits consideration of the whole range of experiences from the initial migration decision through to its impact on family relationships and caring, paid employment and the welfare state and their relationships with other women.

Women who move within the European Union constitute an important group in their own right and the process of moving distinguishes their experience from that of non-migrant women[67]. In this project we are less concerned with issues of nationality, and exclusion on the basis of nationality, than with the impact of geography on caring resources and obligations. The extrication of these women from the 'cushion' of extended family and informal support networks (and also from various associated obligations and expectations) exposes in quite stark terms, the relationship between personal dependency (on male partners) and public dependency (on the state and the labour market).

Peeling away the layers of often invisible family and informal support, and the 'option' of a safety net of social assistance, which forms the basis of many non-migrant women's lives enabling them to exercise some freedom of choice (particularly to secure some modicum of financial autonomy or to escape from oppressive relationships), reveals the opportunities sacrificed on migration. In so doing it also draws attention to the generally hidden nature of the 'private' sphere of women's lives.

A study of the lives of women who migrate also focuses attention on power relations within the family. In practice, most of our lives are moulded

---

[67] These issues are picked up in Chapters Five to Eight.

by the gradual, frequently unconscious, evolution of numerous 'small' decisions as we negotiate our personal relationships over the life-course; often experienced as a progressive erosion of autonomy. While some of these decisions are quite fundamental and often precipitate major shifts in the balance of power within relationships (most notably decisions about caring for children and dependants) these are often milestones in a generally incremental process which shapes the context of women's lives and power relations within the home and which tend to occur within a given cultural context (albeit mediated by class, ethnicity etc). The experiences of migrant women are punctuated by an additional single or series of very significant and conscious decisions which bring into focus and fundamentally alter the course of subsequent life events and relationships. Evaluation of the migration decision-making process thus tells us quite a lot about women's relationships with their family or partner or, indeed, as proved to be the case in the majority of interviews, their exercise of autonomy as individual women.

Debates about commodification and male breadwinning family structures have permeated not only the social policy literature, but quite independently and, in many ways, preceding the latter, have underpinned international migration theory. Indeed, the idea of a male breadwinning nuclear family structure and presumptions about gender roles within the family have dominated traditional models of migration behaviour. Interpreted primarily as economic-maximising behaviour within a rational choice framework, dominant models propose a preliminary phase of male 'pioneer' migration during which time male workers may send remittances home to their wives whose work in the home releases the man from other duties facilitating his commodification. A subsequent 'second phase' of migration is characterised by a period of 'family reunion' as the male secures sufficient funds to enable him to bring over his family and set them up in the country of immigration. International migration theory – and its 'fit' with the reality of migration – particularly in the context of female migration trends, is discussed in detail in Chapter Three. The point to stress here is that theories about international migration are based on assumptions, divorced from empirical reality, about family structure and consensual household decision-making processes. When such models of migration behaviour translate into a framework of legal rights they tend to reflect and reproduce a specific family form which, in the process, renders as either invisible or deviant all those persons whose family situation in any way deviates from that 'norm'.

In the migration context the articulation of public and private dependencies, of commodification and decommodification takes on a new spatial significance. In some cases social reproduction – or caring – may then take place in another geo-political space and in an entirely different welfare context. Migrant women may not only have to negotiate the intermeshing of complex forms of dependency and interdependency within the family and the labour market but, in the process, have to juggle the presumptions and resource frameworks of two or more, possibly quite different welfare systems[68]. The norms embedded within those systems may create enormous pressures and tensions for the women concerned in terms of their own sense of obligation and role and the expectations of those around them, both within the wider family and the State. The simultaneous experience of commodification and decommodification referred to above may be further complicated by its spatial manifestations; a woman may be carer in one country and paid worker and carer in another at the same point in time (or over her life-course)[69]. In this context a woman's social status is highly complex; she may derive certain benefits on an individual basis through employment contribution, on a derived basis via her male breadwinning partner in the country of immigration or, possibly, in recognition of her caring role in the country of origin (should she return to care). In many cases she will lose, by virtue of her migration, the kind of independent needs-based safety net of provision which ultimately protects many women in domestic welfare systems (not only in economic terms but also in sense of enabling her to leave an abusive relationship) reinforcing a polarity of dependency with male breadwinner on the one hand and labour market on the other.

The following chapter turns our attention to the role of the EU, as a policy-making body at supra-national level, to consider the extent to which the development of formal legal rights at EU level are based on gendered assumptions about migration behaviour, family structure and gender roles, effectively replicating – and reinforcing – the hierarchies of entitlement and status evident within domestic welfare systems.

---

[68] Migrant women's exposure to the welfare systems of at least two countries, in itself, makes them a very interesting group to study at comparative level.

[69] This situation was, in fact, quite a common experience and is reported in full in Chapter Eight.

THREE

Evaluating citizenship: the development of a comparative approach

Introduction

This chapter considers some methodological issues surrounding the study of citizenship focusing in particular on the gender dimensions[1]. It begins with a general discussion of approaches to comparative social policy analysis and the limitations of these. It includes in this section the problems of reliance on aggregate data (and the impact of European Union [EU] research funding) and concepts of 'policy' in comparative research (and the relationship between inputs and results). The chapter then goes on to consider, in brief, feminist approaches to social research and their application at comparative level before presenting the approach adopted in the gender and migration project.

Developments in comparative method

Academics, particularly in the social policy field, are increasingly persuaded of the merits of comparative research on the grounds that it removes ethnocentric blinkers[2], permits evaluation and comparison of real policies as opposed to abstract, theoretical, constructs and reduces the tendency to allow national cultural and political myopia to restrict our perception of

---

[1] Chapter Five refers more specifically to the limitations of migration research, building on issues raised here.

[2] Rose, R. (1987) *The methodology of comparative policy analysis*, Cross-national Research Papers No 2 (Research Methods and Problems in Comparative Public Policy), Loughborough: European Studies, University of Loughborough.

policy options[3]. Furthermore, increasing awareness of the impact of global political and economic pressures on domestic policy has called into question the appropriateness of research which fails to take supra-national forces into account. Indeed, Cochrane and Clarke suggest that, "it is perhaps no longer necessary to make the case for a comparative approach to the study of social policy; on the contrary, it may now be single-country studies which need to be justified"[4].

Linda Hantrais defines comparative research as follows:

> ... a study is held to be cross-national and comparative, when individuals or teams set out to examine particular issues or phenomena in two or more countries with the express intention of comparing their manifestations in different socio-cultural settings (institutions, customs, traditions, value systems, lifestyles, language, thought patterns), using the same research instruments either to carry out secondary analysis of national data or to conduct new empirical work. The aim may be to seek explanations for similarities and differences, to generalise from them or to gain a deeper understanding of social reality in different national contexts.[5]

To date, comparative work has generally focused on the first of these two aims, on macro-modelling and the examination of convergence and divergence in whole systems.

In the case of research in the area of international migration, in the context of EU policy, a comparative approach is not simply desirable, but essential. The gender and migration project is not 'comparative' in the traditional sense of a country-by-country comparison of national welfare systems across a range of variables but focuses, instead, on the impact of supra-national policy making on the citizenship experience of women from a variety of national, cultural and socioeconomic backgrounds across international space. In this context the national origin or indeed country of residence of the women concerned are merely two, albeit important,

---

[3] A motivation Hill refers to as 'policy borrowing': Hill, M. (1996) *Social policy. A comparative analysis*, Hemel Hempstead: Harvester Wheatsheaf, p 39.

[4] Cochrane, A. and Clarke, J. (1993) *Comparing welfare states*, Buckingham: Open University Press, p 1.

[5] Hantrais, L. (1996) 'Comparative research methods', *Social Research Update*, no 13, University of Surrey.

variables in a complex interplay of factors shaping their lives and influencing their response to social policies. A focus on national context may indeed mask important processes operating at the level of regional or urban/rural level demanding a finer spatial mesh. In that sense this project is significantly different to mainstream comparative social policy research with its focus on model-building and a generally deterministic systems approach. This project is less concerned with the type of study Hantrais outlines at the start of her definition and more in line with her final point about seeking a deeper understanding of social reality in different national contexts.

Increasing consensus on the need for a comparative dimension to social research does not imply a consensus over methodology, however. Methods of comparative analysis have evolved somewhat independently within firm disciplinary boundaries, very much influenced by the epistemological foundations of the parent discipline. As a result, comparative research is generally hampered by a limited fusion of ideas, theories and objectives. This does not imply a general consensus within disciplines; indeed the comparative social policy literature reflects widespread disagreement on issues of method and approach often resurrecting age-old arguments on the status and place of qualitative or quantitative research and the reliability of different forms of data. To some extent this reflects the problems of doing research on such a scale, in terms of finance, access and cultural and linguistic barriers. The debate has thus moved on from the question of desirability to one of feasibility and the merits of different approaches. The following section briefly maps the evolution of different approaches to comparative study within the discipline of social policy. Where relevant parallels are drawn with approaches in other disciplines, in particular, geography, which has spawned much of the migration research[6] and law, which has witnessed an increasing interest in the implications of developments at EU level for individual rights and citizenship status.

The 'traditional' approach in comparative social policy was that of the detailed, essentially descriptive, 'case study' often involving discrete studies of particular aspects of provision in two or more national contexts. This approach is best exemplified by Richard Titmuss' comparative study of blood donating systems in Britain and the United States which provided the empirical base of his classic theoretical work on altruism[7]. More recent years have seen an explosion in case studies of aspects of social policy in one or more countries, essentially identifying and describing evidence of

---

[6] See Chapter Five for an overview of approaches to migration research.

[7] Titmuss, R.M. (1973) *The gift relationship*, Harmondsworth: Penguin.

difference or similarity in the context of that policy. The limitations of forms of social policy analysis which seek to disaggregate and evaluate discrete areas of policy have been widely acknowledged within the domestic social policy literature on the grounds that all aspects of social policy interact with one another both in a planned and unintended way. Increasing recognition of the interrelationships between areas of public policy extends also to an understanding of broader interactions and interdependencies within the mixed economy of welfare (between statutory provision, fiscal policy, occupational welfare, the voluntary sector and informal care)[8].

Gosta Esping-Andersen's work on welfare regimes[9] represented an important break with the case study tradition and a move in the direction of a more comprehensive attempt to compare whole systems. His model of welfare regimes is based upon the collection and analysis of available aggregate data at national and international level and thus relies quite heavily upon government statistical sources, particularly on matters of public expenditure. The 'commodification index' which forms the basis of his classification system, is derived from a comparison of data on income support, pensions and sickness and unemployment benefits in terms of levels of income replacement, eligibility criteria and population coverage. Not only did he seek to describe and compare social systems, on the basis of this evidence, but also to suggest explanations for policy divergence or convergence. In this way he was able to consider the impact of differences in political culture, social relations and ideology on public policy.

Notwithstanding the importance of this contribution to the development of comparative method, the value of such modelling has been questioned. Spicker, for example, suggests that, "the practice of modelling itself is doomed to failure"[10]; that categories are too static, while policy making is dynamic; that they simply do not work when applied to more detailed policy evaluation; and that, in practice, there is rarely a good 'fit' between countries and the prescribed categories. This chapter concerns itself with two specific areas of criticism; firstly, on 'technical' matters concerning the adequacy of the information utilised in the

---

[8] For more detailed discussion of this point see Ackers, H.L. and Abbott, P. (1996) *Social policy for nurses and the caring professions*, Buckingham: Open University Press.

[9] Esping-Andersen, G. (1990) *The three worlds of welfare capitalism*, Oxford: Polity Press.

[10] Spicker, P. (1996) 'Normative comparisons of social security systems', in L. Hantrais and S. Mangen (eds) *Cross-national research methods*, London: Pinter, pp 66-76 at p 71.

modelling process and secondly, on implicit presumptions concerning the relationship between policy, implementation and outcome on citizenship experience.

Systems analysis clearly demanded the development of an ambitious new approach to comparative method requiring the collection of data across a wide range of indices and a significantly greater geographic scale. The specific indices selected by Esping-Andersen reflect the availability and quality of data which, it has been argued, has limited the model's explanatory potential and lead to explanations of policy divergence which over-emphasise the importance of a limited range of factors (linked to his decommodification index) rather than on the interrelationship of a wider variety of features. One response to the perceived 'technical' limitations of the regime model has been essentially corrective. Feminist researchers, such as Lewis, Glasner and Langan and Ostner[11], for example, used Esping-Andersen's and Leibfried's[12] frameworks as a starting point but introduced new indices into the analyses, selected to present a more accurate representation of women's interests and their structural position in welfare regimes. Essentially replicating the methodology, these analyses have emphasised levels of State provision of childcare and maternity/parental leave and their relationship with women's labour market participation (particularly in terms of part-time work and job segregation). In so doing they have brought into the analysis the complexity of women's relationship with the labour market as a result of the gendered nature of unpaid work. Acceptance of public (as opposed to private) responsibility for various forms of dependency (childcare or care of elderly people, for example) and the degree to which caring functions are socialised thus became a benchmark for the evaluation of citizenship.

This development in comparative method, by feminist researchers, however, tends to reinforce the emphasis on the statutory sector and on a

---

[11] Lewis, J. (1992) 'Gender and the development of welfare regimes', *Journal of European Social Policy*, vol 2, no 3, pp 159-73. Glasner, A. (1992) 'Gender and Europe: cultural and structural impediments to change', in J. Bailey (ed) *Social Europe*, London: Longman. Langan, M. and Ostner, I. (1991) 'Gender and welfare: towards a comparative perspective', in G. Room (ed) *Towards a European welfare state*, Bristol: SAUS Publications.

[12] Leibfried, S. (1992) 'Towards a European welfare state? On integrating poverty regimes into the European Community', in Z. Ferge and J. Kolberg (eds) *Social policy in a changing Europe*, Frankfurt: Campus Verlag, and Boulder, CO: Westview Press.

---

limited period of women's lives (child-bearing and rearing)[13]. In replicating the welfare regime method, it also risks over-simplification masking both important commonalities and differences in women's experiences of citizenship and encourages an approach to social policy analysis in which regime types are compared against each other in the form of 'league tables' and not with broader feminist objectives. In the context of the EU, the emphasis on divergence and the absence of clear objectives limits the possibility of identifying a common feminist strategy across the respective welfare systems. This essentially corrective response by feminist researchers is presumably based on tacit acceptance of the view that analysis of aggregate statistics constitutes the only viable method of empirical enquiry at comparative level. Bussemaker and van Kersbergen express similar concerns, suggesting that, "There is a slight risk that the developing agenda of this research is reproducing a flaw of mainstream welfare state theories, both in terms of basic assumptions and methodologies and in terms of the choice of countries and comparisons"[14].

Moreover, in replicating the methodology of previous approaches, this work compounds the error of presuming a relationship between formal policy and outcome – a point we shall return to in the next section. It is perhaps worth remembering Julia O'Connor's assertion at this stage that a "gender sensitive analysis cannot be achieved by exclusive focus on gender, or by adding gender to the power resources framework of analysis. Some key concepts must be re-examined"[15].

The limitations of secondary analysis in cross-national research

It is evident from the previous discussion that a key weakness of much comparative social policy analysis lies in its reliance on secondary data. Judith Glover concludes her evaluation of the value of secondary analysis in cross-national research with the 'warning' that, "the epistemological

---

[13] A point expanded upon and illustrated by reference to interview material in Chapter Eight.

[14] Bussemaker, J. and van Kersbergen, K. (1994) 'Gender and welfare states: some theoretical reflections', in D. Sainsbury (ed) *Gendering welfare states*, London: Sage, p 15.

[15] O'Connor, J.S. (1993) 'Gender, class and citizenship in the comparative analysis of welfare states: theoretical and methodological issues', *British Journal of Sociology*, vol 44, no 3, pp 501-19 at p 509.

issues arising from secondary analysis are far-reaching and may, indeed, be exacerbated in cross-national research"[16]. These criticisms reflect well-rehearsed arguments over the use of secondary data and official statistics as the basis for social policy analysis[17]. Lisle describes cross-national research as, "the closest approximation to the controlled laboratory experiment of the natural scientist, available to the social scientist ... permitting the stepwise and controlled falsification of hypotheses"[18]. Such language immediately warns us of the dangers, presumptions and limitations of positivist social research: dangers which have long been identified and critiqued by feminist researchers. Some of these messages have been conveniently overlooked, however, when it comes to comparative research, possibly for reasons of expediency. When Hantrais and Mangen suggest that, "cross-national research by its very nature demands greater compromises in methods"[19], they are not inviting prospective comparativists to throw themselves uncritically into secondary analysis but rather to be aware of the problems of transferring traditional tools of social science enquiry to work at comparative level.

A central argument of this chapter is that much existing work at comparative level has tended to compound the problems associated with the secondary analysis of quantitative data. Government statistics are produced with a specific purpose in mind: they are rarely concerned primarily with comparative social policy analysis but focus instead on the relationship between social policy and the regulation of public expenditure and labour markets[20]. Michael Hill stresses the need for constant vigilance in the use of Organisation for Economic Cooperation and Development (OECD) data (which constitutes a key source of data in much comparative research) on the grounds that, "OECD's main concern is the compilation of material on economic performance"[21]. This is the primary purpose for

---

[16] Glover, J. (1996) 'Epistemological and methodical considerations in secondary analysis', in Hantrais and Mangen (1996, p 31) supra, note 10.

[17] May, T. (1997) *Social research: Issues, methods and processes*, 2nd edn, Buckingham: Open University Press (Ch 9, 'Comparative research: potential and problems', pp 179-94).

[18] Cited in Dierkes, M., Weiler, H.N. and Antal, A.B. (eds) (1987) *Comparative policy research: Learning from experience*, New York, NY: St Martin's Press, p 14.

[19] Hantrais, L. and Mangen, S. (1996) 'Method and management of cross-national research', in Hantrais and Mangen (p 10, 1996), supra, note 10.

[20] Ginsburg, N. (1992) *Divisions of welfare: A critical introduction to comparative social policy*, London: Sage, p 19.

[21] Hill (1996, p 40), supra, note 3.

the collection of data and will be reflected in the forms of material collected. Rose similarly points to the limitations of 'output' measures of aggregate public expenditure on the grounds that they "assume that all relevant attributes of government programmes, from the declaration of war to abortion policy, can be reduced to the common measuring rod of money"[22].

This type of data is likely to over-emphasise the role of the State as a provider of welfare (or social goods) at the expense of other players within the mixed economy of welfare. The increasingly important contribution of private provision and occupational welfare (or informal care) to social status is reflected only to the extent that there is some element of State subsidy or regulation[23]. Claire Ungerson points to the weaknesses of 'regime analysis based on modelling' to the extent that the researcher, "loses a sense of welfare states as service deliverers and also fails to indicate fully how the everyday lives of citizens are affected by the structure and objectives of 'their' welfare state"[24].

Increasing interest in comparative work has coincided with an explosion in the availability of on-line data facilitated by the growth in and widespread availability of computing facilities and the Internet. The relative ease and limited costs of using this data, for the comparativist, "carries the danger of forgetting that the concepts used in any research derive from the questions and interests of its original intentions"[25]. Uncritical reliance on official statistics is likely to lead to a comparison of what is comparable; an approach referred to by Castles as following the "primrose path of doing what it was easiest to do on the basis of information gathered by others"[26] thereby distorting analyses of welfare systems and citizenship. Data collected

---

[22] Rose (1987, p 2), supra, note 2.

[23] Comparative information on the role of occupational welfare, for example, is very restricted although it substantially affects the position of women employees. In the UK a survey of 1,100 employers found that 23% offered improvements on statutory schemes (Moss, P. [1990] *Childcare in the European Communities 1985-90*, Commission of the European Communities). Public sector employees, particularly in white-collar positions, for example, often receive enhanced benefits.

[24] Ungerson, C. (1996) 'Qualitative methods', in Hantrais and Mangen (1996, p 63) supra, note 10.

[25] Levitas, R. and Guy, W. (1996) *Interpreting official statistics*, London: Routledge, pp 3 and 63.

[26] Castles, F. (ed) (1989) *The comparative history of public policy*, Cambridge: Polity Press; cited in Cochrane, A. and Clarke, J. (1993) *Comparing welfare states*, Buckingham: Open University Press.

---

by the State for its own purposes may be too limited in scope to provide an adequate basis for comprehensive social policy analysis. Of equal concern, however, is the fact that governments may have certain vested interests to protect when producing such statistics and data may be manipulated to suit political agendas. It is for this reason that Ruth Levitas and Will Guy suggest caution in the use of such data:

> **... it is also abundantly clear that the definitions used in official statistics still produce measures which embody the interests of the state rather than of citizens. It is therefore only with the utmost care that such data can be interpreted for democratic purposes.**[27]

Nowhere is this more evident than in data on unemployment. The dominant use of the 'claimant count' as a measure of unemployment together with progressive changes in the basis of calculation (and in the rules on entitlement to benefit) make it, "virtually useless as an indicator of whether or not unemployment is actually rising or falling"[28]. These problems are profound in all social research but assume a particular significance in analyses concerned with the gendered nature of social systems. Such measures are particularly inaccurate in reflecting female unemployment given the complex rules on benefit entitlement for married women (and women with caring responsibilities[29]) which provide a strong disincentive to women to register as unemployed[30].

---

[27] Levitas and Guy (1996, p 6) supra, note 25.

[28] Levitas, R. (1996) 'Fiddling while Britain burns? The "measurement" of unemployment', in Levitas and Guy, supra, note 25.

[29] In 1987 107,000 women had their unemployment benefit disallowed (and were thereby excluded from statistics) on the grounds that they were unable to demonstrate that they could immediately find full-time childcare for children, by someone other than a relative; N. Whiteside cited in Levitas (1996, p 49), supra, note 28.

[30] The Labour Force Survey may, however, provide a more reliable source of data on matters of employment based as it is on interviews with individuals. Unlike the Census, which relies on the head of household returning a self-completion questionniare on behalf of the entire household, the LFS is a sample survey which relies on trained interviewers visiting the homes of the selected respondents and interviewing them directly. As a consequence of this approach, the LFS samples a high proportion of women (reflecting their more common presence in the household at the time of interview). Moreover it includes, as work, more marginal forms of activity including domestic work, unpaid family work and homeworking as well as self-employment.

In addition to wider concerns about the use of data produced by the State as indicators of citizenship experience, there are often more technical issues relating to problems of definition and the comparability of secondary data: limitations which have been very much evident in the current project. Much of the data was not strictly comparable as different countries have used different definitions (part-time or unpaid family work, for example). In the context of migration data, considerable problems in comparability reflect the varying definitions of the concept of migrant, differing rules on the acquisition of nationality and particular 'arrangements' between certain countries which distort statistics on migration (UK statistics, for example, identify Irish citizens born in the UK as British). Some countries had simply failed to submit any of the relevant data to Eurostat[31] while for other, more recent members of the EU, data was not yet available[32].

In addition to problems of definition are questions of scale. Many public surveys rely on large samples to facilitate statistical analysis. One consequence of this is that minority group experiences are inadequately reflected because the numbers are insufficient to support 'statistically valid' analyses:

> **Data collection in Britain, as elsewhere, is guided by a particular view of what counts as scientific knowledge. It is numerical information derived from large numbers of people and recorded in categories defined by the researcher that is most likely to be accorded the status of scientific knowledge.[33]**

This problem, and the tendency to dismiss the phenomena in question, as a statistical irrelevance, significantly reduces the availability of statistics on intra-Community migration. Data on individual nationality groups in migration flows is often not recorded in European Labour Force Survey (LFS) output due to the relatively small size of the sample (of Swedish migrants in the UK, for example). As a result, it is difficult to compare, on the basis of secondary data, female intra-Community migrants by nationality. In a paper to a recent conference, Anne Singleton, currently employed as expert statistician to the Eurostat Migration Team, Luxembourg, expressed concerns over the limitations and potential misuse

---

[31] There was no data on intra-Community migration for Italy, for example.

[32] Data for Sweden was not available in the 1992 European Labour Force Survey.

[33] Graham, H. (1993) *Hardship and health in women's lives*, Hemel Hempstead: Harvester Wheatsheaf, p 22

of migration data and the extent to which the availability of secondary data has driven research agendas:

> **Policy related research and much academic research in the field of migration has been heavily reliant on the use of statistical data to validate governmental decision-making processes as well as the aims and objectives of government and EU-funded research projects. Data availability or the lack of availability has driven many research priorities whilst there appears to have been a reluctance to acknowledge the limitations imposed by the data themselves. The concerns over numbers of migrants have only relatively recently been matched by concerned efforts in some quarters to understand the implication of uncritical use of the existing data. In the policy areas of migration and asylum a general recognition is long overdue that data are not independent objective measures of reality, but products of the legislative and political processes and priorities which rely on them for legislation.[34]**

In conclusion, Anne Singleton refers to the, "general failure to tackle fundamental questions about the use of statistical data in the social construction of knowledge on migration" and makes a plea for researchers to exercise caution in the use of international migration statistics which, "present only a limited and partial view of a complex and dynamic set of social phenomena".

This problem of migration data is further compounded when we are interested in issues of dual nationality and personal relationships. Hilary Graham refers to the limitations of existing British secondary data on ethnicity and marital status, in particular, arguing that the data on nationality obscures the many relationships in which partners do not share the same ethnic identity. According to LFS data (1984-86), over a quarter of married and cohabiting Afro-Caribbean women and men aged under 30 had a white partner and yet the children of this group are recorded under the

---

[34] Singleton, A. (1997) 'False distinctions: who are migrants and what is the meaning of counting them', Paper to the Immigration Law Practitioners' Association and the Centre of European Law, King's College London Conference, 'The legal framework and social consequences of free movement of persons in the European Union', 27-28 November.

ethnic group in which their father was placed[35]. Similarly, data on marital status is driven by legal classifications and not by the meaning women attribute to personal relationships. Graham gives as an example the treatment of cohabitation as an heterosexual category with no expression, in the statistics, of lesbian cohabitation; such women are classified instead as single, separated, divorced or widowed. The limitations of available European data on dual nationality and marital status are clearly evidenced in Chapter Five and reflect problems with the categories themselves (as above) but also the static nature of the data and the inability of such cross-sectional surveys to trace the evolution of personal relationships over the life-course of women and the implications of these for their legal status and broader citizenship experience.

Jill Rubery and Collette Fagan have devoted much time to detailed analysis of LFS data as editors of the European Commission's (EC) 'Bulletin on Women and Employment in Europe' producing important reports evidencing wage discrimination and activity rates. Despite this work, and the evident advantages of LFS data over Census data for the analysis of gender inequality, they nevertheless conclude that more qualitative research is required to explain the implications of such data. In the case of occupational segregation, for example, they suggest that, in order to determine whether it represents a "bad thing for women ... [we need to] go beyond the labour market data, which in many cases pose more problems and issues than they resolve"[36]. In a similar vein, Veronica Beechey notes the inadequacy of prevailing concepts of economic activity, based on official statistics, for analysing sex discrimination in employment arguing that instead of taking activity rates as given (as indicative of inequality), we need to ask "more sociological questions about ... how discriminatory processes are 'lived' by women"[37]. While quantitative data may raise questions – or even suggest a correlation – they cannot advance our understanding of process. Judith Glover makes a similar point, suggesting that, "Broad-brush harmonised data may allow for the identification of specificity but provide little potential for its explanation"[38].

---

[35] Cited in Graham (1993, p 32), supra, note 33.

[36] Rubery, J. and Fagan, C. (1993) 'Occupational segregation of women and men in the European Community', *Social Europe Supplement*, 3/93, Commission of the European Communities, p 60.

[37] Beechey, V. (1989) 'Women's employment in France and Britain: some problems of comparison', *Work, Employment and Society*, vol 3, no 3, pp 369-78 at p 375.

[38] Glover (1996, p 35), supra, note 16.

Although this shift away from traditional piecemeal case studies which sought to, "simply catalogu[e] different experiences"[39], to a more systematic comparative analysis of aggregated data has met with general approval, the explanatory potential of the welfare regime approach has been questioned on the grounds that the conclusions were, "equally broad and the gaps remained frustratingly large"[40].

Rather than attempting to fine tune the method through the development and refinement of indices, this criticism has lead to the evolution of a new approach which effectively supplements welfare regime frameworks with forms of policy analysis[41]. The work of Cochrane and Clarke and Ginsburg, for example, uses Esping-Andersen's framework as the basis for exploring aspects of policy in individual countries in more depth; a method they refer to as the 'structured diversity' approach. These case studies are not empirically-based as such but seek to, "go below the level of official statistics and explore the content of welfare policies" (with a focus on family policy) in specific historical and cultural contexts[42]. They essentially complement the secondary data with a detailed description of policy evolution in the selected countries, once again focusing on available evidence of 'active' policy, on the assumption that the existence of policy itself makes a difference (in other words, it frames citizenship experience). Micheal Hill describes the 'structured diversity' approach as one which, "dips into specifics about policies by making contrasts between developments in societies at different points in the quantitative 'leagues'"[43]. One of the limitations of this approach is its reliance upon the framework created by systems analysis to, "identify [the] puzzles which need to be explained"[44] and the presumption that these analyses have accurately identified the key structural determinants of welfare regimes. If the framework itself is structurally flawed then the 'puzzles' identified will reflect and reproduce these flaws – and any gendered assumptions or omissions.

Much of the growth in comparative social policy, in the last decade has, however, followed the 'structured diversity' approach. The 'flesh' on the bones of a framework shaped by official statistics has been provided by

---

[39] Cochrane and Clarke (1993, p 6), supra, note 4.

[40] Cochrane and Clarke (1993, p 7), supra, note 4.

[41] Cochrane and Clarke, supra, note 4 and Ginsburg, supra, note 20.

[42] Cochrane and Clarke (1993, p 12), supra, note 4.

[43] Hill (1996, p 57), supra, note 3.

[44] Cochrane and Clarke (1993, p 12), supra, note 4.

teams of 'national experts' reporting, often in country-specific chapters, in edited collections, on the social policy context in their own country. The result is typically a rather disconnected collection of disparate experiences which tend to emphasise diversity with little attempt to draw out and explore similarities and differences effectively. Norman Ginsburg alludes to the inherent weaknesses of this approach before admitting that this criticism applies, in many ways, to his own 'state-by-state' study:

> **Whether this kind of literature deserves the accolade 'comparative' is a matter of debate, since methodical and/or theoretical comparison is often either underdeveloped or absent. Many of these texts devote a chapter to each welfare state, which in itself tends to emphasise diversity and uniqueness, especially if the chapters are written by different people![45]**

This model is quite commonly seen in reports published by the EC where the existence of a 'network of experts' is a prerequisite for much grant funding. At European level the fundamentally economic basis of the Treaty of Rome, and the embedding of the subsidiarity principle in the Treaty on European Union (TEU), has lead to a tight relationship between EU social policy and employment to the extent that the EU can only legitimately claim competence in the social policy field where there is a labour market or employment 'link'. This policy emphasis is, not unsurprisingly, reflected in the availability of secondary data. In common with any other State body, the objective of data collection at EU level is to assist in the evaluation and formulation of its own policy making and is likely, therefore, to reflect dominant interests and perspectives and, in the main, focus on areas of Community competency[46]. On a technical point, European statistics are, in any case, only as good as the sum of national data from which they are extrapolated. Indeed, the harmonisation procedures used as a means of standardising national data sets effectively conceals the social processes underlying the collection of data and blurs distinctions, producing the impression of a "single unseamed reality existing out there"[47]. In that sense harmonised cross-national data needs interpreting with extreme caution.

---

[45] Ginsburg (1992, p 25), supra, note 20.

[46] Although in some areas the Community has the competency to collect and report on social issues, but not to positively intervene.

[47] Stanley and Wise, quoted in Glover (1996, p 37), supra, note 16.

The clamour for scarce funding opportunities at European level has to some extent reinforced this problem. While not imposing a particular methodology as such, adherence to EC guidelines for a successful research application determines both the geographical scope and management structure of projects. Increasingly, large numbers of partners (often between eight and fifteen) are required with one country taking a coordinating role[48]. Indeed, the absolute minimum number of partners admissible under many programmes is three and the success of proposals often requires strategic selection of partnerships to meet with Community objectives to promote research in 'less-favoured regions' or to collaborate with industrial partners. The imposition of quite rigid time and resourcing constraints (with three-year projects the norm in many cases and often shorter deadlines in work undertaken for specific Directorates) often does not allow for the development of genuine collaboration in research design and evaluation[49]. The effect of this approach to funding has been to create a dominant 'model' of comparative research which, for reasons of expediency alone, encourages the use of either secondary analysis or highly descriptive forms of policy evaluation. The product is usually a collection of descriptive or statistical national reports, by partners, on the situation in their country, with little attempt to synthesise these in comparative analysis. Indeed, such a synthesis would, in many cases, prove highly problematic for the coordinator to achieve, from his or her base, given the lack of genuine collaboration in the definition of research parameters and research design and may result in culturally insensitive conclusions based on very limited awareness of the policy context in the participating Member States. The tendency of many of these large projects to be planned and coordinated by partners in Northern Europe, compounds this problem, skewing research in favour of the research interests and perspectives of Northern European social scientists, with Southern European partners often fulfilling the role of dutiful data gatherers, and coordinators exercising considerable cultural hegemony over research agendas[50]. Hantrais and Mangen make a similar observation:

---

[48] A recent call for projects under the 'Training and mobility of researchers' programme (Fourth Framework), for example, required at least eight partnerships.
[49] Another important constraint is the very tight deadlines for receipt of funding applications which, in practice, effectively rule out collaboration in initial research design and careful selection of partnerships. In that sense they also substantially favour academics with already established research links.
[50] This view was recently expressed to me by a researcher in Southern Europe whose institution is a partner in numerous large-scale EC-funded projects.

> Given the imperatives imposed by the European Union to incorporate all Member States or, at least, a broad mixture of them in many of its programmes, researchers have therefore been active in attempts to reduce the sorts of data problems … Many projects never go far beyond data collection and collation since analysis and evaluation are so costly in terms of time and funding and tend to give rise to problems which may be avoided if the study is confined to description … if a Northern dominance is perpetuated, the pressure to create what could be artificial typologies or standardised evaluative criteria may be intensified by the proliferation of research networks funded by the European Union.[51]

Bussemaker and van Kersbergen suggest that one explanation for this Northern dominance, at least in feminist research, reflects the, "understandable, yet problematic preference to study the Nordic countries"[52] which have thus become 'prototypes' in feminist comparative analysis.

Comparative policy analysis – the relationship between policy and outcome

It was noted in the introduction to this chapter that modelling can be criticised not only on more technical grounds concerning the adequacy of data but also on the implied relationship between policy inputs and welfare outcomes. The same argument can be levelled at structured diversity approaches, the value of which depends not only on the data but also on the quality of the policy analysis undertaken to, "put flesh on the statistics"[53]. This 'fleshing out' process raises questions around what constitutes policy in our analyses, how we evaluate policy and what inferences we make, on the basis of this evaluation, about outcomes or effects. What is often lacking in comparative analysis (in common with much social policy analysis) is a clear statement of what constitutes 'policy'. Concepts of

---

[51] Hantrais, L. and Mangen, S. (1996) 'Method and management in cross-national research', supra, note 10, at pp 4 and 10.

[52] Bussemaker, J. and van Kersbergen, K. (1994) 'Gender and welfare states: some theoretical reflections,' in D. Sainsbury (ed) *Gendering welfare states*, London: Sage, p 15.

[53] Hill (1996, p 55), supra, note 3.

---

policy are typically restricted to what can be measured either in terms of expenditure data or gleaned from descriptions of formal policy (such as legislation, for example). Ginsburg provides a very detailed statement of the concept of social policy which is worth restating in full[54]:

> Government action embraces not only direct provision of benefits and services, but also the regulation and subsidy (including fiscal reliefs) of the various private forms of welfare. These latter include occupational welfare provided by employers, welfare provided by for-profit, charitable, trade union, community, religious and other voluntary organisations, as well as that provided informally by family members, friends and neighbours. Clearly the boundaries of social policy extend into areas which are conventionally ascribed to 'economic policy' (eg, employment, industrial, monetary and fiscal policy) and other areas of 'public policy' (eg, immigration, law enforcement, industrial relations and penal policy). The concept of 'policy' is also usefully extended in at least two other directions. First, it must cover the activities of agencies to whom governments and legislation frequently delegate responsibility for social policy – quangos, regional and local government, and so on. Administrative, professional and local government discretion often create enormous complexity in defining what policy actually amounts to. Second, the term 'social policy' should cover areas of inactivity by government and its agencies in relation to social issues. Thus government inaction, or non-decision, becomes a policy when pursued over time in a fairly consistent way against pressures to the contrary. This is particularly apparent in areas such as family policy, where governments uphold the privacy of 'the family' while inevitably, at the same time, intervening in many ways into family life.
>
> From whatever value perspective it is pursued and however its boundaries are defined, the study of social policy involves analysis of three basic elements – the origins, the substance and the impact of policy, or as Heidenheimer put it, 'how, what

---

[54] For more detailed discussion and other definitions see Ackers and Abbott, supra, note 8.

and to what effect ... governments pursue particular courses of action or inaction'.[55]

This extended definition of the concept is useful because it documents the parameters of any comprehensive evaluation of social policy. While any particular study may include consideration of only a small component of policy, it is important to place that research in the context of the wider project and continually remind ourselves of the interrelatedness of all aspects of policy. This is not only the case in comparative research but applies equally to research at national or local level. Comparing the existing body of comparative material against this definition does, however, illustrate the concentration of interest in a very small number of areas and the substantial gaps in coverage. In particular, it calls into question the adequacy of analyses focusing on an increasingly restrictive conception of policy which typically fails to evaluate the impact of policy failure, non-decision or unintended consequences on citizenship.

Before addressing the more problematic issues of how to evaluate outcomes or include within our analyses those dimensions of 'policy' which have no expression in statistics or formal policy statements, it is interesting to consider the effect of the academic 'mode of production' on the policy identification process. Our concern here is not with the social policy-making process 'out there' but with the impact of disciplinary myopia on the very construction of the policy concept. Differences in approach to the 'policy' concept and a failure to develop a genuinely interdisciplinary approach in the socio-legal domain has seriously limited the quality of research[56]. From the social science perspective, the comparative literature rarely includes any reference to the legal status of policies nor to the Courts as active participants in the policy-making process. Grainne de Burca makes a similar point, in the context of European Community policy making:

It seems fair to say that many non-lawyers working in the field of European integration have been unaware of or unwilling to accept the role that law can play in the policy-making process

---

[55] Ginsburg (1992, p 1), supra, note 20.

[56] With some very notable exceptions, including, for example, the work of Meehan, E. (1995) *Citizenship and the European Community*, London: Sage; Gregory, J. (1995) 'Sexual harassment: making the best use of European law', *European Journal of Women's Studies*, vol 2, no 4, pp 421-41; Hervey, T. (1998) *European social law and policy*, Harlow: Addison Wesley Longman Ltd.

> ... Ultimately, it cannot be denied that the Court of Justice is an institutional actor with a considerable degree of autonomy and normative influence, which plays a significant role in the Community's policy-making process.[57]

A cursory examination of the majority of social science texts on European social policy will reveal a fairly common model which includes a broad summary of social policy provisions within the Treaties, and in more enlightened texts, some coverage of key secondary legislation, complemented with a description of the various action plans and Commission programmes. There is rarely any attention to the funding arrangements to give some impression of the scope and potential impact of policies (in the case of the structural funds, for example) nor to the respective legal strength of the instruments.

While detailed analysis of areas of policy developments in childcare, sexual harassment or the poverty programmes may prove very interesting material for a normative analysis of the EC it tells us little about the impact of EU social policy on national systems, or upon citizens. Indeed, it may actually create a misleading impression of a far more proactive and effective intervention than is justified in practice. An interesting example of this approach can be seen in Linda Hantrais' recent book which is widely used as an introductory text in undergraduate courses on European social policy[58]. While providing detailed coverage of the key areas of EU competency in the social field, it pays little attention to the European Court of Justice as a key actor in the European policy-making process, not simply in the implementation and interpretation of 'the law' but in shaping the evolution of individual entitlement. In common with most other work of this nature, it is only in the section on 'Women, welfare and citizenship' that the Court is mentioned as a factor in the development of women's rights and as a precursor to important secondary legislation. Despite the welcome and unusual attention to the right to free movement, as a dimension of European social policy, there is no discussion of how the provisions detailed translate into practical legal rights for migrants. This text is by no means unique; the same could be said for most other key

---

[57] de Burca, G. (1998) 'The principle of subsidiarity and the Court of Justice as an institutional actor', *Journal of Common Market Studies*, vol 36, no 2, pp 217-37.
[58] Hantrais, L. (1995) *Social policy in the European Union*, London: Macmillan.

undergraduate texts[59] and reflects a common limitation of traditional social policy. This failure to draw the role of the Courts into the analysis of European social policy or to consider the legal status of various instruments and interventions, results in a distorted view of EU competency, in some cases leading to a misleading impression of proactivity while in others, to a serious underestimation of its impact[60]. Liebfried and Pierson argue that the general effect of this tendency to focus attention on 'formal' policies has been to reinforce a widespread and mistaken assumption of minimal EU involvement in the social field:

> **The dismissal of claims that a significant EU role now exists in social policy are largely based on examination of 'high politics' ... Lost amidst the noisy fights over Social Charters and Social Protocols has been the quiet accumulation of EC constraints on social policy connected with market integration ... the gradual if incremental expansion of Community-produced regulations and, especially, court decisions that have seriously eroded national welfare-state sovereignties.[61]**

Legal researchers, on the other hand, are often only too ready to dismiss areas of policy as 'soft law' and, therefore, of relatively little consequence despite the influence of these initiatives on future policy development, as a precursor to new legal developments or, at national level, in creating pressures for harmonisation. Despite the undoubted skill of many legal scholars in the painstaking mapping of the scope of individual rights through meticulous analysis of legal instruments and case law, legal researchers often pay scant attention to the social context within which the law is operating and the practical impact of 'theoretical' legal rights. This type of analysis assumes that 'citizenship' can be operationalised through a detailed comparison of formal legal rights which, one assumes, translate into social reality. For such a comparison to have any value,

---

[59] See, for example, Room, G. (1991) *Towards a European welfare state*, Bristol: SAUS Publications, or perhaps the most commonly used text edited by J. Bailey (1992) *Social Europe*, London: Longman.

[60] The role of the European Court of Justice in the evolution of citizenship rights under the free movement provisions is referred to in much more detail in Chapter Four.

[61] Liebfried, S. and Pierson, P. (1996) 'Social policy', in H. Wallace and W. Wallace (eds) *Policy-making in the European Union*, Oxford: Oxford University Press, pp 185-207 at p 193.

however, requires that such policies are fully and effectively implemented (and funded), that citizens are aware of and understand them, are able and willing to exercise them and that they are of some tangible and meaningful benefit to them (and that they do not suffer detriment as a result of unintended consequences). The strength of social policy analysis in identifying problems of policy failure, through lack of resources, non-implementation, professional practice, cultural resistance (or stigma), lack of awareness or problems in the exercise of rights has demonstrated the limitations of much traditional legal scholarship. Unfortunately, however, these lessons are often ignored in comparative social policy analysis where it is often easier to simply document and describe and infer some outcome.

This is one of the key failures of the kind of policy description characteristic of the structured diversity approach which not only adopts a limited definition of policy but also makes little attempt to evaluate the outcome. The very existence of policies such as State-provided nursery places or paternity leave are thus cited as evidence of the normative character of systems (and a reflection of their commitment to gender equality, for example) when, in practice, there is little evidence that this is what women want nor, indeed, that rights are exercised. It may be, for example, that the greater socialisation of care in some countries actually restricts the choices available to women, reinforcing the work ethic and the dual burden of work and care[62]. On the other hand, evidence of high levels of full-time working by mothers (as an outcome measure) cannot be taken as indicative of normative intention when it may, in practice, reflect other social factors such as economic hardship and not autonomy. Without more detailed primary research (and qualitative work) the relationship between formal policy and citizenship is difficult to predict.

Some authors go further and argue that the research focus on, and pursuit of, formal equality (as a political strategy) may actually legitimise inequality, creating a "diversionary tactic for patriarchy"[63]. Such critiques have raised the importance of meaning and outcomes – and of analyses which document the impact of policies on people's lives[64]. A policy which

---

[62] This issue is developed in Chapter Seven.

[63] Forbes, I. (1991) 'Equal opportunity: radical, liberal and conservative critiques' in E. Meehan and S. Sevenhuijsen (eds) *Equality, politics and gender*, London: Sage.

[64] O'Connor, J.S. (1993) 'Gender class and citizenship in the comparative analysis of welfare states; theoretical and methodological issues', *British Journal of Sociology*, vol 44, no 3, September, pp 501-19; Lister, R. (1990) 'Women, economic dependency and citizenship', *Journal of Social Policy*, vol 19, no 4, pp 445-69.

may look particularly progressive on paper (such as a father's entitlement to parental leave in some Scandinavian countries) may not, in practice, make much difference. Furthermore, the unintended consequences of formally adopted equal opportunities policies may result in the evolution of more covert forms of discrimination and strategies of circumvention or avoidance which, when coupled with policy-related backlash, may further embed disadvantage. Julia O'Connor makes a similar point when she says that, "Scandinavian experience points to the fact that policies must be examined not only in terms of formal equality but also in terms of their outcome"[65]. It is worth reminding ourselves at this juncture, that policy 'successes' under Article 119 EEC, in common with other equal opportunities legislation, have often operated to the detriment of women[66].

While this section has focused on the limitations of analyses which presume a relation between statutory policies and the experiences of citizens as consumers (or users), any comprehensive and holistic evaluation of policy must include within it consideration of citizens' experiences as providers. This is particularly important in feminist analyses given the concentration of women in caring work across all sectors of welfare provision (as employees and unpaid carers).

A second major problem with the policy concept, referred to by Ginsburg in the quote above, relates not to the difficulty of selecting aspects of active policy for evaluation but rather to the empirically problematic issue of non-decision or policy omission as a key component of outcome. The availability of official statistics, policy documents and cases encourages a research focus on areas of government *activity*, concealing whole areas of inactivity or non-decision making. It may also obscure important implications of policy withdrawal (or the retraction of funding leaving only a skeletal policy rhetoric in place). These limitations are particularly important in relation to family or gender policy where policy inertia, as well as control through the manipulation of political or popular culture and professional practice, has as much influence on citizenship as 'active' policies. The importance of informal care in the provision of welfare and, consequently, of social status more generally, is emphasised in the following statement by Cochrane and Clarke: "a central feature of social policy in

---

[65] O'Connor (1993, p 509), supra, note 64.
[66] This is particularly evident in cases where compliance is achieved through 'levelling-down' measures. The UK response to the European Court of Justice's ruling on the equalisation of pensionable ages in occupational pension schemes, for example, has effectively reduced women's entitlement.

developed capitalist countries is to be found in the way it defines and constructs families as sources of informal welfare supply"[67]. The collection of public data reflects prevailing public policy (and dominant political ideology) in the countries or regions selected and as such is unlikely to provide comprehensive information on those areas of social life seen to fall outside of the responsibility/interference of the State at that point in time (which will, of course, vary by country). Where governments have questioned the legitimacy of State involvement in family relations and social reproduction[68], there is unlikely to be much information available at national level. The ideology of non-intervention in the private sphere of 'family', and all that goes with that in terms of social reproduction translates into a convenient methodology of concealment. Elizabeth Wilson suggests that social policy making is grounded in deeply embedded assumptions about women, "which sometimes operate at the level of 'taken for granted' and sometimes as part of deliberate planning for women. Sometimes, that is, it seems as if policy makers simply reproduce unthinkingly traditional, unquestioned views about women's role"[69]. A similar point is made by Anne Oakley when she summarises the way in which (masculine) social science, in focusing attention on certain areas of social reality, simultaneously focuses attention *away* from others (those which concern women) in the words, "a way of seeing is a way of not seeing"[70].

Informal care has very limited expression in official statistics and public policy statements and yet is a crucial factor in considering the impact of citizenship. The result is a focus, in comparative research, on statutory welfare (public life) to the neglect of information on informal, voluntary and private provision – areas which dominate welfare provision in all Member States. In his recent text on comparative social policy, Michael Hill introduces his chapter on 'Social care' with a statement referring to the "relative absence of comparative material ... There is a lack of a common

---

[67] Cochrane and Clarke (1993, p 5), supra, note 4.

[68] Forbes, supra, note 63. Scheiwe, K. (1994) 'EC law's unequal treatment of the family: the case law of the European Court of Justice on rules prohibiting discrimination on grounds of sex and nationality', *Social and Legal Studies,* vol 3, no 2, June, pp 243-65.

[69] Wilson, E. (1983) 'Feminism and social policy', in M. Loney, D. Boswell and J. Clarke (eds) *Social policy and social welfare,* Buckingham: Open University Press, p 33.

[70] Oakley, A. (1974) *The sociology of housework,* London: Martin Roberston, p 27.

pool of ideas, data and concepts which facilitate comparison"[71]. The reasons for this vacuum, he suggests, are twofold. Firstly, that social care is less easy to identify in policy terms given its interconnectedness with other services. Secondly, "there are particularly strong problems about identifying the circumstances in which social care problems emerge from that category of issues which are regarded as personal or family concerns to become those of wider society, and especially the state"[72]. The 'guide to further reading' at the end of his chapter is also of interest, expressing once again the dearth of comparative literature on social care. Hill refers the interested reader to Munday's *European social services*[73] which he describes as, "a largely descriptive account of policies in various European countries". He then refers to the growing literature on payments for care[74] which he uses extensively in his chapter. This reference is interesting as it illustrates the fact that, not only does the remuneration of informal care pull an hitherto 'private' matter into the public domain, it also renders it visible by its presence in public expenditure statistics. In many ways this summary provides a good example of the development of comparative method and the dominance of public expenditure related approaches and descriptive case study work.

Measuring 'outcomes'

Recognition of the limitations of both welfare modelling (based on official statistics) and the structured diversity approach, with its emphasis on the evaluation and comparison of 'theoretical' policy inputs, has lead to the development of new research approaches designed to evaluate outcome or impact. One example of such an initiative can be seen in the work of Jonathan Bradshaw et al on child benefit packages in 15 countries[75]. Using public expenditure statistics as a basis for the identification of research questions, these researchers then turned to micro-policy analysis, collecting data via a team of national 'informants' on the range of benefits and services

---

[71] Hill (1996, p 126), supra, note 3.
[72] Supra, note 71.
[73] Munday, B. (ed) (1993) *European social services*, Canterbury: University of Kent.
[74] This literature is refered to in more detail in Chapter Nine.
[75] Bradshaw, J., Ditch, J., Holmes, H. and Whiteford, P. (1993) *Support for children*, Department of Social Security Research Report 21, London: HMSO.

---

for families with children in the countries surveyed[76]. This data is then used to simulate how child benefit packages impact on a range of predetermined 'model' families in each country and to evaluate the redistributive impact of such systems. In designing the research, the team were very aware of the limitations of attempts to classify welfare states on the basis of institutional arrangements alone (that is, policy inputs or formal policies), arguing for more detailed analysis of policy outcomes (on the grounds that successful redistribution may be achieved by a range of system types). In particular, the study stresses the impact of child benefit packages as a mechanism for social redistribution:

> ... family benefits played no part in the Esping-Andersen de-commodification index. But they might have done, for as we have seen child benefits have as one of their possible objectives to reduce pressure for increased earnings. They are a source of income independent of the market which might reduce the need for a second earner in the family and enable lone parents to bring up their children without recourse to the market.[77]

In order to avoid straightforward 'system comparison', which may simply compare the way systems *should* work rather than how they do work, the focus on policy outcome was achieved via the construct of 'model' families which were then used as the basis for comparison in each country. In an interesting comment, Bradshaw et al justify this approach in the following way:

> Choices have to be made about the circumstances and characteristics of the model families and the more choices that are made, the less representative the particular model families are of the range of real families. This problem with the model family method cannot be overcome and has to be faced. It is the cost of achieving comparability, and comparability is a more

---

[76] While reliant on the contribution of a team of national experts, this project avoids the 'state-by-State' format of research based around the kind of networks described above through more detailed analysis and thematic presentation of material in the final report, although arguments about coordination and control of research agendas by Northern European countries may still be present.

[77] Bradshaw et al (1993, p 95), supra, note 75.

important quality in comparative research than representativeness.[78]

The final point in the quote reflects a concern over standardisation and comparability which has, in some respects, stultified comparative research. In reacting against the descriptive case study approach and seeking to develop methods which support a level of theorisation and generalisation, many of us have fallen into the trap identified by Lisle (above, p 53) – of treating comparative research as a form of controlled experiment. My own more recent experience of comparative research suggests that a little more flexibility should be permitted in the research process; while initial project design may endeavour to promote a level of standardisation, as the research unfolds there may be important reasons why particular partners should be encouraged to deviate from the 'blueprint' to take account of the distinctiveness of certain national or local contexts and to avoid researching 'artefacts'. In that sense our commitment to comparability is not to the detriment of relevance.

Notwithstanding its importance in developing a means of studying outcomes, this approach has limitations: researchers were unable, for example, to assess the impact of non-take-up or the response of 'real' families to policies. Furthermore, the construction of the models was undertaken by the UK-based coordinating team and resulted in the design of models which did not translate particularly well into another cultural context. Neither was it possible to take full account of the contribution of the informal sector.

Michaela Schunk uses a similar approach in her comparative qualitative work on care options for elderly people[79]. Focusing again on welfare outcomes, and using the construct of model families, or a 'policy simulation approach', she provides some important insights into the operation of social entitlements from the users' perspectives (including both elderly persons and carers).

This development of the structured diversity approach with its emphasis on policy outcome and effectiveness takes us a step forward in the direction of a more meaningful analysis of citizenship. It stops short, however, of an attempt to evaluate the genuine impact of policies on citizens, their perceptions and exercise of 'social rights' and the meaning they attach to

---

[78] Bradshaw et al (1993, p 56), supra, note 75.
[79] Schunk, M. (1996) 'Constructing models of the welfare mix: care options of frail elders', in Hantrais and Mangen, supra, note 10.

---

them. This type of analysis can only be achieved through more qualitative forms of research involving citizens as active participants in the research process. The translation of formal policies into citizenship experiences cannot simply be measured in terms of crude indices of employment status, labour market participation and numbers of places in State nurseries – or predicted outcomes for 'model citizens' – but must consider how people interpret and negotiate constraints, how they experience welfare systems and how, within those constraints, they make choices. Most importantly of all, we need to develop methods of examining, empirically, how men and women experience and attribute meaning to formal frameworks. Cochrane and Clarke were ready to admit that, despite the collection of rich and important data on family and childcare policy in Sweden, on the basis of information collected, "it is not clear what women want"[80]. The limitations they refer to here may reflect, to some extent, the methodological shortcomings of an approach which stops short of any engagement with women themselves.

Feminist approaches to research: applicability at comparative level

The discussion above has focused on the limitations of existing attempts to operationalise the citizenship concept at comparative level noting, in particular, the tendency of traditional methods to obscure the gender dimension. This was evident not only in the technical and epistemological weaknesses of secondary analysis but also in the discussion about policy vacuums and outcomes. Apart from some attempts to 'add women in' to existing analytical frameworks, largely through a redefinition of indices, the response of feminist research has been somewhat restricted, leading to a situation in which, as O'Connor puts it, "there is an absence of gender analysis in almost all comparative research while most studies that focus on gender are not comparative"[81].

This absence of gender analysis in comparative research (if not in feminist theoretical contribution) is of particular concern given the general trend across European welfare systems in the direction of increased reliance upon informal social infrastructures (the corollary of welfare retrenchment)

---

[80] Cochrane and Clarke (1993, p 196), supra, note 4.
[81] O'Connor, supra, note 15. A point also made in Bussemaker and van Kersbergen, supra, note 14.

and on women as informal care-givers. In this context, and, in spite of considerable theoretical and secondary work on family and gender issues, Prue Chamberlayne and Annette King point to the absence of "primary, cross-national, qualitative research ... conducted into the dynamics of the informal sector"[82]. Furthermore, increasing interest in theoretical work on issues of democratisation and the exploration of agency as well as structure, they contend, calls for new directions in comparative research; "Understanding 'the subject' and relations between the personal and the social in welfare requires a turn to qualitative methods, and their development for comparative purposes"[83].

Outlining their own approach to comparative research centred on the use of individual biographies, Chamberlayne and King attempt to interpret the underlying personal meanings and family dynamics in caring situations and their foundations in informal structures and cultures, identifying not only responses to formal policy but also the unintended consequences of policy.

The important contribution of feminist research, at national level, in casting light on whole areas of social policy, rendering women visible and redefining the citizenship concept, particularly through detailed research on family obligations, informal care and unpaid work has, to some extent, been lost in comparative work. This may, in part, reflect the nature of funding processes (and the fostering of hierarchy and elitism) but also a reluctance to identify the relevance or applicability of feminist epistemology at comparative level. While comparative analysis has promoted the development of hierarchically-managed systems approaches using positivist methods of enquiry, feminist critiques have encouraged the use of more reflexive, qualitative and ethnographic work which seeks to understand and represent women's interpretations of the impact of social structure on their lives; to use research as a means of giving women a voice. These critiques have fostered the use of small-scale, in-depth, studies in which feminist researchers work closely alongside women research participants, often in autobiographical or life-history work. Janet Finch, in her analysis of feminist social policy research refers to the, "Strong and influential arguments in favour of qualitative research ... [and the] major emphasis (within the feminist debate on research methods) upon the value of small-

---

[82] Chamberlayne, P. and King, A. (1996) 'Biographical approaches in comparative work: the "Cultures of Care" Project', in Hantrais and Mangen (1996, p 96), supra, note 10.
[83] Supra, note 82.

scale, qualitative methods for research which seeks to make visible the needs and experiences of women"[84].

To some extent this association of 'good' feminist work with a particular methodological approach (and a preference for small-scale, in-depth qualitative work, with an emphasis on experience and meaning) – together with the widespread rejection of large-scale surveys – discourages comparative work. Not only is it difficult to envisage the applicability of this type of research on a comparative scale, the cost and management implications may seem insurmountable.

While noting feminist criticisms of the survey method on both technical (and in that sense, remediable) and epistemological grounds, Finch suggests that quantitative research may have positive value for feminists in certain contexts, particularly in making visible certain aspects of gender relations (such as low pay or occupational segregation, for example). To seek to understand the processes leading to this situation, however, requires that we ask a different kind of question which may require different research techniques. In that sense, Finch rejects the notion that particular methods are inherently 'sexist' or more exploitative to women, "I do not take the view that we should espouse a single 'correct feminist method'"[85]. Stanley and Wise make a similar point when they say that, "methods in themselves aren't innately anything ... what should be objected to about [positivist methods] isn't quantification or their use of statistical techniques. It is their assumption about the nature of reality, and about the relationship between researcher and researched, which should be rejected"[86].

Hantrais and Mangen conclude their chapter on methods in cross-national research with the statement that, while there is nothing particularly distinctive about the methodology of cross-national research, it may demand "greater compromises in method ... Successful cross-national collaboration is often characterised by the variety of methodologies adopted and the range of disciplinary inputs"[87]. The benefits of multi-method and multi-disciplinary approaches are not unique to comparative method and have

---

[84] Finch, J. (1991) 'Feminist research and social policy', in M. Maclean and D. Groves (eds) *Women's issues in social policy*, London: Routledge, pp 194-205 at p 195.

[85] Finch (1991, p 198) supra, note 84.

[86] A view also expressed by Morgan, D. (1991) 'Men, masculinity and the process of sociological enquiry', in H. Roberts (ed) *Doing feminist research*, London: Routledge and Kegan Paul, pp 83-113.

[87] Hantrais and Mangen (1996, p 12), supra, note 19.

long been recognised in social science research. Rather than constrain the production of feminist social science, through the application of methodological blinkers, it is perhaps more fruitful to consider the objectives of feminist research and then seek to identify a research strategy which takes us in the direction of those goals rather then leaving the field entirely. Stanley and Wise stress the importance of research which consciously seeks to inform policies and advance feminist strategy:

> **Closely associated with the interpretation of feminist research as research on women and by women is the notion that it ought also to be research for women. The product of feminist research should be directly used by women in order to formulate policies and provisions necessary for feminist activities.**[88]

Janet Finch is a little more cautious, accepting that the key criterion, that good feminist research should actively promote women's interests, may be difficult to achieve; indeed even meeting what she calls the "minimum criterion of not damaging other women's interests" can be more difficult than it seems in practice[89]. More specifically, Claire Ungerson, in noting increasing interest in qualitative approaches to comparative work, suggests that this derives in part from shifting objectives reflecting a, "general desire to use research to understand how private lives are affected by, and interact with, public issues and policies ... a commitment to detail ... and to a whole story which includes how private lives relate to structure"[90].

The work referred to by Ungerson, in her analysis of developments in cross-national qualitative research, represents an important departure in comparative method, demonstrating not only the need for qualitative work but also suggesting practical models for its application. By failing to engage themselves in this type of work, feminists are restricting their input into the policy-making process and also missing the opportunity to develop important collaborative liaisons with feminists abroad.

Alternative methods of empirical enquiry, in comparative research, are evidently required, informed by feminist critiques of 'traditional' research methods, which seek to examine not only the formal citizenship context, but also the meaning people ascribe to that, their awareness and subjective

---

[88] Stanley, L. and Wise, S. (1993) *Breaking out again: Feminist ontology and epistemology*, London: Routledge, p 32.

[89] Finch (1991, p 199), supra, note 84.

[90] Ungerson (1996, p 64), supra, note 24.

response to it and the way in which it moulds and shapes their lives. Traditional comparative research, not least because of the financial implications and the geographical scope of the work, has promoted a very hierarchical form of research management with relatively few institutions and researchers dominating the field; precisely the sort of approach to research which has been criticised by feminist academics on the grounds that women, as academics themselves, may find it hard to gain access to the networks and funding opportunities, but also because it increases the tendency to treat women as research objects rather than as subjects and active participants in the design, execution and dissemination of research. An approach is therefore called for which adopts a less hierarchical research strategy, involving the development of genuinely collaborative research partnerships working together in the planning and execution of research, thereby overcoming some of the limitations traditionally ascribed to comparative work (in terms of culture, ethnocentrism and linguistic problems).

The following section outlines the approach used in the gender and migration project. It considers issues of project management, the methods employed in data collection and analysis and reflects upon the benefits and limitations of these.

The gender and migration project

This research project has attempted to respond to some of the weaknesses of previous approaches discussed above. In particular it has attempted to combine a variety of techniques including formal policy-evaluation (of case law and legislation), the analysis of aggregate secondary data at national and European level and in-depth interviewing creating both quantitative and qualitative output. In this way the aggregate data creates a tentative framework for the research, giving some indication of the representativeness of the sample. At the same time, the validity of the secondary data is itself subject to testing against national statistics and the interview data. This approach achieves a breadth of information without sacrificing depth and permits women's own perceptions and experiences to be taken into account. It also illuminates areas of women's lives, of key importance to their citizenship experience, which are concealed in statistical sources (such as the interaction of caring with employment, for example).

In addition to responding to some of the limitations of previous comparative research in the broad field of social scientific enquiry (and comparative social policy analysis, in particular), this project has also attempted to develop a framework for genuinely interdisciplinary, socio-legal research combining some of the approaches of traditional legal research with the techniques of social science to maximise the range of skills, breadth of knowledge, insight and, hopefully also, the policy relevance and impact of the research. In that sense it is both multi-disciplinary and multi-method in its approach[91].

Project management and the role of partners

In order to undertake the research, partnerships were developed in the four partner countries. The first stage of the research involved the identification of suitable partners and preliminary discussions with each partner, individually, over project objectives, timetables, and approach. These meetings played an important role in finalising the funding proposal. Once funded, a team meeting was organised, involving all partners, to plan the research and discuss methods and reporting procedures. The partners were responsible for the organisation and supervision of empirical work in the Member States. Although each partner undertook to present an interim report based on national migration data they were not responsible for data analysis nor production of the final report as funding did not allow for this and it proved 'expedient' for this to take place in one location. Partners were free, but not obliged, to disseminate findings at national level and to comment on the reports. A second team meeting took place following the piloting of the interviews to discuss issues of sampling and our respective experiences of interviewing (and transcribing etc) and to make any changes in the topics covered.

A multi-method approach

In terms of method, the research involved work at three levels. The first stage involved an examination of the legal framework (in European Community law) underpinning the development of European citizenship through an analysis of the relevant legislation and case law to determine both the formal legal context and also the role of the European Court of Justice in the policy-making process and its interpretation of the gender

---

[91] See the project outline in Chapter One or, for a summary of the research approach, see Ackers, H.L. (1995) 'Women, citizenship and European Community law: the gender implications of the free movement provisions', *Journal of Social Welfare and Family Law*, vol 17, no 4, pp 498-502.

dynamics. In this type of research, cases essentially constitute a form of imperfect primary textual data. While not verbatim reports, as such, they nevertheless reveal much about the thought processes underpinning specific judgments. The primary purpose of this phase of the research, which took place prior to the empirical work in Member States, was not only to detail the formal or theoretical legal position but, through an examination of the cases, to identify the presumptions about social relations and migration behaviour that were guiding the Court in its deliberations. The purpose of the subsequent empirical work was twofold: to evaluate the relationship between formal rights and citizenship experience (the material impact of law and policy) and also to assess the empirical basis of those presumptions.

The second element of the study examined the extent to which the dominant model of migration – as male breadwinning, profit-maximising, behaviour evident in both the academic literature and the Court's decision making – is founded on sound empirical evidence or is simply a convenient ideological construct. Evidence was collected from tables commissioned from Eurostat, based on the European LFS (1992)[92]. While the previous section has gone to some effort to caution extreme vigilance in the use of official statistics in comparative analysis, this does not imply that such data has no valid use in research. In rejecting outright the potential offered by secondary data, social researchers cut themselves off from important sources which may both contextualise their research and raise key questions, in the initial stages of a project, for subsequent appraisal[93].

---

[92] Specific sources used include the following: the Guarini study (1994), which involved both static and time-series analysis (based upon data from the previous three LFSs, 1983, 1986 and 1991). The 1991 LFS excluded figures for Italy as Italy did not collect data on foreign residents in Italy although data on the presence of Italians in other countries was available; Eurostat (1994) *Demographic statistics* (Population and Social Conditions); Eurostat (1993a) *Results of the Labour Force Survey, 1991*, Luxembourg: Office for Official Publications of the European Communities; Eurostat (1993b) *Population by citizenship in the EC*, Population and Social Conditions Rapid Reports No 6; Eurostat (1993c) *Female population by citizenship in the EC*, Population and Social Conditions Rapid Reports No 8; OECD (1994) *Trends in international migration*, SOPEMI Annual Report 1993, London: HMSO; Salt, J., Singleton, A. and Hogarth, J. (1994) *Europe's international migrants*, London: HMSO.

[93] Bulmer, M. (1980) 'Why don't sociologists make more use of official statistics?', *Sociology*, vol 14, no 4, pp 505-23, reprinted in Bulmer, M. (ed) (1984) *Sociological research methods: An introduction*, London: Macmillan.

The European Labour Force Survey (ELFS) has been described by Hakim as, "the most important single source of socio-economic data on the European Community as a whole"[94]. The Statistical Office of the EU (Eurostat) is responsible for publishing EU-wide statistics on the population of working age and particularly on the workforce. The data is not collected by the EU directly but by national statistical offices. The EU sets out certain requirements and standards but Member States collect the data in a variety of ways. Some countries do not collect all the requisite data; the 1991 data, for example, does not include migration data for Italy and more recent ELFS data does not include a gender breakdown for at least five of the Member States. There are also problems in ensuring that each country defines and measures phenomena in the same way. Eurostat itself adds a cautionary note:

> The data must be interpreted with circumspection: they are based on varying national definitions and practices. Some data are drawn from the census, others from administrative records; yet others from the [national] Labour Force Survey. Further complications arise because the procedures for acquiring citizenship of the host country also vary from one Member State to another.[95]

Some of the problems of using ELFS data, particularly on migration-related topics have been referred to above. Because the ELFS is primarily concerned with the labour force, it does not provide data on unpaid work such as informal care and unpaid domestic work (apart from 'unpaid family work'). To that extent it is unable to tell us very much about the lives of women, many of whom are involved in this area of informal, invisible work. Published Eurostat data includes very little information on internal migration. Special tables were therefore commissioned from Eurostat for this research. Where possible the reliability of these figures has been ensured through cross-checking with data from the Guarini report which includes time-series data over a number of years[96]. What this data gives us is some indication of the characteristics of nationals compared to the EU migrants

---

[94] Hakim, C. (1991) 'Cross-national comparative research on the European Community: the EC Labour Force Surveys', *Work, Employment and Society*, vol 5, no 1, pp 101-17 at p 101.

[95] Eurostat (1993b), supra, note 92.

[96] Hakim (1991), supra, note 94.

resident in that country. We are thus comparing, for example, UK nationals with EU migrants in the UK, by gender. In many cases it is difficult to break down the data further, by nationality, as the numbers are considered too small to be statistically significant and are not, therefore, provided. Because this data is based on country of residence it is not possible to make comparisons between nationals and nationals who have migrated (for example, Irish women resident in Ireland compared to Irish women residing in other EU countries). Neither does it give us any indication of the characteristics of return migrants as these would be classified as nationals by the ELFS.

Such data is, however, useful if only to provide a broad framework for further study giving us a broad picture of migration flows between Member States and regions, by gender, together with some general background information on the characteristics of EU migrants. The range of indices available includes material on labour force participation, occupational status, educational background, socioeconomic group, demography and fertility, marital status and length of residence. Although this data was collected, much of it proved less than useful for a broad analysis of the characteristics of the population of migrant women[97]. The data on migration flows and the broad demographic characteristics of the EU migrant population did, however, raise very interesting questions which were subject to more detailed analysis in the following phase of primary data collection.

The central empirical focus of the project was on the detailed life-history interviews with migrant women in the five Member States. Given the problems of defining a population from which to sample in a project of this nature, the project team used a variety of approaches (contacting employers, Embassies, colleges and migrant organisations etc) to find a sample. Once a number of contacts had been made a snowballing method was used. We were careful to select women from a range of income groups, from both core and peripheral areas[98] and across as broad a range

---

[97] The data on occupational status and social class was not used in the final analysis as the categories were very complex and static and reflected all the problems of assigning women into pre-set groups. The data on educational qualification was also finally disregarded as it proved very difficult to compare, in any meaningful way, different forms of qualifications across Europe. The ELFS data is reported in more detail in the Interim Report to the European Commission: 'Internal migration within the European Union: the presence of women in migration flows and the characteristics of female migrants' (H.L. Ackers, 1995).

[98] Census data enabled us to identify regions in the UK, for example, that received large or small proportions of this population.

of nationalities as possible. A total of 341 women were interviewed. The interviews were designed to collect both quantitative and qualitative data. In relation to the former the type of data collected was comparable to that represented in the ELFS. The qualitative dimension is concerned with women's experiences of migration and its impact on their autonomy. During the interviews women were encouraged to talk about their migration history, their experiences of the migration process and its impact on:

- family/informal care networks
- career and financial autonomy
- identity (including a sense of feeling 'European')
- general quality of life (including experience of welfare systems)
- awareness and exercise of Community rights.

The interviews also covered discussion of household decision-making processes and any conflicts that arose at the time, or subsequent reappraisals. The interview schedule took the form of a list of topics. In most cases it was not necessary to ask any specific questions but merely to set women on the track, recounting their life-history from the point of leaving school or migrating (where they migrated as a child) and simply intervening at certain points to seek clarification and checking, towards the end of the interview, that all relevant topics had been covered. On many occasions women would ask for more information, either specifically about their rights or to enquire about the experiences of other women interviewed. There was no attempt to deflect such questions and all attempts were made to answer queries or get back to women with answers where these could not be provided 'on the spot'. This was discussed in the team meetings and proved an important means of ensuring that interviewees had access to the wider range of expertise, in such a multi-disciplinary project, than that of the interviewer alone. Team meetings were also used as a means of disseminating information, mainly on the EU legal framework, which could then not only inform partners, but also filter through to respondents[99].

The quality and character of the interviews varied quite considerably, largely reflecting the commitment or interests of the woman concerned and, on occasions her work, family commitments or the presence or

---

[99] In the two current projects, on children and migration and retirement migration, this aspect of team meetings as a means of sharing information across the team is being built in much more explicitly with partners contributing via presentation of papers.

impending presence of her partner or children. Some women had very clear views about what an 'interview' should be like and expected to be asked structured questions. In some cases they were relieved not to have this structure imposed. While all attempts were made to ensure that language problems did not prevent women being selected, in practice it often shaped their responses, particularly if the language used was not their first language. In some cases women insisted on being interviewed in their second language, making a statement about their identity.

The 'problem' of language was compounded by the need to translate the interviews; the significant burden of translation and transcription meant that final transcripts were not verbatim reports as such but the product of a 'filtering' process. Each filter was a woman in her own right, a subject, with ideas and values which doubtless coloured their perception of what the respondent was attempting to convey, what priority to attach to issues and how to articulate them. In that sense the project could not be said to be genuinely, 'letting women speak for themselves'. The greater the geographical scope of a project and the more actors involved in the research process the further we get from each individual woman. This problem is particularly difficult in comparative research where it is less easy to have regular 'debriefing' sessions. To some extent we can attempt to control this through restricting the number of research workers involved in the process[100].

In addition, each interviewer was asked to record her subjective responses to the interviews – or indeed any particular events or contexts which affected the process in any way (such as having a child or husband present, for example) – in a memo preceding the actual transcript. In attempting to render these factors explicit, rather than sanitising the product through a policy of concealment, we are producing a more honest and valid research output. Criticising the tendency even of 'naturalism' to present research as orderly, coherent and logically organised (or 'hygienic'), concealing the 'messiness' of empirical work, Stanley and Wise refer to the tendency

---

[100] The use of 'contract researchers' to undertake interviewing, for example, complicates processes and reduces information flows, even if such a practice may reflect attempts to dismantle the professionalism and mystique of research and empower women as researchers. My experience of this project suggests that minimising the number of researchers in each country improves the overall quality of communication and facilitates limited standardisation. A policy of ensuring that all partners conduct at least a proportion of the interviews personally similarly promotes quality. This may of course prove difficult where time-scales are short, academic schedules onerous and funding limited.

within feminist research to, "systematically downgrade the importance of the personal and of experience"[101]. One example of this is the attempt to deny or conceal the personal, subjective, response of the interviewer herself.

The recording of 'contextual' material in the memo preceding the interview transcript proved a very useful aid to the interpretation of the transcript itself. In some cases it simply stated that the interview was interrupted by noise or the arrival of friends – or the fact that the respondent had a short lunch hour – whereas, in others, it recorded more interesting facets of the research process. The following 'memos' give some indication of the type of detail recorded by interviewers:

> **The interview took place in the interviewee's home, and from the minute I got there the interviewee's husband didn't leave my or his wife's side, which did effect the interview process, not least because he constantly interrupted and took over when the interviewee tried to explain or elaborate her answers. This was very frustrating. He also tended to correct the answers his wife gave me, which resulted in her acceptance of his description of the reality of her emotions and experiences. Also the 15-year-old son was at home at the time of the interview and he sat next to his mother, clinging on to her, hugging and padding her all the time.[102]**

> **The interview was held in her apartment (which recently had been renovated in an Italian style), at the request of the interviewee, since she had her baby to look after.[103]**

> **She was very suspicious and extremely conscious of the tape to the extent that she said more about her life and her feelings once I had switched off the recorder. I think she accepted to be interviewed mainly because she wanted or needed someone to talk to and show her beautiful garden to.[104]**

In some cases much more detail was given, reflecting not only the context

---

[101] Stanley, L. and Wise, S. (1993) *Breaking out again: Feminist ontology and epistemology*, London: Routledge, p 160.

[102] Interviewee D240 (Sweden).

[103] Interviewee D205 (Sweden).

[104] Interviewee D026 (UK).

of the interview but also the interviewer's subjective response to the situation and its impact on the research process. The following memo is reproduced in detail to reflect the relationship between the two women involved:

> The interview was conducted in the respondent's own house and no one else was present. Louise lives on the fifth floor of a housing association/council block estate and she has minimal possessions. Louise was sewing when I arrived. The more interesting information was not recorded on the tape because Louise got very upset and I turned off the recorder. The interview lasted one and a half hours but only forty minutes is recorded. At first I thought this interview was a complete disaster and in many respects it could have been conducted with greater skill. Louise started crying on a couple of occasions near the beginning when I made reference to family members and this threw me and I felt completely out of my depth and out of control. I just wanted to leave as soon as possible. Who was I, more than half of Louise's age, to come to her home and intrude on what were obviously very sensitive issues. I didn't feel confident to probe but in retrospect I could have done so as Louise really wanted to talk about her story and didn't mind my asking personal questions. However, it was really difficult to gauge the situation. What surprised me was that what I considered to be factual questions actually evoked sensitive issues. Louise didn't want me to leave and encouraged me to stay for something to eat or drink. I learnt that her husband mentally abuses her and makes her life a misery. He verbally attacks her by calling her a prostitute, a whore etc ... Her tears made me feel that I was imposing and I felt awkward although Louise did reassure me that she was glad to be able to reveal her story to me and apologised for telling such a sad tale. I felt it a privilege to be privy to Louise's story.[105]

Stanley and Wise, in their discussion of inter-subjectivity, refer to the 'dishonesty' of much feminist interactive methodology which claims to have broken down research hierarchies and to be undertaking research, not on but 'with' women. Rejecting what they call the 'fictitious sympathy'

---

[105] Interviewee D053 (UK)

approach as similar, in many respects, to positivism in its failure to acknowledge the importance of the "situated nature of the researcher [which] should form the very beginning and basis of social science work", they suggest that:

> **The best alternative is that researchers should present analytic accounts of how and why we think we know what we do about research situations and people in them. The only way we can avoid overriding other people's understandings as 'deficient' in some way is not to attempt to present these within research. Instead we should be much more concerned with presenting *ourselves* and *our* understandings of what is going on.**[106]

The recording of as much detail as possible in the memos, although this again varied depending on the response of the interviewer to different situations, constantly reminded us, in the analysis phase, that the transcript reflected a relationship and an interpretation of another woman's reality which is then further 'filtered' by the 'understandings' of the women involved in the data analysis and writing-up process and finally by the reader.

It was not possible, in this piece of research, given the geographical scale, and the separation of collection and analysis, together with the time and cost implications of a second phase of translation, to return transcripts to the women interviewed. This is, undoubtedly, an important means of not only ensuring that the interviewee is happy with the representation of her feelings, but also of triggering fresh responses, viewed by many feminist researchers as essential to the process; unfortunately the resources and time were not available to permit this[107].

Once translated and transcribed, the interviews were imported directly into a software package for qualitative data analysis (Nud*ist)[108] in order to preserve the quality of the findings while enabling various cross-tabulations to be made. With a sample of this size and the quantity of

---

[106] Stanley and Wise (1993, p 166), supra, note 101.

[107] In a recent trial on one of our current projects I found this process of returning transcripts both useful and problematic; in one case, for example, the respondent wished to rephrase her comments in order to promote a more 'respectable' image of her husband whom she had referred to as 'racist' in the first interview. I was thus obliged to do as she suggested and remove this reference.

[108] Non-numerical Unidimensional Data: Indexing, Selecting and Theorising.

---

qualitative data it would have been extremely cumbersome to have attempted to evaluate the women's responses manually.

The decision to analyse all the data in the UK was taken primarily for resource reasons (there was insufficient funding to pay researchers to undertake the analysis and also to buy multiple copies of the program). In practice, however, none of the members of the team had used computer-assisted analysis before and substantial investment of time was required to develop the necessary skills[109].

'Indexing' is the term used, in the Nud★ist program, to describe the organisation and categorisation of text. Rather than the researcher imposing a structure on the data, she starts with the first transcript and allows that to suggest key issues or categories. The relevance and appropriateness of this form of categorisation is subsequently tested against other transcripts and continually refined until it provides a meaningful, comprehensive and workable template against which to compare the interviews. The indexing process in the Nud★ist system thus supports a 'grounded theory' approach to the extent that it permits the data to suggest relevant categories for analysis. In practice, of course, the researcher comes into the process with various ideas about the data, reflecting both something about themselves as a person, their values and feminism, and their own experience in undertaking interviews. This latter fact, unchecked, can introduce a source of bias when the person involved in the analysis has undertaken a specified group of interviews (in one country or region, for example, as was the case in this project). Even after reading all the transcripts beforehand, my personal experience of interviewing migrant women in the South West of England and the specific issues these women raised undoubtedly coloured my approach to the indexing process. A considerable amount of time was spent in 'piloting' various forms of indexing, scrapping them (in the light of subsequent interviews) and starting again from scratch. This process was important in terms of 'theory-building' but proved far more time-consuming than we had envisaged. While this method of analysis avoids the problems associated with deductive forms of positivism where empirical data is used essentially to test predetermined hypotheses, it does not support the notion, implicit within 'grounded theory'

---

[109] In current projects preliminary training in the use of Nud★ist is being provided to partners in the team meetings. The recent availability of a new programme (for use with Nud★ist) enabling partners to work simultaneously on the programme from different locations and 'merge' the findings, potentially opens the way for collaborative analysis.

approaches, of the existence of theory-untainted 'facts'. Rather it accepts the reality of a constant interplay between theory and all aspects of the research process. While our preconceptions based upon our own experiences and reading – or secondary analysis – may suggest the importance of certain categories, empirical data may redefine these: the point is to permit a flexibility into the process and resist 'closure' for as long as time schedules permit[110].

This chapter has attempted to draw out certain issues concerning the methods of comparative analysis, particularly in gender-sensitive or feminist projects. In general terms it has identified a gulf between comparative research orthodoxy and feminist critical approaches to social research. In practice this gulf or impasse has meant that the contribution of feminist epistemology has been lost in much cross-national work and feminist researchers have avoided developing a comparative dimension to their work. Not only does this restrict the basis of social science knowledge but also the development of feminist praxis in general. In so doing, feminists have eschewed both the opportunity of learning from women's experiences abroad and also the prospect of closer personal relationships with other feminists and the potential to build political alliances and advance, politically, the interests of all European women. Learning to research together teaches us important lessons in humility, understanding, cooperation and compromise providing important 'transferable skills' for the building of a united feminist politics at supra-national level.

The final part of this chapter has briefly detailed one possible research approach with the aim, not of presenting a model of good practice, but simply to demonstrate that good feminist research is both possible and useful without massive budgets and may advance the interests of women without objectifying them.

---

[110] The point about closure refers, in this instance, to the final 'decision' to adopt an indexing 'system'. Such a decision must be made eventually in order to subject all the interviews to broadly similar analysis.

FOUR

Legal spaces: the free movement of persons provisions

Introduction: 'citizenship of the Union'

The purpose of this chapter is to map out the legal framework within which intra-Community mobility has been and is currently taking place. As such it does not present a comprehensive review of all aspects of Community law in this area but rather seeks to give a flavour of the quality and extent of the 'basket' of Community goods and systems of entitlement accruing to those persons who take up their right to move within the European Union (EU).

In seeking to give effect to the Treaty commitment to promote the free movement of persons, the drafters of secondary legislation and the European Court of Justice (ECJ) are required to interpret Treaty objectives (define the policy goals) and to develop measures for their implementation. Effective policy design and implementation require a conceptualisation of the migration process and an understanding of the specific barriers to mobility.

In the process of charting the evolution of social entitlement in this area, I have thus sought to examine the extent to which existing theories or ideas about the process of intra-Communty mobility and the identification of impediments to mobility are informed by gendered assumptions about migration behaviour which may, in turn, give rise to gendered material outcomes.

The research project on which this book is based commenced prior to the ratification of the Maastricht Treaty and the explicit introduction of the concept of 'citizenship of the Union' in Community law. Nevertheless, the concept of citizenship has been used increasingly as a tool to evaluate the progressive evolution of social entitlement accruing to those Community nationals who exercised their right to move within the Community.

The formal introduction of 'citizenship of the Union' in Article 8 of the Treaty on European Union (TEU) has implications for how we research citizenship; rather than teasing out and piecing together evidence of the evolution of a social status for this group of EU nationals and assessing whether this collection of measures and entitlements can be analysed in terms of citizenship, we are now presented with the formal status of citizenship and left to determine what that really means in concrete terms.

Until relatively recently the legal framework governing intra-Community mobility had evolved somewhat incrementally, tracing and nudging at the parameters of a series of fairly established trajectories. The emergence of Community citizenship was thus achieved through numerous 'small' and scattered developments re-defining the material and personal scope of entitlement. The recent deliberations of the Court of Justice in a number of cases and, in particular the judgment in *Martinez Sala*[1], suggest the possibility of a more fundamental shift, asserting Article 8 TEU as the basis of an over-arching social status, the implications of which are, as yet, somewhat uncertain.

The extent to which Community nationals can now appeal directly to Article 8 as the basis of their citizenship entitlement (in conjunction with the non-discrimination principle contained in Article 6) or whether they need to continue to base their claims against pre-existing established principles remains unclear. For this reason, while I have tried to identify, throughout the chapter, areas of Community law directly affected by these decisions (particularly in relation to the rights of jobseekers, for example), more general concerns about the potential impact of recent cases concerning Article 8 on citizenship entitlement will be discussed in the final chapter.

Citizenship and mobility

Couched in the language of rights and obligations traditionally associated with citizenship, Article 8 TEU states that, "every person holding the nationality of a Member State shall be a Citizen of the Union" and shall, as a consequence, "enjoy the rights conferred by this Treaty"[2]. Despite the symbolic importance of Article 8, not least in terms of building a popular European identity and securing public support for the development of European integration, these provisions have little real meaning or consequence for those European citizens residing in their country of nationality[3].

---

[1] *Martinez Sala v Freistaat Bayern*, Case C-85/96.

[2] Paragraph Two.

[3] Apart from the right established in Article 8d to petition the European Parliament.

The close link between Community citizenship and mobility is reflected in Article 8a TEU which outlines the fundamental right, "to move and reside freely within the territory of the Member States"[4]. The importance of intra-Community mobility or migration as the lynch-pin of citizenship leads D'Oliveira to identify the right to free movement as, "the central element around which other rights crystallise"[5]. This relationship, between mobility and citizenship, has a long tradition reflecting the historical evolution of entitlement from an initially quite narrow concern to promote labour mobility to its subsequent metamorphosis, in recent years, into a more holistic concept of citizenship. In that sense the status of 'citizenship of the Union', although formally established quite recently, has developed over the past three decades as evidenced by the following discussion about free movement written in 1972:

> **The system of freedom of movement for workers represents a truly remarkable advance into one of the most sensitive areas of every modern nation-state. Whereas hitherto the migration of workers was handled by the authorities of the receiving country, freedom of movement has since become a Community affair ... The same Commissioner who in 1961 saw free movement in terms of a factor of production, proclaimed in 1968 that it constituted 'an incipient form – still embryonic and imperfect – of European Citizenship.**[6]

---

[4] The legal effect of Article 8a is contestable and currently forms the focus of considerable debate. On the one hand, the European Commission has argued that the inclusion of the right to mobility for all EU nationals, in the Treaty itself, has provided a new conceptual basis for the development of European citizenship (European Commission Report: 'Citizenship of the Union', COM(93)702). On the other hand, it could be argued that Article 8a introduces no new rights but essentially reaffirms pre-existing Community legislation, in particular, the general right of residence introduced two years earlier (Council Directive 90/364) for all persons who do not enjoy this right under other provisions of Community law. For more detail, see O'Leary, S. (1997) 'Citizenship of the Union', *European Law Review*, October, pp 436–43.

[5] D'Oliveira, J. (1995) 'Union citizenship: pie in the sky?', in A. Rosas and E. Antola (eds) *A citizen's Europe: In search of a new order*, London: Sage, p 65.

[6] Bohning, W.R. (1972) *The migration of workers in the United Kingdom and the European Community*, London: Oxford University Press, pp 18–19.

During this early phase in the development of the European Economic Community (EEC), the free movement of workers was viewed primarily in economic terms, as a means of removing barriers to labour mobility – a point made by Brian Wilkinson:

> **The real interest of the Member States was not to establish free movement and residence rights for all citizens of the Community, rather it was to establish free movement for workers as one of the factors of production. Consequently from the outset any incipient form of European citizenship was only to be enjoyed by those who would contribute economically through their labour to the economy of the host Member State.[7]**

Nevertheless, the social and political significance of evolving Community rights under the free movement provisions was not lost to commentators. On a more pragmatic level, in the period before the expansion of a pro-active regional development policy, measures to encourage labour mobility constituted an important means of regulating discrepancies in the demand for and supply of labour in the regions of the Community and, in the process, ameliorating the worst effects of unemployment in peripheral areas. To that extent, within the confines of a free market approach, labour mobility already fulfilled an important social function central to the integrationist strategy, albeit with tragic consequences for the depopulated rural areas concerned. The symbolic significance of free movement to the wider European project was, however, acknowledged in the early years as the following quote from Commissioner Levi-Sandri demonstrates:

> **This, in the last analysis, must be and will be the most important political and social result of the liberalisation of the labour market: to the extent to which it is attained, we shall all be made to appreciate the effective range of European solidarity and the progress of the *idea of unity* in the minds of our peoples.[8]**

---

[7] Wilkinson, B. (1996) 'Free movement of workers: nationality, discrimination and European citizenship', in J. Dine and B. Watt (eds) *Discrimination law*, London: Longman, pp 123-34.

[8] Commissioner Levi-Sandri (1961) 'The free movement of workers in the countries of the European Economic Community', Bulletin EC 6-1961, 5, cited in P. Craig and G. de Burca (1995) *EC law. Text, cases and materials*, Oxford: Clarendon Press, p 653.

The continued tension over the interpretation of the provisions since their inclusion in the Treaty of Rome as an instrument of economic policy, on the one hand, and as the basis of a more fundamental project to shape and legitimate, in the minds of the public, a European social space, on the other, is reflected in the secondary legislation and the case law of the ECJ. The following section begins by outlining some of the main areas of Community legislation and then moves on to analyse the role the ECJ has played in interpreting the provisions and determining the direction and meaning of European citizenship. It first details the substantive basis of entitlement for migrant workers[9] in order to demonstrate the significance – and tangible material benefit – accruing to Community workers and, in that sense, the appropriateness of using the language of citizenship.

Neither the status of Union citizenship nor the general right of residence conferred on all Community nationals currently give rise to uniform entitlement, however; some groups of migrants have more limited status in the host State. The chapter thus considers the personal scope of the free movement provisions and the relationship between individual status and social entitlement. In particular, the chapter examines the gender implications of Community law and the extent to which it institutionalises an inferior and dependent status for female 'citizens of the Union'.

The provisions

The main Treaty provisions of concern to us here can be found under Title III of the Treaty which contains chapters on the free movement of workers (Chapter One); the right of establishment (Chapter Two) and the freedom to provide services (Chapter Three). The basic source of the right to free movement for workers is set out in Article 48 EC which refers exclusively to 'workers' and provides for a right to move freely and reside in another Member State, for the purposes of employment:

ARTICLE 48 EC

1. Freedom of movement for workers shall be secured within the Community by the end of the transitional period at the latest.

---

[9] Parallel provisions exist for self-employed persons under the Right of Establishment and the Right to Provide Services. These are not discussed in detail here.

---

2. Such freedom of movement shall entail the abolition of any discrimination based on nationality between workers of the Member States as regards employment, remuneration and other conditions of work and employment.

3. It shall entail the right, subject to limitations justified on grounds of public policy, public security or public health:

(a) to accept offers of employment actually made;

(b) to move freely within the territory of Member States for this purpose;

(c) to stay in a Member State for the purpose of employment in accordance with the provisions governing the employment of nationals of that State laid down by law, regulation or administrative action;

(d) to remain in the territory of a Member State after having been employed in that state, subject to conditions ...

4. The provisions of this Article shall not apply to employment in the public service.

The non-discrimination principle

Paragraph two of Article 48 EC contains the fundamental principle underpinning the right to freedom of movement opening up domestic labour markets to Community nationals. In practice, the provisions amount to a specific application of the non-discrimination principle (Article 6 EC) which states that, "Within the scope of application of this Treaty, and without prejudice to any special provisions contained therein, any discrimination on grounds of nationality shall be prohibited".

What this means in practice, is that any EU national[10] employed in a Member State other than that of his or her nationality is entitled to the same treatment in matters of employment as a national *of that State*. The provisions referred to in paragraph three of Article 48 EC suggest a narrow

---

[10] The issue of nationality is discussed in more detail below.

---

application of this principle to matters connected with employment and 'conditions of work'. The rights associated with the freedom of movement have been clarified and extended by Community secondary legislation, in the form of Directives and Regulations. Of particular importance have been Regulation 1612/68[11] on the freedom of movement of workers, Regulation 1408/71[12] on social security rights and Council Directive 68/360[13] which sets out the right of residence for workers and their families. Referring once again specifically to 'workers' and echoing the gendered language of the Treaty, Regulation 1612/68 reaffirms the basic Treaty right to equal treatment in matters of employment, remuneration and conditions of work. It broadens the material scope of Article 48 quite considerably, however, by introducing a range of educational and social entitlements for favoured EU citizens (paid workers and their families with 'settled residence').

Of particular importance in the evolution of Community rights, from those narrowly concerned with removing barriers to employment-related mobility towards a fuller recognition of the migrant worker as, "a citizen integrated with the citizens of the host Member State"[14] has been Article 7(2) which states that, "*He shall enjoy the same social and tax advantages as national workers*". While the Treaty provisions make no explicit reference to worker's families[15], Title 3 of Regulation 1612/68 boldly extends the rights granted to workers to members of their families. This includes the extension of the right to take up employment (Article 11) and important educational entitlements for the children of migrant workers, who should be given the same rights of access as national children in the host Member State (Article 12)[16].

---

[11] Council Regulation 1612/68, Articles 1-12 as amended (Workers' and Workers' Families' Rights).

[12] Council Regulation (EEC) 1408/71 on the application of social security schemes to unemployed persons and to members of their families moving within the Community.

[13] Council Directive 68/360, Articles 1-10 (Free Movement and Residence).

[14] Pollard, D. and Ross, M. (1994) *European Community Law. Text and materials*, London: Butterworths, p 430.

[15] Apart from the mention of dependants under the social security provisions in Article 51.

[16] In addition to these basic provisions, other measures have been taken to deal with more specific barriers to mobility, particularly of skilled and professional labour (mutual recognition of diplomas etc).

Non-discrimination or harmonisation?

It is important to stress at this juncture that access to social and tax advantages (and other forms of educational or employment benefit) under the free movement provisions is based on the non-discrimination principle and, as such, does not represent an explicit attempt to harmonise national social policy although it doubtless creates an impetus for convergence – not least to inhibit the perceived growth in aspects of 'welfare tourism'[17]. The social status of any intra-Community migrant will thus mirror that of a national in the host State (and may, indeed, be less advantageous than the country they have left depending on the relative merits of the respective systems). The provisions do not, therefore, explicitly seek to create a uniformity of experience between migrant workers, or between workers in general within the EU. Nevertheless, the prohibition on discrimination in the host State constitutes an important soure of social protection.

The residency directives

Perhaps the most basic right available to Community workers is the right to enter and reside in another Member State. It is easy, from a national perspective, to overlook the importance of residency to citizenship. Hans

---

[17] 'Welfare tourism' is a term coined by the popular press to refer to the movement of persons motivated by reasons other than employment, to the detriment of the receiving State. The most common variant of which is 'benefits tourism' which occurs when persons are attracted to migrate to countries with more generous social security arrangements. Concern has also been raised over the prospect of 'educational' tourism where students are attracted to study in countries with the most advantageous educational package. The suffix 'tourism' is increasingly utilised to refer, generically, to all forms of migration motivated by other than strictly economic considerations with an unwritten presumption that all such migrations are to be discouraged. The origin of the term may lie in the notion of transient – or semi-permanent – forms of migration. It is, however, increasingly used to refer to presumptions about migrants' motivations and, indeed, the legitimacy of their migration. Only those migrants who are individual economic agents (paid worker or self-employed person) it seems, are legitimate beneficiaries of citizenship status despite the very real economic contribution of some of the other 'tourists'. The author is currently directing a project on retirement migration within the EU which raises important concerns about the impact of this migration on local economies.

---

van Amersfoort notes the absence of any reference to the right of abode in Marshall's work on citizenship, suggesting that this right is central to concerns about social citizenship, both as an entitlement in itself, but also as the trigger to other forms of entitlement[18]. Certainly, in an EU context the right of residency, is a key determinant of social status. Josephine Steiner sets out the importance of a worker's residency entitlement under Council Directive 68/360[19] as follows:

> **The question of whether a worker or a member of his family is entitled to 'settled' residence in a Member State is of fundamental importance because ... their right to equal treatment in the host State, and all that that involves, has been held to flow not so much from the claimant's status as a worker, although it originates there, as from the worker's, and his family's 'lawful residence' in a Member State.**[20]

We have already discussed the right of residence inferred in Article 8 EC suggesting that all citizens who hold the nationality of a Member State have the right of entry and abode. Arguably, the introduction of the 'General Right of Residence' in Council Directive 90/364[21] already extended the right to enter and reside to all nationals, irrespective of economic status, who failed to qualify under pre-existing measures[22]. This extension of the Right of Residence has been applauded by commentators as representing a shift in the direction of a more inclusive approach to citizenship leading D'Oliveira to assert that:

> **The mobility of economically active persons has now been elevated to the core of European citizenship and expanded into mobility for persons generally. In other words, the**

---

[18] Professor Hans van Amersfoort (1997) 'International migration and civil rights: the dilemmas of migration control in an age of globalisation', Paper presented at the Immigration Law Practitioners' Association and the Centre of European Law, King's College London Conference, 'The legal framework and social consequences of free movement of persons in the European Union', 27-28 November.

[19] Supra, note 13.

[20] Steiner, J. (1996) *Textbook on EC law*, London: Blackstone Press, p 261.

[21] Council Directive 90/364 (General right of residence).

[22] With the exception of persons caught by the public policy derogations.

> economically irrelevant people have been promoted to the status
> of persons.[23]

The inference of uniformity was, however, misplaced. This new Directive did not replace existing measures but created an additional tier to the hierarchy of entitlement, access to which depends on a migrant's status. The Right of Residence was thus implemented, in Community law, through a cluster of Directives which together grant a Right of Residence to all nationals. In that sense, at least, there is some common status deriving from Community nationality. The fact of residence does not, however, confer a broad equality of status but rather sets out different terms and conditions for different categories of citizens. Separate Directives apply to different groups depending on their motives for migration; it is thus not so much the right of residence that is at issue here but the social rights this gives rise to in the host State.

The general rights of residence for economically inactive persons, including the right of residence for students, persons who have ceased their occupational activity and all other persons who do not enjoy the right under other provisions, are all subject to a resources requirement[24]. In each case the right of residence is conditional upon the claimant demonstrating self-sufficiency in order to, "*avoid becoming a burden on the social assistance system of the host Member State*".

This requirement of financial autonomy for the duration of residence severely restricts the scope of citizenship. Indeed, for those relying on these provisions as the source of their citizenship status in another Member State, there is effectively no Community entitlement in terms of social rights; citizenship has failed to develop beyond limited political rights (to vote and stand for election at local level)[25]. The limitations contained

---

[23] D'Oliveira, J. (1995) 'Union citizenship: pie in the sky?', in A. Rosas and E. Antola (eds) *A citizen's Europe: In search of a new order*, London: Sage, pp 65-6.

[24] Article 1, supra, note 21.

[25] The social status of such persons will vary depending on the domestic policy of the host Member State. In some cases, Member States may grant extensive access to public welfare. Indeed research in coastal regions of Spain has found that retirement migrants have good access to local health and social services (Betty, C. and Cahill, M. [1995] 'British expatriates' experience of health and social services on the Costa Del Sol', Paper to the Nation and Migration in Southern Europe Conference, University of Greenwich, December). The spatial concentration of these communities, and their consequent electoral significance, may also increase the scope of provision.

within the secondary legislation and carried forward via Article 8a EC thus severely circumscribe the scope of the new citizenship. While apparently universal in coverage, the general right of residence has not, of itself, given rise to an equality of citizenship entitlement; in the Marshallian sense it has failed to provide for even a basic modicum of welfare[26]. As such it is difficult to endorse the optimism in D'Oliveira's assertion. Indeed, it is not without reason that Directive 90/364 has become known as the 'playboy Directive'[27].

Other categories of persons, in particular workers and their families and persons exercising their right to remain after employment in another Member State, do not have to rely on the general rights of residence discussed above but can claim a broader entitlement under Council Directive 68/360 which contains no requirement of financial autonomy[28]. The scope of rights available for this group of 'favoured' EU citizens forms the basis of the following discussion.

The evolution of substantive rights for migrant workers and their families

The impact of Community law

It is neither possible nor desirable in a text of this nature to discuss in detail general issues about Community law. Nevertheless, it is necessary to consider the effect of Community law and its applicability in domestic legal systems before we examine the substantive content. This is important as it determines the extent to which persons or organisations can rely upon Community law to enforce their rights in domestic courts. The

---

[26] Marshall, T.H. (1964) *Class, citizenship and social development*, Westport: Greenwood Press.

[27] The Martinez Sala case has raised important new questions about the relationship between the residency Directives and the new Article 8a. The Commission, in this case, argued that Martinez Sala's claim to residency (giving rise to her material entitlement to a non-contributory child allowance) derived not from the residency Directive 90/364 (which contains the resources requirement) but directly from Article 8a. For a discussion of the potential implications of Article 8a as an a priori general right of residence, see Fries, S. and Shaw, J. (1998) 'Citizenship of the Union: first steps in the Court of Justice', *European Public Law*, vol 4, no 4, p 12.

[28] Parallel provisions exist for the self-employed and retired Community workers.

ECJ has established, in a series of cases[29] that Article 48 EC is binding on all parties in the Member States and creates individual rights and responsibilities for persons and organisations which are enforceable in national courts without any need for implementing legislation at national level. In addition, Regulation 1612/68[30] has been held to have direct effect[31]. Furthermore, the prohibition of discrimination on grounds of nationality applies to both direct and indirect or covert forms of discrimination. Article 3 of Regulation 1612/68 refers specifically to its application to practices or actions which, although not directly discriminatory, have the effect of restricting the opportunities of other EU nationals. The Court confirmed this position in *Sotgiu* stating that Article 7 of Regulation 1612/68, prohibited, "not only overt discrimination by reason of nationality but also all covert forms of discrimination which, by the application of other criteria of differentiation, lead in fact to the same result"[32].

In some cases, however, indirect discrimination, may be justified. One of the most common incidences of indirect discrimination – which consitutes a significant obstacle to labour mobility – arises in relation to the language requirement. Article 3 of Regulation 1612/68 specifically exempts linguistic knowledge from the general prohibition where this is a *requirement* of the post. The scope and application of this exemption was, however, subject to an ECJ ruling in *Groener*[33]. This case involved a Dutch woman who had been teaching art on a part-time basis in an Irish school for a number of years and applied for a permanent position. The language of instruction was exclusively English. Despite being recommended for the post, she was rejected on the grounds that she failed an oral test in Gaelic. Although a clear case of indirect discrimination the Court found that such discrimination could be objectively justified given the special constitutional status of the Irish language and its importance to national identity and culture[34].

---

[29] *Commission v France (the Merchant Seamen Case)*, Case 167/73 [1974] ECR 359; *Van Duyn v Home Office*, Case 41/74 [1975] ECR 1337; *Walrave/Koch v AUCI*, Case 36/74 [1974] ECR 1405; *Dona v Mantero*, Case 13/76 [1976] ECR 1333.

[30] Supra, note 11.

[31] *Rutiliv Minister for the Interior*, Case 36/75 [1975] ECR 1219.

[32] *Sotgiu v Deutsche Bundespost*, Case 152/73 [1974] ECR 153, para 11. This approach to the issue of covert discrimination was recently reaffirmed in *Christos Konstantinidis*, Case C-168/91 [1993] ECR I-119.1.

[33] *Groener v Minister of Education*, Case C-379/87 [1989] ECR 3967.

[34] The impact of this ruling on migrant women will be discussed in more detail in Chapter Six.

The ECJ has not only been influential in establishing the effectiveness of Community law in a domestic context and the enforceability of rights. The key role played by the ECJ in shaping the evolution of both the material and personal scope of Community protection can be witnessed in its generally integrationist approach to the free movement provisions. On the whole, it has interpreted the provisions constructively, strengthening and widening the personal and material scope and restricting the parameters of the derogations which permit Member States to limit entitlement. Indeed, it has been suggested that the Court has gone beyond a literal interpretation of the provisions conferring upon itself a "hermeneutic monopoly"[35]. This view is also expressed by Nielsen and Szyszczak:

> **The ECJ has provided a broad interpretation of Community law in this area and has elevated the principle of free movement of persons into one of the fundamental rights of Community law. The completion of the Internal Market has led to the development of free movement ideas beyond those linked to the economic activities outlined in Articles 48-66 EEC.**[36]

As such the ECJ has become a key player in the development of Community rights. The evolution of the law in this area has not, however, been uniform nor even. The Court's apparent generosity and willingness to acknowledge the impact of changing socioeconomic and cultural conditions on the scope of the legislation in some areas (in its interpretation of part-time work, for example), can be contrasted with narrowly legalistic judgments elsewhere (on the status of cohabitants or entitlement to educational grants). This tension which exists between the various dimensions of the right to free movement reflects to some degree the wider political context of European integration and the battle over competency in the new social Europe, as well as more pragmatic concerns about the economic impact of Community law. In practice, the uneven development of Community law may also rest upon gendered notions about the social and political priority of issues with important implications for women migrants. The following section considers the effect the ECJ has had on the scope of Community entitlement to give a clearer impression of the nature and meaning of European citizenship. It begins with an

---

[35] G.F. Mancini, cited in Craig and de Burca, supra (1995, p 662), note 8.

[36] Nielsen, R. and Szyszczak, E. (1993) *The social dimension of the European Community*, Copenhagen: Handelshojskolens Forlag, p 55.

examination of the material scope of the provisions, mapping out the nature of the social rights 'on offer'. Having established that the EU is indeed the source of some significant and enforceable material rights for Community migrants, and the legitimacy of use of the language of citizenship to describe those rights, the chapter then goes on to consider issues of personal entitlement.

Material scope

The provisions themselves refer to the progressive abolition of discrimination with regard to employment, remuneration and conditions of work (Article 48), giving EU nationals an equal opportunity in the employment market. Article 51 EC provides for the development of measures to enable workers to aggregate and transfer *contributory* or insurance-based benefits, but does not extend to forms of social assistance (means-tested or needs-based benefits etc) which were generally believed to fall outside of Community competence. These employment rights have been extended by the implementing of legislation to include the right, for workers and their families, to remain in the host State after employment has ceased (Regulation 1251/70)[37] and important substantive rights under Regulation 1612/68[38] covering equality of access in relation to training in vocational schools (Article 7(3) and, most importantly, via Article 7(2)), to the same social and tax advantages as workers. The Court has interpreted these provisions broadly, extending entitlement to all forms of social assistance leading Weatherill to the conclusion that, "The worker stands in a uniquely favourable position in claiming a wide panoply of social rights available under national law"[39].

Craig and de Burca[40] note how the Court "departed silently" from its earlier, more restrictive, approach in *Michel S.*[41] where it held that Article 7(2) only applied to benefits connected with employment to assume a more expansive approach. In *Fiorini v SNCF* the Court ruled that the term 'social advantages' could not be interpreted restrictively:

---

[37] Commission Regulation 1251/70, Articles 1-8 (Rights to Remain).

[38] Supra, note 11.

[39] Weatherill, S. and Beaumont, P. (1993) *EC law*, London: Penguin Books, p 484.

[40] Craig and de Burca, supra, note 8.

[41] *Michel S. v Fonds national de Reclassement handicapés*, Case 76/72 [1973] ECR 457.

It therefore follows that, in view of the equality of treatment which the provision seeks to achieve, the substantive area of application must be delineated so as to include all social and tax advantages, whether or not attached to the contract of employment, such as reductions in fares for large families.[42]

This case involved a claim, by the widow of an Italian migrant worker, for a fare reduction card granted to workers on the French railway who had 'large' families. The Court held that this right was available not only to the worker but, by virtue of Regulation 1251/70[43], which gives workers and their families a right to remain in the host State after employment has ceased, extended also to the surviving family members who had been residing with the deceased worker. In *Ministère Public v Even*, the Court defined the material scope of Article 7(2) in what has become known as the 'social advantages formula' to include:

... all those [advantages] which, whether or not linked to the contract of employment, are generally granted to national workers primarily because of their objective status as workers or by virtue of their residence on national territory and the extension of which to workers who are nationals of other Member States therefore *seems suitable to facilitate their mobility within the Community*.[44]

This broad 'facilitating mobility' test, which has superseded the more restrictive non-discrimination principle, was adopted in *Reina*[45] in a claim, by an Italian couple working in Germany, for a discretionary interest-free childbirth loan. The State-financed loans system was introduced in Germany, for low-income families, as part of its demographic policy to increase the birth rate and reduce the number of abortions. The defendant bank refused the loan to the Reinas on the grounds that there was no link between the granting of the loan and the recipients' status as workers. Furthermore, refusal of such a loan in no way impeded the mobility of

---

[42] *Fiorini (née Christini) v Société Nationale des Chemins de Fer Français (SNCF)*, Case 32/75 [1975] ECR 1085 [1975] 1 CMLR 573 at para 13.

[43] Supra, note 37.

[44] *Ministere Public v Even*, Case 207/78 [1979] ECR 2019.

[45] *Reina v Landeskredit Bank Baden-Wurttemberg*, Case 65/81 [1982] ECR 33 [1982] 1 CMLR 744.

workers within the Community. The Court cited the 'social advantage formula' and held that, in view of the objectives of the loan, to alleviate the financial burden of parenthood on low-income families, the loan should be granted to workers of other Member States on the same conditions as those which applied to nationals. Furthermore, in *Castelli v ONPTS*[46] on similar reasoning the Court found that an Italian widow who moved to live with her migrant worker son in Belgium was entitled to a minimum income allowance paid to all elderly persons under Belgian law. Since she had a right under Article 10 Regulation 1612/68 to install herself with her son, she was also entitled to the same social and tax advantages as Belgian workers and ex-workers. Applying the Even formula the Court held that Castelli was entitled to the old age benefit by virtue of her 'settled residence'[47].

Nielsen and Szyszczak argue that it is in the field of educational rights that the Court of Justice has contributed most to the development of a 'People's Europe'[48]. Article 12 of Regulation 1612/68 provides that children of migrant workers are to be admitted to educational courses and vocational training under the same conditions as nationals of the host State. Designed to promote the integration of children in the host country, this provision covers all types and levels of education (not just vocational training) on the basis that failure to do so would impede labour mobility[49]. In *Casagrande*[50] the Court held, in the context of a claim by a child, under Article 12 of Regulation 1612/68, that this right included not only admission but general measures to facilitate attendance, which in this case included a maintenance grant. Article 12 has also been found to encompass 'special' educational arrangements for disabled children[51]. The concept of

---

[46] *Carmella Castelli v Office National des Pensions pour Travailleurs Salariés (ONPTS)*, Case 261/83 [1984] ECR 3199.

[47] The 'facilitating mobility' approach to defining social advantages has been further supported in *Peter de Vos v Stadt Bielefeld*, Case C-315/94 [1996] ECR I-1417, para 20 and in *Schmid v Belgian State* [1993] ECR I-3011, para 18.

[48] Nielsen and Szyszczak (1993, p 100), supra, note 36. For a more detailed and recent discussion of educational rights see Shaw, J. (1998) 'From the margins to the centre: education and training in law and policy', in P. Craig and G. de Burca (eds) *European Community law: An evaluationary perspective*, Oxford: Oxford University Press.

[49] *Echternach* and *Moritz v Netherlands Minister for Education*, Joined Cases 389 and 390/87 [1989] ECR 755.

[50] *Casagrande v Landeshaupstadt Munich*, Case 9/74 [1974] ECR 773.

[51] *Michel S.*, Case 76/72 [1973] ECR 437.

social advantage has thus been implied into Article 12 giving the dependent children of migrant workers full access to educational finance[52]. The Court has further extended these rights to cases where the working parent has died. Furthermore, a child was not to be regarded as having lost its status as a child of the family benefiting from the rights under Regulation 1612/68 merely because its family had moved back to its State of origin[53].

In another case involving a claim for a form of disability allowance, the Court held that such an allowance fell within the concept of social advantages and should therefore be awarded to the disabled son of a migrant worker[54]. The rationale for this generous approach was given by the Court in *Deak*[55] where the Court submitted that, in that failing to extend the non-discrimination principle to dependant descendants of a worker (in this case payments to young persons seeking employment), the worker would be induced to leave that Member State.

Although Article 12 does not, as such, give the spouse a right to equal access to educational or vocational training courses, a spouse was successful in claiming such rights in *Forcheri v Belgian State*[56]. The Court held that the right arose under the Treaty, given her position as a favoured EEC citizen (as a spouse). Such a case may now be taken under Article 7(2) Regulation 1612/68[57].

Article 9 of Regulation 1612/68 entitles a migrant worker to enjoy all the rights and benefits accorded to national workers in matters of housing, including ownership of the housing he needs. Restrictions on migrants' rights to acquire property are therefore unlawful[58]. This right extends to private and public housing although Denning was reluctant to apply the principle in the context of a claim under the 1977 Housing (Homeless

---

[52] *Echternach*, supra, note 49.

[53] *Commission v Belgium*, Case 42/87 [1989] 1 CMLR 457; *Echternach* and *Moritz*, note 49. See also, *Matteucci v Communaute Francaise de Belgique*, Case [1989] 1 CMLR 357 (migrant workers can be the beneficiaries of bilateral agreements between Member States).

[54] *Inzirillo*, Case 63/76 [1976] ECR 2057.

[55] *Deak*, Case 94/84 [1985] ECR 1873.

[56] *Forcheri v Belgian State*, Case 152/82 [1983] ECR 2323.

[57] *Bernini*, Case C-3/90 [1992] ECR I-1071. Although this case involved a dependant child, the principle would seem to apply to all dependant family members.

[58] *Commission v Greece*, Case 305/87 [1989] ECR 1461.

Persons) Act[59]. Steiner, however, submits that all statutory protection in this field must apply equally to favoured EEC citizens (those with 'lawful residence')[60]. These rights would also constitute social advantages under Article 7(2). Following the impact of these, and many other cases[61], Meehan describes the Court's approach as having, "...blurred customary distinctions between security and assistance so much that discrimination in almost any welfare benefit might be regarded as contravening Community law"[62].

As such, it is fair to say that the Community has moved beyond the extension of limited economic and political rights (and specific measures to facilitate the transfer of insurance-based benefits) to claim competency over key areas of needs-based social provision with very immediate and tangible implications for the social status of Community migrant workers and their families over the life-course. While Community law cannot guarantee any individual a standardised platform of social entitlement, it does provide for a very broad application of the non-discrimination principle giving migrant workers full and equal access to welfare benefits in the host Member State, including forms of social assistance. Robin Allen QC has recently documented the evolution of social entitlement under the social advantages concept as reflecting a 'cradle-to-grave' approach echoing references in the social policy literature, to the development of the post-war welfare state[63].

To analyse these developments in terms of 'citizenship', however, requires not only an examination of the substantive content of social rights but also analysis of the concept of 'Community' itself (defining who are to be the fortunate beneficiaries of these 'rights', and who are to be excluded). The following section considers in more detail the impact of ECJ decisions

---

[59] *De Falco v Crawley Borough Council*, Case [1980] QB 460.

[60] Steiner (1996, p 268), supra, note 20.

[61] For more discussion refer to O'Keefe, D. (1988) 'Equal rights for migrants: the concept of social advantage in Article 7(2), regulation 1612/68', *Yearbook of European Law*, vol 5, p 93.

[62] Meehan, E. (1993) *Citizenship and the European Community*, London: Sage, p 93.

[63] The notion of a 'cradle-to-grave' approach is developed from a paper given by Robin Allen QC, Chairman of the Employment Law Bar Association, entitled, 'Equal treatment, social advantages and obstacles: in search of coherence in freedom and dignity' and presented at the Immigration Law Practitioners' Association and the Centre of European Law, King's College London Conference, 'The legal framework and social consequences of free movement of persons in the European Union', 27-28 November 1997.

on the personal scope of entitlement. It focuses, in particular, on gendered assumptions which underpin and guide the Court's interpretation of the legislation, reinforcing and reproducing inequality and dependency. The discussion is divided into a number of sections dealing with the Court's role in the definition of a hierarchy of entitlement based around the concepts of 'nationality', 'worker' and 'family'[64]. We have already identified a broad distinction between 'economically-inactive' migrants (whose residency status gives rise to a highly circumscribed social status) and those Community workers able to rely on the more generous framework provided by Council Directive 68/360[65]. The following discussion moves on to consider finer distinctions within this relatively privileged group of citizens.

The protected persons: the nationality question

Any person seeking to enjoy the rights of free movement must qualify, in the first instance, as a Community citizen. The question of nationality circumscribes the personal scope of the free movement provisions defining who is to be included within the broad concept of citizenship and who is excluded. Nationality, writes D'Oliveira, provides the "ticket to Union Citizenship"[66]. While the wider issue of Community competence in the area of immigration policy falls largely outside the scope of this book[67], the following section is concerned with examining which persons qualify as Community citizens.

Third country migrants (non-EU nationals) working or legally residing in the EU at present derive few rights under existing Community law as Member States have strongly defended their competence in relation to external immigration policy[68]. As Nielsen and Szyszczak put it, "Even the

---

[64] Articles 48(3), 56 and 66 EC allow Member States, in certain restricted circumstances, to prevent the entry of Community nationals into another Member State. The grounds on which a Member State can refuse entry include concerns about public policy, public security and public health.

[65] Supra, note 13.

[66] D'Oliveira (1995, p 60), supra, note 5.

[67] For detailed discussion of immigration policy, see Handoll, J. (1995) *Free movement of persons in the EU*, Chichester: John Wiley and Sons; Schermers, H.G., Flinterman, C., Kellermann, A.E., van Haersolte, J.C. and van de Meent, G.W.A. (eds) (1993) *Free movement of persons in Europe. Legal problems and experiences*, Dordecht: Martinus Nijhoff Publishers or Rosas, A. and Antola, E. (1995) *A Citizens' Europe*, London: Sage.

[68] The notion of extending free movement rights to legally resident third country migrants is currently under discussion in the review of Regulation 1408/71.

ECJ which normally interprets the free movement provisions liberally has found it difficult to ascribe Community competence in this area"[69]. The general non-discrimination principle contained in Article 6 EC makes no specific reference to nationality but simply states that, "*any discrimination on grounds of nationality* shall be prohibited".

The section of the Treaty (Title III) concerned with free movement leaves some room for interpretation, however. Chapter Two (Articles 52-59 EC), which provides for the progressive removal of restrictions on the freedom of establishment, refers explicitly to 'nationals of a Member State'. The preceding chapter, on the other hand, which sets out the right to free movement of workers, refers to 'workers within the Community' (Article 48 EC) and does not make specific reference to issues of nationality. It could be argued that the express reference to nationality in Chapter Two and its omission from Chapter One indicates an intention not to circumscribe the provisions for workers in the same way. If this were the case, then the personal scope of Community protection under the provisions would extend to third country nationals legally resident and working in a Member State. This line of argument is further supported by Plender's suggestion that the contrast between Article 69 of the pre-existing European Coal and Steel Community (ECSC) Treaty which expressly refers to, "workers who are nationals of the Member States" and the conspicuous absence of reference to nationality in Article 48 EC, implies that, "the draftsmen of the EEC Treaty intended to establish a common policy for all workers in the Community, irrespective of their nationality"[70].

Whatever the initial intention, the situation has been clarified in secondary legislation and through the case law. All the implementing legislation specifically restricts the application of Article 48 to "nationals of a Member State"[71]. Furthermore, Article 8 explicitly states that, "Every person *holding the nationality of a Member State* shall be a citizen of the Union". The provisions, at present, thus protect only Community migrants, who have been referred to, in consequence, as 'privileged aliens'[72]. Despite the central importance of the nationality issue to the functioning of the free movement of persons, and the Court's insistence that the concept of

---

[69] Nielsen and Szyszczak (1993, p 56), supra, note 36.

[70] Cited in Craig and de Burca (1995, p 661), supra, note 8.

[71] Cf Article 1, Regulation 1612/68 above.

[72] Baldwin-Edwards, M. (1992) 'The socio-political rights of migrants in the European Community', in G. Room (ed) *Towards a European welfare state*, Bristol: SAUS Publications, p 212.

---

worker, and the public policy derogations, should be governed by Community law, Member States have retained sovereignty over the issue of nationality. It is, in the main, for Member States to define the parameters of nationality – to decide who is a national for the purposes of the free movement of persons. The autonomy of Member States in decisions concerning the ascription of nationality was further reinforced by a declaration annexed to the Maastricht Treaty, which states that:

Wherever in the Treaty establishing the European Community reference is made to nationals of the Member States, the question of whether an individual possesses the nationality of a Member State shall be settled solely by reference to the national law of the Member State.

The *Micheletti* case[73], however, raised some doubts about the absolute and exclusive competency of Member States in matters concerning nationality. In this case, a person of dual Argentinian and Italian nationality was refused a card identifying him as a Community national enabling him to work as an odontologist in Spain. The refusal by the Spanish authorities was based upon an article of the Spanish Civil Code which required that dual nationals (in cases where neither nationality was Spanish) should be accorded the nationality of the country of their habitual residence prior to their entry into Spain (in this case Argentina). The ECJ held that, although it was for Member States to define conditions governing the acquisition of nationality, a Member State could not apply additional conditions of recognition of that nationality. So, if a person can produce evidence that they hold the nationality of a Member State, other Member States cannot dispute their status as a Community national[74]. The consequences of *Micheletti* for Community citizenship are remarked upon by Handoll who refers to the Court as having, "adopted a 'more the merrier' approach, promoting, within the confines of national determinants of nationality, an inclusive rather than exclusive, view of citizenship"[75].

---

[73] *Micheletti and others v Delegacion del Gobierno en Cantabria*, Case C-369/90 [1992] ECR 1-4239.
[74] This case was concerned specifically with the right of establishment (Council Directive 73/148/EEC). In the case, however, the Court held that the ruling also applied to the provisions for workers.
[75] Handoll, J. (1995) *Free movement of persons in the EU*, Chichester: John Wiley and Sons, p 67.

Although Member States have exclusive competence in determining which persons are classed as nationals for the purposes of Community law, the consequences of possession of nationality may be subject to rules of Community law.

One important exception to the exclusion of third country nationals concerns the status of members of workers' families. Article 10 Regulation 1612/68 clearly states that the provisions for workers' families apply, "irrespective of their nationality". The implications of this exception are discussed in the section on family rights (below). It does, however, give rise to some surprising anomalies in the ascription of citizenship which may, by virtue of the non-application of the provisions to host nationals, contravene the principle of equal treatment giving third country nationals who are members of a Community worker's family, greater protection than that afforded to family members of national workers. The concept of 'reverse discrimination' has been used to describe such cases where Community migrants are positively advantaged, in comparison to nationals[76]. This situation arises because of the requirement for some 'Community dimension' typically evidenced by some connection with cross-border activity, which 'triggers' entitlement under the free movement provisions. Non-migrant nationals cannot, therefore, use the provisions to claim equal treatment with EU migrant workers[77].

While the present exclusion of third country migrants from the benefits of European citizenship leads to a pronounced polarisation of status between those migrants within the Community who do not possess Community nationality and those 'privileged aliens' who do, it is a mistake to infer, as is often the case, a universality of status among the latter group. Indeed, many Community nationals can claim no more than a simple, and conditional, basic right of residence. Citizenship status alone does not

---

[76] For further discussion see Kon, S. (1981) 'Aspects of reverse discrimination in community law', *European Law Review*, vol 6, p 75; Pickup, D. (1986) 'Reverse discrimination and freedom of movement for workers', *Common Market Law Review*, vol 23, p 135; and D'Oliveira, J. (1990) 'The Community Case: is reverse discrimination still permissible under the Single European Act?', in *Forty years on: The evolution of postwar private international law in Europe*, Deveneter: Kluwer. The concept could be applied to unequal status of women in Ireland, for example, where nationals have had restricted rights to receive abortion services in other Member States compared to EU migrant women (see Chapter Seven).

[77] *R v Saunders*, Case 175/78 [1979] ECR 1129; *Moser v Land Baden-Wurttenberg*, Case 180/83 [1984] ECR 2539.

---

confer a broad equality of condition as the concept suggests, but simply a general and restricted right of residence. Having satisfied the condition of nationality, a Community citizen's access to rights and benefits in the host Member State depends on them demonstrating membership of one or more 'classes' of persons, the membership of which gives rise to a distinctive citizenship status based upon an identifiable body of Community law. There are essentially three broad classes (subject to the derogations):

- **Business class**: Paid workers and self-employed persons (and those exercising their right to remain after occupational activity has ceased) with full, independent entitlement.
- **Club class**: Family members of the above with derivative rights.
- **Tourist class**: Students, retired persons and 'other' economically-inactive persons[78].

The concept of 'worker' in community law.

In the beginning there were workers ... The essence of freedom of movement for workers is that restrictions are abolished for, and rights are granted to, human factors of production who cross Community national borders to work or to seek work in the situations envisaged by Community law, in other words, freedom is for migrant workers.[79]

In the language of citizenship, Article 8 EC bestows on citizens of the Union both rights and 'duties'. In practice, put the other way around, any rights derived from citizenship are dependent upon forms of social contribution and contribution is interpreted in essentially economic terms. The most highly 'rewarded' form of contribution is through individual economic endeavour or, more precisely, paid work. It is in matters concerning the rights of paid workers that the EU generally adopts its most self-confident approach to social policy, secure in the knowledge that its actions fall well within its legitimate competency and do not contravene the politically sensitive principle of subsidiarity (Article 3b EC). The paid worker and employment-related matters, broadly construed,

---

[78] The impact of the *Martinez Sala* case on this hitherto fundamental distinction between economic and non-economic migrants has already been referred to.

[79] Pollard, D. and Ross, M. (1994) *European Community law. Text and materials*, London: Butterworths, p 429.

are legitimate areas for Community action. This confidence has led to broad and expansive rulings under the free movement provisions pushing the boundaries of EU competence beyond the apparent intention of Article 48. In so doing, the EU has extended its social policy role, in a largely unnoticed fashion, 'through the back door'.

We have already seen how Article 48 and Regulation 1612/68 refers specifically to the 'freedom of movement for workers'. The concept of 'worker' and 'activity as employed person' is not defined in Community legislation but has been left to the Court to interpret. In contrast to the concept of nationality, the Court has insisted upon a Community-wide definition to ensure even application of the law and to avoid a situation in which Member States adopt their own definition[80]. The Court's insistence on a Community definition can be seen in its ruling in *Levin*[81]. Here, a British woman married to a third country national and residing in The Netherlands was refused a resident's permit on the grounds that the wages derived from her employment, as a chambermaid, fell below the minimum legal wage and did not, therefore, provide her with adequate financial support. The Court held that the enjoyment of the rights for workers could not be made subject to national legislation on minimum wage levels, "so that the field of application ratione personae of the Community rules might vary from one Member State to another". Although, in this case, Levin was not claiming social assistance in the host State (her husband was working full-time), the key concern of Member States was to restrict the entry of persons who were not financially independent and may, as a result, seek welfare support in the host country. This desire, on the part of Member States, to insulate national welfare systems, particularly in relation to needs-based benefits, from the consequences of labour mobility, illustrates the tension between economic and social policy and the impossibility of separating the two. The Levin case also illustrates the implications of the articulation of nationality with marriage for citizenship status. For Levin herself, as the spouse of a worker of third country nationality (from whom she derives no Community entitlement), her status as a Community worker is an essential source of personal social entitlement. For her spouse, on the other hand, the case illustrates the importance of a 'Community link' for a third country national who, by virtue of his marriage to a Community worker can then derive entitlement under Regulation 1612/68.

---

[80] *Unger v Bestuur*, Case 75/63 [1964] ECR 1977.
[81] *Levin v Secretary of State for Justice*, Case 53/81 [1982] ECR 1035.

The Court attempted to resolve this problem (of Levin's low wage) by arguing that a person's status as a Community worker depended not so much on their financial self-sufficiency, but on their economic contribution. Referring to Article 117 EC and the Treaty commitment to an, "improved standard of living for workers", the Court argued that part-time work was an important and effective means of achieving that objective. In an interesting judgment, which may be contrasted with its subsequent ruling in *Reed*[82] (below), the Court showed itself prepared to take account of changing socioeconomic and cultural conditions arguing that restricting eligibility to full-time employees would jeopardise Treaty objectives by, "excluding very large, and probably increasing numbers of persons [including] women, the elderly and disabled".

The Court also considered, in this case, the issue of motive, responding to the suggestion that Levin should be disqualified on the grounds of instrumentalism (she only sought work as a means to securing residency). Preferring an 'objective' definition, the Court found that motive or purpose was irrelevant provided that the person was engaged in the pursuit of effective and genuine activities, to the exclusion of activities on such a small scale as to be regarded as purely marginal and ancillary. Member States' concerns that the extension of rights to free movement would both increase incentives to benefits tourism and undermine sovereignty in matters of domestic social policy were further exacerbated by the Court's subsequent ruling in *Kempf*[83]. Here, a part-time music teacher sought to supplement his meagre income (which fell below the minimum subsistence level) by claiming social assistance from public funds in the host State. In ruling that reliance on social assistance did not, automatically, undermine Kempf's status as a worker, the Court further blurred the distinction between a citizen's economic status as paid worker and benefit recipient. Such forms of work qualified, provided they were not 'purely marginal and ancillary', by virtue of their economic nature, even when they were

---

[82] *The Netherlands v Reed*, Case 59/85 [1986] ECR 1283.
[83] *Kempf v Staatsecretaris van Justitie*, Case 139/85 [1986] ECR 1741.

to the economic detriment of the receiving state (something of a tautology)[84].

The Court extended its definition of 'worker' still further in *Raulin* to include employment in irregular, 'on-call' contracts:

> **The conditions of employment under a contract which provides no guarantee as to the number of hours to be worked, with the result that the person concerned works only a limited number of days per week or hours per day ... do not prevent the employed person in question from being regarded as a worker within the meaning of Article 48 of the Treaty, in so far as the activities pursued are effective and genuine activities to the exclusion of activities on such a small scale as to be regarded as marginal and ancillary ... [However] ... National courts may, when assessing the effective and genuine nature of the activity pursued by the worker, take account of the irregular nature and limited duration of the services actually performed under an on-call contract.[85]**

Under pressure from Member States to provide more concrete guidance, the Court, in ruling that a trainee teacher qualified as a 'worker', set out a formula detailing the defining features of an employment relationship:

> **The essential feature of an employment relationship, however, is that for a certain period of time a person performs services**

---

[84] The questions here are further complicated by the Court's recent judgment in *Martinez Sala* (supra, note 1). In a somewhat counter-intuitive argument, the Court suggested that reliance on social security benefits may actually provide the source of a claim to the status of worker under Regulation 1408/71. In this case, Martinez Sala had worked in Germany prior to 1986 after which time she was dependent upon social welfare. The Court suggested that her status as an employed person (under Regulation 1408/71) did not require the existence of an employment relationship but rather proof that she was covered, even if only in respect of a single risk, by a general or special social security scheme. Fries and Shaw (1998, p 16), supra, note 27, conclude on this point that: "It seems all the more likely given that those who are on social welfare in Germany are automatically insured against sickness, and this provides the leverage to bring Martinez Sala within the scope of Regulation 1408/71".
[85] *Raulin v Netherlands Ministry of Education and Science*, Case C-357/89 [1992] ECR 1-1027, para 1.

for and under the direction of another person in return for which he receives remuneration.[86]

This 'silent' inclusive approach broadened the net of Community protection which was cast still further in *Steymann*[87]. Here, a German national, residing once again in The Netherlands, was refused a residence permit by the relevant authorities on the grounds that his contribution to the life of a religious community could not be regarded as 'economic' for the purposes of Community law. In consideration for his contribution, the religious community provided for his keep, including an element of 'pocket money'. In a judgment which strained even a purposive approach, the Court held that, under the *Lawrie-Blum* formula, Steymann provided services of value to the religious community which would, otherwise, have had to be performed by someone else (and presumably paid for); on that basis, he qualified as a worker. The Court found that Steymann's contribution to the community via some plumbing work, general housework and participation in the outside economic activities of the organisation (a disco and laundry service), while unremunerated nevertheless, "constitute economic activities in so far as the services which the community provides to its members may be regarded as the *indirect quid pro quo for genuine and effective work*".

The ruling in Steymann is clearly good news for those workers engaged in more marginal forms of 'work', the majority of whom will be women. Furthermore, if the concept of remuneration, under the *Lawrie-Blum* formula, can be strained so substantially to include pocket money and the notion of indirect economic 'savings' as opposed to income, then the only thing which sets Steymann's 'work' apart from that of the average housewife/carer is the reference to plumbing. Indeed, recognition that the work done by carers would otherwise have to be performed (and paid for) by someone else underpins the explicit recognition of carers' rights in the 1990 Disabled Persons Act (in order to promote the viability of the British government's policy of 'Care in the Community'). The significance of the plumbing work is unclear, and the extent to which it may be interpreted as distinctively different to other forms of domestic or caring work may simply reflect yet another example of the ways in which women's unpaid work is accorded low status.

---

[86] *Lawrie-Blum v Land Baden Wurtemberg*, Case 66/85 [1986] ECR 2121, para 17.
[87] *Steymann v Staatssecretaris van Justitie*, Case 196/87 [1988] ECR 6159.

Recent developments in social policy across Europe may, however, require some clarification from the ECJ. The pressure on the voluntary sector as a key provider of social welfare, for example, has resulted in the growth of 'paid volunteering' schemes. The fact that the overwhelming majority of 'paid volunteers' are women reflects the typically low level and exploitative nature of the payments and the 'attractiveness' of this type of work to women with family commitments (in that they can work 'flexibly'). Women working in such schemes would thus arguably qualify as 'workers' under Community law. In addition to the changing nature of work in the voluntary sector, the combination of demographic and economic pressures on welfare systems has prompted an interest in mechanisms which might increase the supply of caring labour while, at the same time, reducing the unit cost. The UK and Finland, for example, have seen the introduction of schemes involving cash payments to informal care-givers[88]. These pressures to increase reliance on informal care (and on women as carers) raise questions about the citizenship status and quality of life of dependants and carers. They also blur traditional boundaries between unpaid and paid work and between women's roles as carers and earners, raising interesting questions in relation to Community competence in areas hitherto outside the public sphere. While the relative generosity of the Finnish Home Care Allowances scheme has been welcomed as recognition of the importance of this form of work, concern remains that the workers concerned may be denied the kinds of rights associated with paid work, such as occupational pensions and paid holiday entitlements. These shortcomings have recently been challenged in the Finnish labour and insurance courts on the grounds that the relationship between the municipality (responsible for paying the carer) and the care-giver is equivalent to a normal employment contract, and that the care-giver should therefore enjoy the same rights as other municipal employees. This has resulted in proposals for a form of contract to be drawn up specifying the tasks the care-giver is expected to undertake, the rate of pay and the period of time for which the contract is operative.

In relation to the present discussion, at least, it could be argued that the development of even minimal quasi-employment rights for carers where a carer is in receipt of remuneration either as a form of social assistance, as in the UK, or as a form of compensation for labour market 'withdrawal',

---

[88] Glendinning, C. and McLaughlin, E. (1993) 'Paying for informal care: lessons from Finland', *Journal of European Social Policy*, vol 3, no 4, pp 239-53. For more discussion see Chapter Eight.

as in some Scandinavian schemes, would enable them to qualify as 'workers' under Community law. Certainly it would be very difficult to justify, in the context of *Steymann*, the exclusion of paid carers or volunteers.

One year later, however, the Court applied a more restrictive approach in relation to a person who was undertaking therapeutic 'work' as part of a Dutch social employment scheme (aimed at re-integrating people into the workforce)[89]. The Court began by examining the facts in the light of the *Lawrie-Blum* formula and found that the 'work' was carried out under supervision and in return for remuneration (in contrast to Steymann) and the fact that the pay came from public funds did not, in itself, disqualify Bettray. The opinion of the Advocate General in the case, however, stressed that, "if the elements of the normal employment relationship are indeed merely incidental to the social aims of the scheme, then the activity in question might be regarded as purely ancillary".

Taking care not to rule out the possibility of work undertaken by disabled workers in private organisations, he described the 'sole decisive criterion' as follows:

> **The concern exists solely and specifically to give those who are unable to work in normal conditions an activity similar to that which a person might be engaged if he were able to work in a normal environment. In such a situation, the activity is created for the person, and it is not a case of access to employment at all.**

Departing from its judgment in *Levin* and its insistence on an objective definition, the Court examined the purpose of Bettray's 'work' and found that, "Work under social employment law cannot be regarded as an effective and genuine economic activity if it constitutes merely a means of rehabilitation or reintegration".

This questionable judgment, read in the light of Article 117 and the European Community's apparent support for the integration of disabled persons and women into the labour market, represents a brake on its hitherto expansionary approach. Indeed, the Advocate General referred to the judgment in *Levin* which emphasised the purpose of the free movement of workers in the promotion of, "an harmonious development of economic activities and [to raise] the standard of living"[90].

---

[89] *Bettray v Staatssecretaris van Justitie*, Case 344/87 [1989] ECR 1621.
[90] Para 27.

It would appear that, following this decision, work in sheltered employment schemes does not constitute genuine and effective economic activity. Concern over the implications of this notion of 'work' was expressed by the European Commission (EC) in its submission to the case:

> **The claim that the activity pursued by Mr Bettray is not an economic activity but has a purely social purpose anounts to refusing to regard as workers within the meaning of Community law those who are employed in foundations, associations or other non-profit organisations.**

The return to a more subjective approach, through the admission of motive or purpose as a relevant factor, potentially restricts the scope of the concept to the possible exclusion of voluntary or informal care. To the extent that informal care can be distinguished from other forms of social care on grounds of motivation then any move in this direction may seriously restrict the possibility of pulling into the frame, forms of work undertaken by women, even when remunerated on the grounds that these are motivated by altruism or familial obligation (hence the reference to caring as a 'labour of love'[91]) as opposed to financial reward.

The thorny problem of motive, not least in terms of safeguarding the general principle of legal certainty and the problems of operationalising the concept, has been compounded by a series of rulings concerned with the development of educational rights under Regulation 1612/68. Faced, once again, with the tension between a more expansive and inclusionary interpretation of the free movement provisions and Member State concerns about the distributional impact of social costs (particularly the encouragement of educational tourism), the Court has effectively blurred the boundaries and introduced, unwittingly, a quasi-worker status by creating fine distinctions based upon motive. The growing sense of confusion and uncertainty can be illustrated by reference to the following decisions which, when taken together, apparently undermine the principles of both equality and legal certainty.

It follows from the discussion above (of the substantive scope of the provisions) that educational grants and loans may now fall within the 'social advantages' formula. The matter of educational grants has caused

---

[91] Finch, J. and Groves, D. (1983) *A labour of love. Women, work and caring*, London: RKP.

---

considerable anxiety among Member States concerned to prevent 'educational tourism'. The relative ease of qualifying as a Community worker, coupled with the widening material scope, together open up the possibility of persons gaining entitlement to educational maintenance grants simply by taking up limited forms of part-time work. This prospect was raised in the cases of *Lair* and *Brown* and resulted in a re-definition of the worker concept[92]. Sylvie Lair was a French woman who had worked, on a part-time basis, in Germany for over five years with some periods of involuntary unemployment. Lair then gave up work in order to study and claimed a maintenance grant. The Court found that, in deciding whether or not she qualified for such a grant, as a worker, a distinction should be drawn between those workers who become involuntarily unemployed in the host Member State who would be entitled to equal treatment with nationals and those workers who *voluntarily* give up paid work in order to study. In such cases, although the person concerned retains her status as a worker, she would not be entitled to a maintenance grant unless there was a 'link' between the course of study and her previous employment. This decision, designed to inhibit benefits tourism, and appease those Member States anticipating a deluge of claims, has the unfortunate, and in the context of the internal market, undesirable effect of restricting opportunities for re-skilling.

In *Brown*, a student of dual French/British nationality had been domiciled in France when he secured a place at Cambridge University to study engineering. Brown also obtained sponsorship from a Scottish firm which involved him working for the firm for seven months prior to commencement of the course. During this time he applied for a maintenance grant from the British authorities and was rejected. The Advocate General in the case suggested that a distinction could be made between those who migrated genuinely in their capacities as workers and those who move for other reasons. Only the former, he suggested, could invoke Article 7(2) and (3) of Regulation 1612/68. The Court, however, ruled that, although Brown clearly was a worker, he was not entitled to claim the grant since his employment was "*merely ancillary*" to the studies to be financed. This decision can be contrasted with the outcome in *Bernini*[93] where an Italian woman who had only worked in The Netherlands

---

[92] *Lair v University of Hanover*, Case 39/86 [1988] ECR 3161 and *Brown v Secretary of State for Scotland*, Case 197/86 [1988] ECR 3205.

[93] *Bernini v Minister van Onderwijs en Wetensc happen*, Case C-3/90 [1992] ECR 1-1071.

for 10 weeks nevertheless retained the status of worker when she left the employment and, after a period of time, took up a full-time course. These decisions, based on the subjective question of motive, have resulted in important inequalities in substantive entitlement and fine, if confusing, distinctions between groups of workers leading Craig and de Burca to refer to a new, "semi-status between worker and non-worker"[94]. Not surprisingly, this is a situation in which many EU migrant women find themselves.

Jobseekers and the 'voluntarily' unemployed

Another grey area concerns the status of persons looking for work in another Member State. We saw, in *Levin*, how the Court extended its ruling to include those persons "seriously wishing to pursue" a genuine economic activity. Regulation 1408/71[95] introduced measures enabling unemployed persons to retain their right to benefit in their country of nationality when they move to another Member State to look for work (for a period of up to three months). In another attempt to limit the social responsibility of receiving Member States, the ECJ has ruled that, while jobseekers *are* workers, their citizenship status is highly circumscribed. In *Antonissen*[96] the Court held that although persons seeking work *were* covered by Article 48 and had the right to move freely in search for work, such a right was not, however, unlimited and Member States retain the power to expel a person who has failed to secure employment after an (unstated) period of time. The importance of 'full' status as a worker was emphasised in another case involving a claim under the social advantages formula by the unemployed son of a migrant worker. Here, the Court found that, "Those who move in search of employment qualify for equal treatment *only as regards access to employment*"[97]. Jobseekers, as well as those

---

[94] Craig and de Burca (1995, p 670), supra, note 8.

[95] Supra, note 12.

[96] *R v IAT ex parte Antonissen*, Case C-292/89 [1991] ECR 1-745. The Court found that it was not contrary to EC law to find that a person who has entered a Member State in search of work and has not found any after six months, may be required to leave, subject to appeal, unless that person provides evidence that he is continuing to seek work and has genuine chances of being engaged. The Court decided not to impose a time limit as such.

[97] *Centre Public d'Aide Sociale de Courcelles v Lebon*, Case 316/85 [1987] ECR 2811.

---

whose work is considered to be ancillary to education, are apparently denied access to substantive social rights under Article 7(2) Regulation 1612/68.

A further restriction on the personal scope concerns those unemployed persons whose predicament is classed as 'voluntary' by the competent employment authorities. The impact of unemployment on worker status was raised in *Unger*[98]. The Court found that the status of worker extended to those persons who, having lost their job, are capable of taking another. However, Directive 68/360[99] expressly provides that a worker's right of residence cannot be withdrawn as a result of *in*voluntary unemployment (Article 7(1)), implying that that right will be lost if the unemployment is construed as 'voluntary'. The distinction between *in*voluntary and voluntary unemployment was considered by the Immigration Appeal Tribunal in *Giangregorio*:

> **The distinction between voluntary and involuntary unemployment is critical to the curtailment [of the appellant's residency] and in our view any exercise of the power to curtail must be based on 'voluntary unemployment'.**[100]

This definition of 'voluntary' unemployment may disadvantage migrant women who take time out of paid employment for family reasons and raises the question of whether interruptions in a woman's employment, as a result of her domestic responsibilities, may be interpreted as periods of 'voluntary' unemployment resulting in the removal of important social rights. Pauline Jackson's study of migrant women in the Republic of Ireland[101] notes the 'vigorous enforcement' of a rule denying unemployment payments to married women with young children, who had previously been in paid work, on the grounds that they are not genuinely available for work. The UK operates a similar policy of requiring married women with young children to demonstrate that they have adequate provisions for childcare before they can register as available for work. In the UK, at least, unemployed mothers may be refused Jobseeker's Allowance if they

---

[98] *Unger v Bestuur*, Case 75/63 [1964] ECR 1977, para 26.

[99] Supra, note 13.

[100] *Giangregorio v Secretary of State for the Home Department*, Case [1983] 3 CMLR 472, para 28.

[101] Jackson, P. (1987) 'Migrant women: the Republic of Ireland', Commission of Europe, DGV/139/89.

have caring responsibilities which prevent them being able to take up an offer of work within 48 hours[102].

Even the involuntarily unemployed, however, must have attained the status of Community worker in the host State before becoming unemployed in order to qualify for full residency rights under Directive 68/360. The ECJ made this clear in *Raulin*, where it introduced a new yardstick which both broadens the scope of the 'worker' concept and represents a significant restriction for many migrant women:

> **In assessing whether a person is a worker account should be taken of all the occupational activities which the person concerned has pursued within the territory of the host Member State but not the activities which he has pursued elsewhere in the Community.** [103]

In view of women's relationship with paid work, the problems of discontinuity, the predominance of women in what is euphemistically referred to as 'flexible' work and the high incidence of female unemployment following migration, this lack of recognition of previous employment status particularly disadvantages women. Traditional 'rational' economic models of migration behaviour, based on principles of economic maximisation, would regard the prospect of de-skilling and downward career mobility as insurmountable barriers to labour mobility – and yet for women this is a common experience[104].

.

Citizenship, jobseekers and the impact of Article 8a

I referred in the introduction to this chapter to current uncertainty over the effect of Article 8a. Recent discussions about Article 8a have crystallised around the issue of residency entitlement of jobseekers – as a specific category of citizens whose rights will very much depend upon the Court's

---

[102] Barnes, M., Ravell, M. and Lakhani, B. (1998) *Jobseeker's allowance handbook*, 2nd edn, London: Child Poverty Action Group. This represents an improvement on the previous scheme which required that such persons were available to start work at 'a moment's notice'.

[103] *Raulin v Netherlands Ministry of Education and Science*, Case C-357/89 [1992] ECR 1-1027, para 2.

[104] A point discussed further in Chapter Six.

interpretation of the new concept of citizenship. We have seen that, following *Antonissen*[105], it is not unlawful for a Member State to revoke the residency rights of unemployed persons who have exercised their right of entry on the precept that they are actively seeking employment, after a certain period of time. The question is whether Article 8a creates a free-standing, independent, source of citizenship entitlement (at least in the context of a claim for residency) or whether this right is subject to pre-existing conditions and restrictions under Article 48 and associated secondary legislation. Peter Duffy QC, examining the recent case of *Vitale*[106], sets out the issue as follows:

> **The decision in *Antonissen* rested solely on Article 48 EC, and the rights given to 'workers' by that provision. In issue is whether or not the legal framework has been altered by the introduction of the new Article 8a, which makes the political category of citizenship, rather than the economic categories of employment or self-employment, the foundation of free movement rights.**[107]

The issue at stake in *Vitale* was whether the Home Office had been entitled to decide that Mr Vitale was not lawfully present in this country when, after more than six months presence as a work seeker, he had failed to find work and, in the opinion of the Home Office, did not show reasonable prospects of securing employment. The Home Office position was that his *stay* thereafter was *unlawful* because he was dependent on public funds and thus fell outside the scope of Directive 90/365[108].

The question was thus whether Article 8a had created a new foundation for European citizenship, extending the right of residence to non-economically active persons and effectively replacing the right, established in *Antonissen*, of Member States to require jobseekers to leave if they have

---

[105] Supra, note 96.

[106] *R v Secretary of State for Home Department ex p Vitale*, Case [1995] All ER EC 946 affirmed by the Court of Appeal at [1996] All ER EC 461.

[107] Peter Duffy QC (1997), 'Workers and work seekers – an incomplete legal agenda in the light of Citizenship of the Union'. Paper to the Immigration Law Practitioners' Association and the Centre of European Law, King's College London Conference, 'The legal framework and social consequences of free movement of persons in the European Union', 27-28 November.

[108] Council Directive 90/365 (Residence Rights for Ex-employees and Self-employed).

not found work after six months (that is, to revoke their residency entitlement). The Court of Appeal held that Article 8a EC does not give rise to a directly effective general right of residence and insisted that it was subject to the limitations contained in the Treaty and secondary legislation. In the event, the case was suspended as Mr Vitale decided to return home, leaving the status of Article 8a unclear.

In a recent discussion of the effect of the Treaty's citizenship provisions, Siofra O'Leary refers to the Opinion of Advocate General La Pergola in another case where he suggests that the ultimate objective of the Treaty provisions was to found a "growing assimilation between the Citizens of the Union"[109]. For the time being, the effect of Article 8a and the status of jobseekers, among others, is open to question.

Family rights

We saw, in the previous section, how the most favoured citizenship status derives from forms of 'economic' contribution via paid work. The extension of substantive rights to members of workers' families may thus, at first analysis, appear to contradict this principle and mark a genuine departure in the direction of a more holistic, universal and meaningful citizenship. The extent to which the explicit recognition of family policy as a legitimate area of Community intervention represents such a shift away from the narrow individualism of free market economics – and an advancement of women's interests – depends, however, on our conceptualisation of 'family'. Although women's experience and autonomy is very much tied up with family matters, it would be a grave mistake to interpret public recognition and intervention in family policy as indicative of a more collectivist or, indeed, 'woman friendly' approach. Whatever the ultimate motivation, whether it be Catholic public morality (as in Mediterranean countries and Ireland), pro-natalist, nationalistic, demographic policy (as in France and Germany), or simply the fiscal demands of social-democratic regimes (demanding full employment, as in Sweden), very rarely does the development of family policy reflect an explicit concern to advance women's interests. More commonly it reflects the further entrenchment of forms of public and private patriarchal control. In the British context, Margaret Thatcher's now infamous enunciation of liberal individualism –

---

[109] *Stober and Pereira v Bundesanstalt fur Arbeit*, Joined Cases C-4/95 and C-5/95, judgment of the Court of 30 January 1997, Opinion of the Advocate General of 6 June, 1996 unreported.

---

that there is no such thing as society but simply a collection of individuals – underpinned the 'New Right' strategy of welfare retrenchment, the rejection of post-war 'rational' social planning and a return to individual responsibility. Concealed by the rhetoric of methodological individualism, the fundamental economic unit of the new free market regime was not to be individuals at all, but 'families' in a bid to replace the 'culture of [public] dependency' on State welfare with a culture of [private] dependency within families. The 'family' in Britain, both as a unit of consumption and reproduction, became the invisible vehicle for the promotion of a new decollectivised liberal vision.

Matters which may be swept under the carpet as convenient policy vacuums or non-decisions become, all of a sudden, economically relevant as the imperative of labour mobility demands the removal of barriers to the movement of factors of production in European and global markets. Thus, that which was functional to subject to the subsidiarity principle in a non-migration context becomes dysfunctional when economic expediency demands 'footloose' labour. Given the Court's interpretation of the purpose of free movement as essentially one of 'facilitating mobility'[110] and its assessment of migration behaviour (and perceptions of barriers to labour mobility), such incursions into the family policy may be justified on the grounds that the migrant worker's family provides the essential "infrastructure for men's mobility"[111].

Welcome though it is, the extension of entitlement to workers' families does not represent a significant departure away from a fundamentally market-oriented social policy, but simply a recognition that desired economic objectives may not be realised in the absence of limited incursions into family policy. Scheiwe sets out the policy agenda as follows:

> **Provisions on the free movement of workers allow interventions into the family sphere and related areas of law, despite their market connections being rather indirect, in order to guarantee the stabilising function of the existing gendered division of labour and to augment the male migrant's mobility. In this model, a (male) worker's family is clearly a market-related issue that matters. The woman is dealt with only as a subordinated**

---

[110] The formula adopted in *Even*, supra, note 44.

[111] Scheiwe, K. (1994) 'EC law's unequal treatment of the family: the case law of the European Court of Justice on rules prohibiting discrimination on grounds of sex and nationality', *Social and Legal Studies*, vol 3, pp 243-65 at p 251.

> part of the family unit not as a 'head of household' or an
> individual of equal importance. This is also shown by the wide
> lack of special provisions or structural policies that could
> augment female worker's mobility through the improvement
> of childcare facilities or other infrastructures which would
> reduce obstacles to the free movement of the female workforce.[112]

The male breadwinning family model has thus permeated not only the domestic social policy of Member States but is also enshrined in analyses of migration. Notions of family structure and the apportionment of roles within families translate into a convenient model of migration behaviour. Thus, the male breadwinner family model takes on a spatial and temporal dimension. The extension of social rights under the free movement provisions, generous as they are, is founded upon an ideologically-loaded conceptualisation of the family, and of migration behaviour which both presumes and reinforces high levels of dependency within families and ignores the barriers to labour mobility facing women migrants. The 'family', in policy terms, becomes simply an appendage of the male breadwinner, facilitating his commodification, consuming the fruits of his labour and securing the survival of the system through reproduction. The only individual in this fundamentally economic 'unit' is the breadwinner and it is only he who, by virtue of his direct economic contribution (via waged labour) derives independent social entitlement. The contribution of the spouse is of an indirect nature and is thus rewarded indirectly. This is the case in those Member States whose domestic social provision is characterised by Lewis' 'strong male breadwinning model' (such as Ireland and the UK)[113]. The evolution of 'family' entitlement, at Community level, under the free movement provisions to a large extent replicates this model, restricting independent entitlement to paid workers thus reinforcing patterns of dependency:

> Members of the worker's family are only indirect beneficiaries
> of the right to equal treatment accorded to the worker under
> Article 7(2) of Regulation 1612/68; social advantages can only
> be granted to members of the family under Article 7(2) as
> advantages to the *worker*.[114]

---

[112] Scheiwe (1994, p 251), supra, note 111.

[113] Lewis, J. (1992) 'Gender and the development of welfare regimes', *Journal of European Social Policy*, vol 2, no 3, pp 159-73.

[114] Steiner (1996, p 271), supra, note 20.

The rights of the family, therefore, depend on their relationship with the worker and are coterminous with the worker's rights unless they themselves are Community nationals who qualify in their own right as 'workers' or have acquired a right of residence in some other way (such as the right to remain under Regulation 1251/70). It is for this reason that Steiner refers to spousal rights as 'parasitic'[115].

The protected persons: the concept of family in Community law

This limited and functional approach to family rights can be seen in the Court's restrictive interpretation of the concept of family. The legislation refers to the migrant worker and 'his' family suggesting a male breadwinning model and the ECJ has made it clear that these measures are less concerned with the rights of family members per se but exist to, "assist his [the worker's] integration in the host State and thus to contribute to the achievement of the freedom of movement of workers"[116]. Families are defined in Regulation 1612/68 as, "his spouse and their descendants who are under the age of 21 years or are dependants and, dependent relatives in the ascending line of the worker and his spouse". The rights afforded to Community workers thus extend to 'his spouse', their children and dependant parents[117] or grandparents, irrespective of nationality[118]. The following section considers the Court's interpretation of the concept of 'spouse' in some detail before going on to address the derivative nature of the rights (in that they are ultimately the rights of the worker and not independent rights for family members).

The concept of 'spouse' in Community law

Regulation 1612/68 simply refers to 'his spouse'. This definition leaves scope for some ambiguity with important implications for the rights of

---

[115] Steiner (1996, p 260), supra, note 20.

[116] *Netherlands State v Reed*, Case 59/85 [1986] ECR 1283.

[117] In *Castelli v ONPTS*, Case 261/83 [1984] ECR 3199, the Court found that an Italian mother who moved to join her migrant worker son in Belgium was entitled to a minimum income allowance on the grounds that she had 'settled residence'.

[118] The right of residence and associated social rights can thus be claimed by a parent of a Community worker even when they do not possess Community nationality.

the partners of migrant workers. In particular, concern has arisen over the definition of 'spouse' in Community law, the entitlement of cohabitants and the implications of separation and divorce on spousal rights. In future we may also see cases involving the rights of homosexual and lesbian partnerships throwing traditional notions of the family into further disarray[119].

The rights of cohabitants

In *Netherlands State v Reed*[120] the Court of Justice was asked whether the term 'spouse' included a cohabitant. Ms Reed, a British national, accompanied her partner, of five years standing, when he took up employment for the subsidiary of a British company based in The Netherlands. After a period spent looking for work, Ms Reed applied for a residence permit on the basis of her relationship with her partner (claiming her derived entitlement). Her application was dismissed on the grounds that she was not the spouse of a Community national. The case was then referred to the ECJ. In its judgment the Court emphasised the importance of a Community-wide definition drawing parallels with its case law on the concept of worker:

> **The term 'spouse' has a specific meaning in Community law – [therefore] divergence in the application of the law on an issue important for freedom of movement, would be just as unacceptable as divergence with regard to the term 'worker'.**

Ms Reed argued that, in the light of legal and social developments, in applying Article 10 of Regulation 1612/68, and in particular the word 'spouse', to circumstances such as those of this case, unmarried partners must, in so far as possible, be treated as spouses. Failure to adopt such a

---

[119] The implications of recent changes in Dutch law granting legal recognition of same-sex marriages was reported in *The Guardian* (20 April 1996, p 27) in an article which considered the status of these marriages in Community law and the prospect of 'marriage tourism' where same-sex couples travel to The Netherlands to marry and then demand Community recognition of those partnerships in other Member States. For more detailed discussion, see Waaldijk, K. and Clapham, A. (eds) (1993) *Homosexuality: A European Community issue*, Dordrecht: Martinus Nijhoff.

[120] *Netherlands State v Reed*, Case 59/85 [1987] 2 CMLR 448.

broad interpretation would have the effect of restricting the free movement of persons on the grounds that many couples who live together today would have been married in 1968 when the Regulation was drafted. Changes in social circumstances would, therefore, result in a more limited application of the principle contained within Regulation 1612/68 than it had a number of years ago (contrary to the original intention of the Regulation). The Court rejected Ms Reed's argument in favour of a broad interpretation of the concept and found that:

> **When, in support of a dynamic interpretation reference is made to developments in social and legal conceptions, those developments must be visible in the whole of the Community; such an argument cannot be based on social and legal developments in only one or two Member States.**

The term 'spouse' in Article 10 thus, "applies to marriage partners only and does not include cohabitation". However, a Member State which grants such an advantage to its own nationals cannot refuse it to workers who are nationals of other Member States without being guilty of discrimination on grounds of nationality contrary to Articles 6 and 48 EC (Dutch law permitted 'aliens' with stable relationships with Dutch nationals in similar situations to reside in Holland). Ms Reed would, therefore, have been entitled to remain in Holland.

It is difficult to assess whether, in practice, this decision relates to the empirical difficulty of establishing evidence of a 'general social development' nor, indeed, whether the Court actually considered any empirical evidence of this kind. The wording of the judgment, however, suggests that, presented with sound empirical evidence of a 'general social development' of this kind, it would consider a broader construction:

> **In the absence of any indication of a general social development which would justify a broad construction and in the absence of any indication to the contrary in the Regulation, it must be held that the term 'spouse' in Article 10 of Regulation 1612/68 refers to a marital relationship only. There is no reason, therefore, to give the term 'spouse' an interpretation which goes beyond the legal implications of that term, which embrace rights and obligations which do not exist between unmarried companions.**

D'Oliveira suggests that, when sufficient evidence is available to demonstrate the increased incidence of cohabitation across all Member States, the Court's approach will change. This optimism presumes an underlying 'rationality' in the Court's jurisprudence in this area, however, suggesting that sound evidence of a European trend in cohabitation could bring about a change in the law – and may indeed be extended to cover same-sex relationships[121].

This raises two questions, however, the first of which concerns empirical evidence, and the second, the impact of culture and ideology on the Court itself (which in practice, like all institutions, consititutes a collection of individuals [mainly men] reflecting dominant societal values). In statistical terms, it is always difficult to collect data on what is construed as 'deviant' behaviour, or, indeed, behaviour which results in forms of discrimination, where it may be in the interests of those concerned (the persons themselves or the State) to conceal their status[122]. Furthermore, where there is no benefit, or purpose, and, indeed, where it may be positively detrimental to reveal such information, then the prevalence of 'alternative', culturally sanctioned, family forms will be concealed in established sources of secondary data[123]. Having said that, considerable amount of data does exist, and has been reproduced by the EC, to evidence the rise in cohabitation and other new family forms[124]. How this presumption of impartiality or 'disinterest' on the part of the Court sits alongside what smacks of a devaluation of cohabitation (in its reference to marriage as embracing 'rights and obligations which do not exist between unmarried companions') is unclear. It does, however, appear that some value judgments are in evidence!

---

[121] D'Oliveira, J. (1995) 'Lesbians and gays and the freedom of movement of persons', in Waaldijk and Clapham, supra, note 119.

[122] For an example of the way in which cohabiting women in Ireland reported concealing their relationships see Chapter Seven.

[123] The difficulty of using this analogy in the case of same-sex relationships is discussed in Harrison, V. (1996) 'Using EC Law to challenge sexual orientation discrimination at work,' in T. Hervey and D. O'Keefe (eds) *Sex equality law in the European Union*, Chichester: John Wiley.

[124] Eurostat publications which cover this issue include, *Women in the European Community* (1995); *Digest of statistics on social protection in Europe* (vol 4 on 'the family'); *Demographic Statistics* (1995).

The implications of separation and divorce

There is, as yet, very little case law concerning the effect of divorce and separation on a spouse with Community citizenship. The cases discussed below all involve non-Community spouses. Some uncertainty exists over whether a spouse with Community nationality would be dealt with similarly. A Community spouse would, for example, have a general right of residence under Council Directive 90/364[125] although she would have to be financially independent and would not have access to social advantages. The cases raise broader issues, however, concerning the relationship between marital status and entitlement to social rights under Article 7(2) Regulation 1612/ 68. The English High Court considered the impact of separation on the rights of a non-Community spouse of a migrant worker in *Sandhu*[126]. Sandhu was a male of third country nationality who gained entry into the UK by virtue of his status as the spouse of a Community migrant worker. Some years later his German spouse left to return (apparently permanently) to Germany, along with their son. Mr Sandhu then applied for unrestricted leave to remain in the UK where he held a full-time job. The judge in the case (Comyn J.) described the issues as follows:

> **Can an EEC national admitted to this country as such together with her non-EEC husband deprive him of EEC protection by, for example, deserting him, separating from him, by going to live elsewhere in this country, by going back to her native State or by going somewhere else abroad? If she can automatically and over any interval of time do that, it would ... add a new terror to marriage.**

Comyn J. argued that there cannot be a hard and fast rule either way; it must always depend upon circumstances – whether it was a marriage of convenience or whether the parting took place after a fairly short period of time – in which case, "it might well be proper to say that the EEC protection was lost by the non-EEC member". He then referred to the commitment of the EC under the free movement of persons provisions to, "... take into account family and other commitments of the person involved ... in particular as regards the worker's right to be joined by his

---

[125] Supra, note 21.

[126] *R v Secretary of State for the Home Department (ex parte Amarjit Singh Sandhu)*, Case [1982] 2 CMLR 553.

family and the conditions for the integration of that family into the host country". This commitment, he argued, should not be, "construed as meaning that there is a permanent cloak thrown around the non-EEC partner; a cloak of a general permanent condition. But it gives him a status of which, in my judgement, the other party by a unilateral act cannot deprive him."

Despite constant reference to the 'family', however, neither the legislation nor the judge attempt to define the term. We are, therefore, left to conclude that by 'family' reference is to some notional 'nuclear' family norm; a family form which is more of an ideological construct than a reality and has been in steady decline across Europe for many years (as Ms Reed argued). Comyn J. argued by analogy to the right of family members to remain following the death of a worker that divorced or separated spouses should be entitled to remain. Referring then to the preamble to Council Directive 73/148 on the abolition of restrictions on movement and residence, he notes, "that is again a clear indication of the EEC law gathering the family of a spouse under its cloak, not the spouse's cloak".

The Court held that Mr Sandhu should be allowed to stay indefinitely and permanently; separation and divorce did not automatically extinguish spousal rights. The Court of Appeal, however, took a different view on the grounds that the worker's right to be joined by his family did not imply:

> ... the family's right to join the worker. There is a right given to a spouse as a member of the family, it is a right not to come here independently of the other spouse, but a right to install themselves with a worker who ... and note it is in the present tense ... is employed in the territory of another member State ... in the present case the husband can only make a claim to a right for permission to stay in this country as long as the wife herself is exercising it.

Steiner suggests that if the matter had been referred to the Court of Justice, its conclusions would have been closer to those of the English High Court on the grounds that:

> Policy reasons in favour of giving some security of residence to divorced or abandoned spouses of a bona fide marriage, especially when there may be children of that marriage who will still remain members of the worker's family surely require

that the law be construed to ensure that a spouse's EC rights do not necessarily cease on divorce or when the worker leaves the country.[127]

The ECJ considered the impact of separation in another case involving the Senegalese wife of a French Community worker living in Germany, who had separated with the intention of seeking a divorce (*Diatta*)[128]. The question of whether the spouse of a migrant worker is required to live with the migrant worker in order to retain her rights was referred to the Court of Justice. Ms Diatta claimed that the provisions of Regulation 1612/68 (Article 10)[129] do not impose an express obligation to cohabit. The requirement of a migrant worker to make available to his family, housing "considered as normal ... in the region where he is employed" is based on requirements of public policy and does not infer that married couples should live together. Moreover, "a worker who is a national of a member State cannot be allowed to cause the expulsion of a spouse in whom he has lost interest merely by refusing to continue to share his accommodation with her".

Finally, it is possible that the couple may be reconciled. Both the German Court and the intervening Member States considered that the question should be answered in the negative on the grounds that the provision was intended to facilitate the implementation of Article 48 by allowing migrant workers to live with their families and was not intended to cover the case of spouses who are separated on a permanent basis. The Commission proposed a broader interpretation arguing that, "the severance of the family relationship – in this instance the marital relationship – should not have the effect of automatically withdrawing 'the protection of Community law' from the members of the family who benefit from it".

The Court interpreted EC law to the effect that the marriage subsisted until divorce; there was no requirement to live under the same roof, and consequently Ms Diatta was still a member of her husband's family. The Court was, however, insistent that any right of residence, for a spouse, derived from their relationship with the Community worker, and was not an independent right:

The members of a migrant worker's family, as defined in Article

---

[127] Steiner (1996, p 257), supra, note 20.

[128] *Aissatou Diatta v Land Berlin*, Case 267/83 [1986] 2 CMLR 164.

[129] Supra, note 11.

10 of Regulation 1612/68, are not necessarily required to live permanently with him in order to qualify for a right of residence under that provision and Article 11 of the same Regulation does not establish a right of residence independently of that provided for in Article 10.

The Court avoided any discussion of the question of divorce. In a subsequent case involving a couple who were part way through divorce proceedings (they had already obtained a decree nisi)[130] the Court held that the protection of Community law protected a spouse up until the point at which the marriage was finally dissolved – but, once again failed to clarify the impact of divorce itself on spousal rights. The failure of the Court to consider the effect of divorce in a case in which divorce proceedings had already commenced may reflect its reluctance to deal with this issue.

The case was of particular interest as it involved an Indian national who had married a British citizen and then travelled with her to Germany where they worked for some years before returning to the UK. In other words, it took place in an 'internal situation'. The Court, however, found that the period of working in Germany 'made all the difference' and qualified Singh as a Community worker thereby extending important rights to him in the UK (which he would not have had if he had not migrated!)[131].

The problem in relation to a spouse's rights is clearly most acute where the spouse is not a national of a Member State, as in the above cases. A spouse who is a 'citizen of the Union' may derive an independent right of

---

[130] *R v IAT and Surinder Singh ex parte Secretary of State for the Home Department,* Case C-370/90 [1992] ECR 1-4265.

[131] The importance of a Community 'link' was emphasised in *Morson and Jhanjan v Netherlands,* Cases 35 and 36/82 [1982] ECR 3723 where the Court ruled that two Dutch nationals resident in The Netherlands, 'who had never exercised the right to freedom of movement within the Community' had no rights under Regulation 1612/68 to bring their Surinamese parents into The Netherlands. This decision can be compared with that in *Dzodzi v Belgium,* Joined Cases C-297/88 and C-197/89 [1990] ECR 3783 where the ECJ confirmed the right of a non-Community spouse to install themselves with a Community worker with full access to social advantages in the host State. In such cases, a non-migrant national may be in a less favourable position than the beneficiaries of Community rules.

residence under Directive 90/364. While protecting such a spouse from the risk of expulsion, however, this new Directive does not provide for access to the panoply of social rights available to migrant workers and their spouses. The law in relation to the rights of divorced and separated spouses is currently under review by the EC with a proposed new Directive; the position of cohabitants is not, however, in question.

The parasitic nature of family rights

We have seen, in the discussion above, how the benefits accruing to workers under the free movement provisions (including access social advantages) extend to those persons who fall within Community definitions of 'family'. Such 'specifically included family members'[132] have broadly similar substantive rights to those of the worker. The status of family members and workers differs, however, in a fundamental sense, in that the former only have derived entitlement. Families thus gain their social entitlement indirectly through the economic contribution of the worker. The problems of financial dependency within marriage are summarised by Lister:

> **When married or cohabiting women do not have a wage or other source of personal income in their own right, their male partners have enormous power (potential or realised) over the resources at these women's disposal.**[133]

Where marriage determines not only the allocation of resources within the family (the breadwinner's wage), but also access to key social goods, then this problem is clearly compounded. The availability of social advantages to members of migrant workers' families depends on the existence and subsistence of marriage or, in the case of a dependant child, the continuance of a relationship of dependency. This has significant implications for the autonomy of family members reinforcing relationships of dependency within families and vulnerability. Where, for example, a worker loses his or her employment – and where this is construed as being 'voluntary', thus losing important residency rights – the family's derivative rights are also lost. This 'subjective' interpretation of the worker's motivation has dramatic implications for any family members. The Court

---

[132] Craig and de Burca (1995, p 695), supra, note 8.

[133] Lister, R. (1990) 'Women, economic dependency and citizenship', *Journal of Social Policy*, vol 19, no 4, pp 445-69 at p 450.

---

made it clear in *Lebon*[134] that, once a child of a migrant worker reached the age of 21 and was no longer dependent on the worker, benefits to that child could not be construed as an advantage to the worker:

> **However, the members of a worker's family, within the meaning of Article 10 of Regulation 1612/68 qualify only indirectly for the equal treatment accorded to the worker himself by Article 7 of Regulation 1612/68. Social benefits ... operate in favour of members of the worker's family only if such benefits may be regarded as a social advantage, within the meaning of Article 7(2) of Regulation No 1612/68, for the worker himself.**

The Court has made it clear that the rationale for this extension of entitlement to workers' families hinges on the interpretation of the 'facilitating mobility' test; the 'right' must therefore be of some direct or indirect benefit to the worker and does not amount to an independent right for family members. In *Reed* the Court, in ruling that unmarried companions were not 'spouses' under Community law, nevertheless found that while unmarried companions did not fall within the Community concept of 'spouse', the right of residence of such a person could fall within the social advantage concept on the grounds that:

> **The possibility for a migrant worker of obtaining permission for his unmarried companion to reside with him ... can assist his integration in the host state and thus contribute to the achievement of freedom of movement for workers.**[135]

The wording of this judgment is highly indicative: the Court makes no attempt to disguise its fundamental concern with labour mobility and disinterest in the implications of this situation for the families of Community workers.

Summary

This chapter has summarised the evolution of social entitlement under the free movement provisions. On the one hand, the development of the

---

[134] *Centre public d'aide sociale de Courcelles v Lebon*, Case 316/85 [1987] ECR 2811, para 12.
[135] *Netherlands State v Reed*, Case 59/85 [1986] ECR 1283.

non-discrimination principle to cover virtually the whole spectrum of substantive material rights, extending well beyond those narrowly connected with the employment relationship, does, indeed represent an important extension in the evolution of a social Europe. In this context the term 'citizenship' can be used in a meaningful and tangible way to describe the relationship between the EU and 'mobile' Community nationals. On the other hand, the development of a complex and confused set of rules governing the personal scope of the provisions raises fundamental questions concerning the nature of this evolving citizenship status which is evidently anything but universal. The Court of Justice has contributed significantly to the broadening of the parameters of 'favoured' EU status through its interpretations of the 'worker' concept to include almost any form of lawful remunerated work – even that which leaves the person concerned reliant on State welfare (and is to that extent to the economic detriment of the host State). The exclusion of forms of social employment does, however, raise serious concerns for disabled people, voluntary workers and informal carers. Someone undertaking caring or domestic work in the 'formal' labour market can thus claim worker status while an unpaid domestic worker cannot.

Membership of the exclusive 'worker' club does seem to turn on some rather arbitrary distinctions between different types of work. Limited domestic work in the labour market gives rise to worker status – even when it does not involve direct remuneration (but 'savings') – while full-time caring or domestic work in the home apparently does not. Even within this highly privileged group of Community 'workers', entitlement is not universal but depends on subjective motivational judgments concerning the voluntariness of unemployment and the worker's primary locus of interest. Although, in general, good news for women, the inability to take into account work done prior to migration, the potential for discrimination in the determination of 'voluntary' unemployment, the exclusion of voluntary and informal work and potential problems in the definition of 'purely marginal' activities all threaten to restrict entitlement. That such distinctions exist in many Member States should not, in itself, provide a justification for such exceptions.

Of particular concern to women is the concept of 'family' in Community law and notably, the restrictive interpretation of 'spouse' to the total exclusion of cohabitants, same-sex partners and divorcees. This exclusion will increasingly limit the personal scope of the provisions as marriage declines in popularity. Of greater concern is the prospect of women being under pressure to marry, as a result of migration, in order to safeguard their entitlement. While marriage is recognised in Community law as an indirect form of social contribution, facilitating the mobility of breadwinning partners, it is rewarded on a similarly indirect basis, resulting in high levels of personal dependency within families and a highly vulnerable position for the non-working partner. In its interpretation of the concept of 'family', the Court has based its deliberations on presumed patterns of gender relations and interdependency and failed, in the process, to recognise the structural barriers facing women both as independent migrants and as the partners of migrant men.

It is conceivable that Article 8 TEU, following the *Martinez Sala* case, constitutes a turning point in Community law, simplifying the rules governing the personal scope of Community entitlement – and possibly removing discriminatory consequences of existing provisions (in particular the distinction beween economic and non-economic migrants). For the time being, however, and for the purposes of this research, we have to work on the basis that the law is, as yet, unchanged.

There is little concrete evidence to assess the impact of this area of Community law on migrant women. Scheiwe, on the one hand, argues that the concern of Community law is essentially with members of male workers' families, "since migrant workers are predominantly male"[136] while Steiner, on the other, suggests that, following *Kempf*[137], an estranged spouse or cohabitant, who has Community nationality, can avoid loss of entitlement by undertaking paid work which, "even for a spouse with family responsibilities ... should not prove too daunting a prospect"[138]. Both of these comments are based on levels of conjecture, as opposed to empirical evidence. The following section moves on to consider the position of women in migration flows and some of the characteristics of female migrants as the basis for assessing the material impact of the formal citizenship status of migrant women.

---

[136] Scheiwe (1994, p 249), supra, note 112.

[137] *Kempf*, supra, note 83.

[138] Steiner (1996, p 212), supra, note 20.

FIVE

Women on the move in the European Union

"There was an interesting job for him in Oporto and me, as his wife, I followed him, I had to follow him ...."[1]

Introduction

The interpretation of intra-Community migration expressed by Kirsten Scheiwe[2] in the closing paragraph of Chapter Four, as a predominantly male activity, certainly echoes the migration literature. Castles and Miller, for example, have recently identified the "feminisation of migration" as an important new feature in international population movement: "in the past most labour migrations were male-dominated, and women were often dealt with under the category of family reunion"[3]. It is not the absence of women, however, but their invisibility in the research that is at issue here – and the increased awareness brought about by feminist researchers. As Silvia Pedraza notes in her study of Dominican settlement in the United States:

> Despite the overwhelming presence of women in migration flows (internationally) until recently the role of women in migration has been totally neglected ... we have yet to develop a truly gendered understanding of the causes, processes, and consequences of migration.[4]

---

[1] Quote from interviewee D343 (Portugal).

[2] Scheiwe, K. (1994) 'EC law's unequal treatment of the family: the case law of the European Court of Justice on rules prohibiting discrimination on grounds of sex and nationality', *Social and Legal Studies*, vol 3, no 2, pp 243-65.

[3] Castles, S. and Miller, M.J. (1993) *The age of migration*, Basingstoke: Macmillan, p 8.

[4] Pedraza, S. (1991) 'Women and migration: the social consequences of gender', *Annual Review of Sociology*, vol 17, pp 303-25 at p 303.

The tendency to obscure the gender dimension of migration flows and to analyse migration patterns in terms of male breadwinner, profit-maximising, behaviour has dominated much migration research both internationally and at European level. Paula Jackson's study of Irish migrant women notes the manner in which the position of women in migration is concealed within this dominant paradigm:

> **The volume of literature on Irish migration or emigration is prolific, yet with rare exceptions, one is left with the overwhelming impression that Irish emigration has been a purely male phenomena.[5]**

This chapter considers some of the existing work on international migration and, in particular, those studies which have considered women's presence and role in migration. It begins by looking at the way in which migration has been defined and the problems this poses for an understanding of internal migration. A brief overview of mainstream migration accounts follows, which argues that such accounts have perpetuated a dual myth of migration as male-dominated and economically-determined. Women are largely obscured by such analyses. Mainstream migration theory, and its applicability in the European Union (EU) context, is then challenged by the presentation of secondary data documenting the presence of women in the population of intra-Community migrants. In addition to statistical evidence on the gendered nature of migration flows and stocks, we also present data on marital status and the migration experiences of migrant women, both from European statistical sources and from our own empirical work, which further challenges mainstream migration theory.

The chapter then reviews a number of studies which have looked explicitly at women and the migration decision. Material from the interviews with migrant women is introduced to examine their motivations for migration. It will be seen that women are not passive agents in the migration process, as is so often portrayed in the mainstream migration literature. Furthermore, the decision to migrate is a complex issue. It cannot be attributed to one factor alone and rarely involves a simple linear move from an individual's country of origin to their country of destination.

---

[5] Jackson, P. (1987) 'Migrant women: the Republic of Ireland', Commission of Europe, DGV/139/89, p 5.

Levels of intra-Community migration

In the main, migration research is either concerned with international movements between countries or with patterns and processes of internal migration within a country. The distinction between international and internal migration is somewhat confusing, however, when considering the movement of Community nationals within the EU. It can be defined as a subset of international migration since it is concerned with mobility between the Member States. On the other hand, it can be regarded as internal to the extent that the EU constitutes a distinctive geo-political entity. As Salt and Kitching remark, "it is in the European context that the distinction between internal and international migration becomes most blurred"[6].

The very thrust of European integration has led to a distinction between nationals, EU nationals and third country nationals, thereby adding a new dimension to migration analyses. The development of 'Fortress Europe' implies a distinction between what Salt and Kitching call migration within the 'ring fence' and migration from those outside its perimeters. In practice, most research has focused on the latter form with, as Rees et al suggest, "relatively little attention ... paid to date to a proper comparative examination of internal migration within the European Union"[7]. Indeed, studies of migration within the EU such as those by Baldwin-Edwards[8] and Ireland[9] have focused on third country immigration: the role of internal migration is barely mentioned. Salt and Kitching note how, "the field of international migration has been characterised especially by issues relating to ethnicity and the position of minority groups"[10]. This lack of research interest in internal migration reflects, in part, presumptions about the relative privilege of this group of migrants but also the relatively small

---

[6] Salt, J. and Kitching, R. (1992) 'The relationship between international and internal migration', in T. Champion and T. Fielding (eds) *Migration processes and patterns volume 1: Research progress and prospects*, London: Belhaven, p 158.

[7] Rees, P., Stillwell, J., Convey, A. and Kupiszewski, M. (1996) 'Introduction: migration in an integrated Europe', in P. Rees, J. Stillwell, A. Convey and M. Kupiszewski (eds) *Population migration in the European Union*, Chichester: John Wiley and Sons, p 2.

[8] Baldwin-Edwards, M. (1991) 'Immigration after 1992', *Policy & Politics*, vol 19, no 3, pp 199-211.

[9] Ireland, P. (1991) 'Facing the true "fortress Europe": immigration and politics in the EC', *Journal of Common Market Studies*, vol 24, no 3, pp 572-80.

[10] Salt and Kitching (1992, p 148) supra, note 6.

numbers involved. Figure 5.1 shows that, of the 4.2% of the European Community[11] population made up of non-nationals, only one third were EU nationals. This picture, however, masks some important differences between Member States, with some 'exporting' much larger numbers and some receiving a disproportionate share, as Figures 5.2 and 5.3 illustrate.

While Ireland, Spain and Portugal export a larger share of their nationals to other Member States, Germany, France and the UK together receive some three quarters of all EU migrants. Moreover, within these countries, particular historic patterns are reflected in the flows from specific exporting States; migration into Germany, for example, is dominated by Italian and Greek nationals while in the UK two thirds of EU nationals have moved from Ireland, as illustrated in Figures 5.4 and 5.5.

Figure 5.1: Population by citizenship (1 January 1991 - EC12)

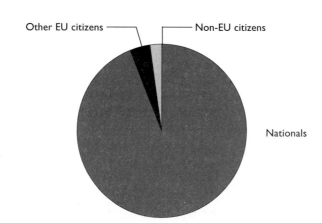

Source: Eurostat Rapid Reports (1993)

---

[11] The term European Community is used wherever the reference period is prior to the Treaty of European Union.

Figure 5.2 Key labour exporters in the EU

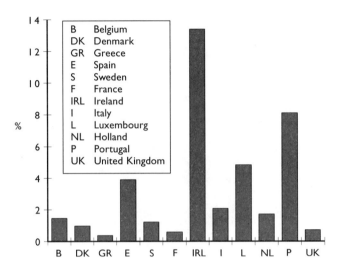

B   Belgium
DK   Denmark
GR   Greece
E   Spain
S   Sweden
F   France
IRL Ireland
I   Italy
L   Luxembourg
NL   Holland
P   Portugal
UK   United Kingdom

Source: Eurostat Rapid Reports (1993)

Figure 5.3: Key destinations

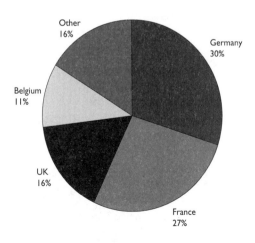

Source: Eurostat Rapid Reports (1993)

Figure 5.4: Nationalities of key EU immigrant groups in Germany

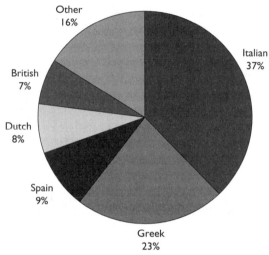

Source: Eurostat Rapid Reports (1993)

Figure 5.5: Nationalities of key EU immigrant groups in the UK

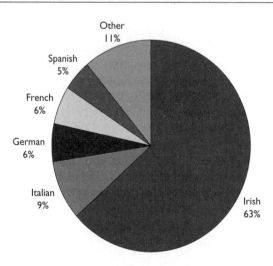

Source: Eurostat Rapid Reports (1993)

Explaining migration: why people move

In response to the empiricist nature of much migration research (focused on the 'numbers game') which has limited explanatory potential, some accounts have attempted to explain the phenomenon of migration – and what motivates a person to move. Commentators such as Willis[12], Molle and Van Mourik[13] and Fotheringham[14], for example, utilise a series of mathematical models of migration to explain the circumstances in which a migrant will decide to move. Analyses have generally adopted one of two theoretical frameworks, both of which have stressed the economic nature of migration. Firstly, macro/micro-economic theory[15], considers the 'demand-pull' factors which attract a migrant to a particular country and the 'supply-push' factors which encourage the decision to move away from their country of citizenship. Rooted in development economics, migrants are generally assumed to be male and are viewed as 'utility-maximising subjects' where economic determinants (such as employment opportunities and higher wages) are the main considerations when deciding whether or not to migrate.

Family resource theory[16], on the other hand, has responded to calls to include the household rather than the individual as the basic unit of analysis since some negotiation among family members is inevitable in a household's decision to migrate. It is assumed that some cost benefit analysis takes place within the household to determine the overall benefit of migration to the family as a whole. These theories

---

[12] Willis, K.G. (1974) *Problems in migration analysis*, Farnborough and Lexington, MA: Saxon House.

[13] Molle, W. and Van Mourik, A. (1988) 'International movements of labour under conditions of economic integration: the case of Western Europe', *Journal of Common Market Studies*, vol 26, no 3, pp 317-42.

[14] Fotheringham, S. (1991) 'Migration and spatial structure: the development of competing destinations model', in J. Stillwell and P. Congdon (eds) *Migration models: Macro and micro approaches*, London: Belhaven.

[15] Sjaastad, L.A. (1962) 'The costs and returns of human migration', *Journal of Political Economy*, vol 70, pp 80-93; Lansing, J.B. and Morgan, J.N. (1967) 'The effect of geographical mobility on income', *Journal of Human Resources*, vol 2, pp 449-60; DaVanzo, J. (1978) 'Does unemployment affect migration?', *Review of Economics and Statistics*, vol 60, pp 504-14.

[16] Blood, R.O. and Wolfe, D.M. (1960) *Husbands and wives: The dynamics of married living*, Glencoe, IL: Free Press.

---

typically assume that migration is driven by the male head of household's employment trajectories and that women follow their partners for family reasons, identifying a two-stage migration process precipitated by male pioneer migration and subsequently followed by family reunion migration[17]. Of these two approaches, family resource theory most closely approximates the ideas underpinning the EU's approach to promoting labour mobility and the rationale behind the facilitating mobility test; as a model of migration behaviour it evidently does take account of wider family concerns but stops short of seeing women (and children) as active agents in the migration process, viewing them instead as passive appendages of male breadwinners.

The way in which both of these models seek to explain migration as an objective economic choice and migrants as rational actors, however, reflects a simplistic view of migration. In addition, the assumption of 'the household' as a single, uncomplicated, unit, within family resource theory ignores the dynamics of decision making between family members and potential conflicts of interest.

In addition to concerns over the (gendered) presumptions underpinning these forms of economic modelling, other authors have noted the importance of non-economic factors in migration decision making. Bogue[18], for example, refers to the tendency in migration research to deny the 'social psychological variables'. For Bogue the choices, perceptions, feelings and beliefs of individuals are pivotal elements in the decision to migrate. Fielding identifies similar problems with 'statistical modeling' approaches:

> **There is something strange about the way we study migration ... It is one of those events around which an individual's biography is built. The feelings associated with migration are usually complicated, the decision to migrate is typically difficult to make, and the outcome usually involves mixed emotions ...**

---

[17] Houstoun, M.F., Kramer, R.G. and Barrett, J.M. (1984) 'Female predominance of immigration to the United States since 1930: a first look', *International Migration Review*, vol 18, pp 908-63; Lichter, D. (1983) 'Socio-economic returns to migration among married women', *Social Forces*, vol 62, no 2, pp 487-503.

[18] Bogue, D.J. (1977) 'A migrant's-eye view of the costs and benefits of migration to a metropolis', in A.A. Brown and E. Neuberger (eds) *Internal migration: A comparative perspective*, New York, San Francisco and London: Academic Press.

And yet when we study migration scientifically, we seem to forget all this.[19]

Researchers such as Pooley and Whyte[20], Gordon[21] and Grundy[22] warn against statistical modeling and suggest a combination of both theoretical and empirical work as the best approach to understanding migration:

Modelling should thus be a bridge between migration theory and empirical explorations of actual movements – feeding off, and contributing to both, and ultimately to the telling of 'stories' about the role of migration...[23]

Together these researchers emphasise the fact that migration cannot be appreciated by analyses based on large datasets alone; such approaches need to be supplemented by a more qualitative, in-depth, understanding of the migrant's perception of their actions and the impact migration has had on their (and their family's) lives.

Of those studies that have distinguished between EU and third country nationals, giving some indication of mobility by nationality and identifying popular destinations, few have considered the gender composition of intra-Community population movements[24]. Economic models of migration behaviour have generally failed to examine female geographic mobility

---

[19] Fielding,T. (1992) 'Migration and culture', in T. Champion and T. Fielding (eds) *Migration processes and patterns volume 1: Research progress and prospects*, London: Belhaven, p 201.

[20] Pooley, C. and Whyte, I. (eds) (1991) *Migrants, emigrants and immigrants: A social history of migration*, London: Routledge.

[21] Gordon, I. (1992) 'Modelling approaches to migration and the labour market', in T. Champion and T. Fielding (eds) *Migration processes and patterns volume 1: Research progress and prospects*, London: Belhaven.

[22] Grundy, E. (1992) 'The household dimension in migration research', in T. Champion and T. Fielding (eds) *Migration processes and patterns volume 1: Research progress and prospects*, London: Belhaven.

[23] Gordon (1992, p 119) supra, note 21.

[24] Rees, Stillwell, Convey and Kupiszewski, supra, note 7; Martin, P. (1990) 'Europe 1992: effects on labor migration', *International Migration Review*, vol 24, pp 591-603; Straubhaar,T. (1988) 'International labour migration within a common market: some aspects of the EC experience', *Journal of Common Market Studies*, vol 27, no 1, pp 45-62.

or the relationship between women's employment experiences and family migration despite the increasing labour force participation of single and married women. Mainstream migration literature has thus perpetuated a dual myth that migration is male–dominated and that motives for migration are exclusively economic; women do not migrate as individuals, in their own right, and when they do move, they do so as passive escorts of male partners.

Morokvasic attributes this concealment of women in migration theorising to the fact that women's migration is subsumed within the category of 'family' and therefore not worthy of investigation[25]. Lichter makes a similar point suggesting that a key explanation for the neglect of women in migration research stems from a presumption of 'passivity': married women are considered to be secondary migrants implying that they do not initiate family moves and are merely "... passive participants in family decisions"[26]. Although women are economically active, their contribution has been looked upon as secondary and as supporting the income of the head of the family: "... the activities of migrant women are considered as an accidental and marginal phenomenon. Looked upon first of all as mothers and wives, housewives, they are only considered as subsidiary workers"[27].

Part of the problem undoubtedly lies in the methodology and, in particular, the reliance upon aggregate data which fail to capture the complexity of women's lives and the subjective factors influencing the migration decision[28]. Notwithstanding the limitations of secondary data, however, it is interesting to examine what evidence exists, within European data sources, on the presence of women in migration flows. The following section presents material from the European Labour Force Survey (ELFS), suggesting that inadequacy of data alone is an insufficient explanation for the neglect of the gender dimension in migration research[29].

---

[25] Morokvasic, M. (1983) 'Women in migration: beyond the reductionist outlook', in A. Phizackleas (ed) *One way ticket: Migration and female labour*, London: Routledge and Kegan Paul.

[26] Lichter (1983), supra, note 17.

[27] DeTroy, C. (1987) *Migrant women and employment*, Brussels: Commission of the European Communities, V/928/87-EN, p 10.

[28] Points discussed in more detail in Chapter Three.

[29] Full details of these findings are reported in Ackers, H.L. (1995) 'Internal migration within the European Union: the presence of women in migration flows and the characteristics of female Migrants', Interim report to DGV, European Commission [Project SOC-94-101784-05A03].

Women in internal migration: examining the 'evidence' from the European Labour Force Survey

The most recent Eurostat data[30] challenges the myth that migration is predominantly male and that where females do migrate, their primary purpose is for family reunion (to join male breadwinning partners)[31]. While just below 50% of all EU migrants are women, Figure 5.6 indicates the variation between Member States both in terms of the gender breakdown

Figure 5.6: Women as a proportion of out-going and in-coming EU migrants, by nationality (1992)

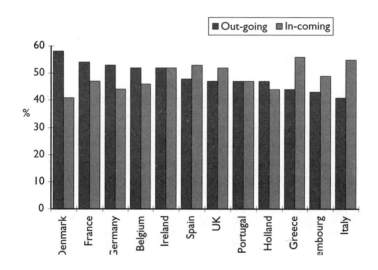

Sources: Eurostat Rapid Report (1993) and Eurostat Demographic Data (1994)

[30] Most of the data presented here is based on the 1992 ELFS. The most recent ELFS provides very limited disaggregation of migration stocks by gender. We therefore decided to stick with the most comprehensive source.

[31] DeTroy states that the phenomenon of female dominated migration flows is also true for a section of Spanish, Yugoslav, French and German women; DeTroy, C. (1987) *Migrant women and employment*, Brussels: Commission of the European Communities, V/928/87-EN.

of in-coming EU migrants and for out-going nationals migrating to another Member State.

Five countries[32] 'export' a greater proportion of females than males (Belgium, Denmark, Germany, France and Ireland), while four other countries import a greater proportion of women (Spain, Greece, Italy and the UK). This comparison raises important questions about migration; of particular interest is the situation in three Mediterranean countries (Greece, Italy and Spain) and the UK, all of which export more males but import a greater proportion of women. Belgium, Denmark, France and Germany, on the other hand, export a greater proportion of women and receive a higher proportion of men.

Closer analysis of the nationality of female migrants in particular countries shows even greater differences. Migration into the UK, for example, is dominated by females for all nationalities except The Netherlands (marginal), Italy and Greece. No less than 72% of Belgian migrants in the UK are female, as shown in Figure 5.7.

Figure 5.7: The proportion of female EU migrants in the UK by nationality (1992)

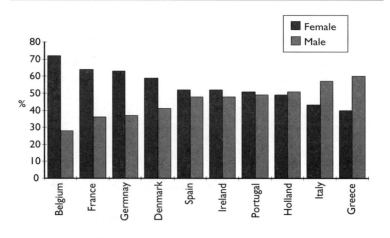

Source: Eurostat Rapid Report (1993) and Eurostat Demographic Data (1994)

---

[32] Based on EUR 12 Statistics for the 12 Member States.

Similar patterns can be seen in Italy, where 57% of all 'other EU' citizens are female, as shown in Figure 5.8. Once again females dominate the migration flows from every Member State apart from Greece. Figure 5.9 shows that, in the case of Greece, women form some 56% of EU migrants, dominating all migration flows apart from Italians. EU migration into Ireland, illustrated in Figure 5.10, is dominated by females in some cases and males in others.

Figure 5.8: The proportion of female EU migrants in Italy by nationality, 1992

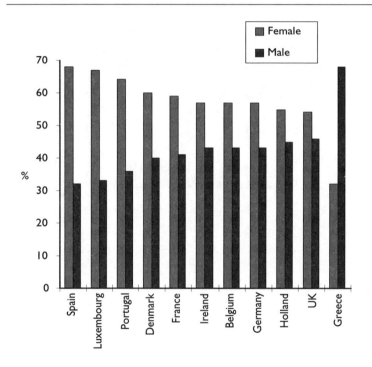

Source: Eurostat Demographic Statistics (1994) and Eurostat Rapid Report (1993)

Figure 5.9: The proportion of female EU migrants in Greece by nationality (1992)

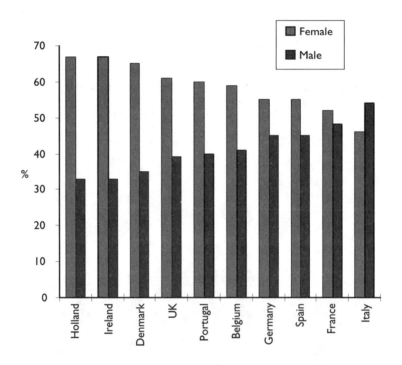

Source: Eurostat Demographic Statistics (1994) and Eurostat Rapid Report (1993)

Figure 5.10: The proportion of female EU migrants in Ireland by nationality (1992)

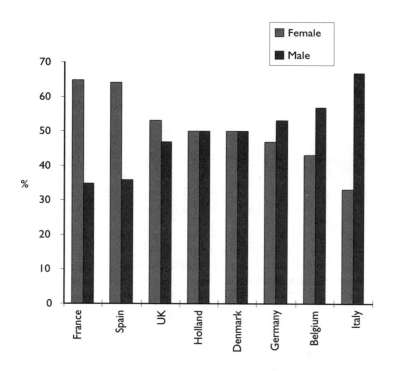

Note: no figures for Greece, Portugal or Luxembourg.

Source: Eurostat Demographic Statistics (1994) and Eurostat Rapid Report (1993)

The following two figures look at the gendered nature of population *outflows* (as opposed to inflows) in two countries. Figure 5.11 shows that the majority of UK migrants resident in another EU country are male; in the destinations of Greece, Italy and Ireland, however, women out-number men. The situation in the UK can be contrasted with that in Ireland where women dominate migration outflows in all but three destinations, as Figure 5.12 shows. Female migration to Greece and Italy is again particularly marked and women also dominate migration into the UK (representing over 95% of Irish migration within the EU). The dominance of females in migration outflows from Denmark is even more stark; here the proportion of men exceeds that of women in only one case, as illustrated in Figure 5.13.

Despite the relatively small numbers of persons involved, intra-Community migration does not appear to fit very easily within traditional theories of international migration. The male breadwinning model of migration behaviour is further undermined, in an EU context at least, by the available data on marital status.

Figure 5.11: Females as a proportion of UK citizens residing in another Member State (1992)

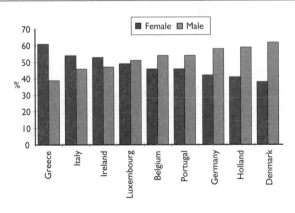

Source: Eurostat Demographic Statistics (1994) and Eurostat Rapid Report (1993)

Figure 5.12: Females as a proportion of Irish citizens residing in another Member State (1992)

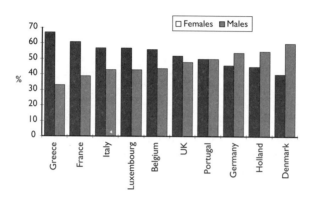

Source: Eurostat Demographic Statistics (1994) and Eurostat Rapid Report (1993)

Figure 5.13: Females as a proportion of Danish citizens residing in another Member State (1992)

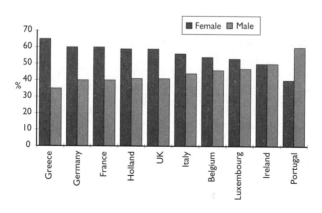

Source: Eurostat Demographic Statistics (1994) and Eurostat Rapid Report (1993)

The marital status of EU migrant women

Research which has acknowledged the role of women in migration has been primarily concerned with married women. This is understandable given the sacrifices that many of these women have to make, sacrifices which have been swept under the carpet in most migration research. Nevertheless, this is at the expense of recognising the volition of many single women. Irish women are perhaps a unique case in their domination of emigration patterns from Ireland, which can be traced as far back as the 'Great Famine' in 1845. A study by Mary Lennon et al of Irish women in Britain was inspired by the lack of awareness of the migration of single women[33]. Many Irish emigrants have been young, single, women who have fled from not only poverty but from a patriarchal hereditary system.

A breakdown of data on marital status based on the ELFS (Eurostat, 1994) suggests that around a half of all women surveyed were married, with a slightly higher proportion of EU migrants falling into this group. These figures must be interpreted with some caution, however, due to a very high non-response rate to the question on marital status in France and Ireland[34].

The European figures mask considerable variations between Member States with some 52% of EU women in Portugal recorded as 'single', compared to only a quarter of those in the UK, for example. The divorce rate for EU migrant women is also considerably higher in The Netherlands (9%) and the UK (7%). The 1992 ELFS did not publish figures for

Table 5.1: Marital status of nationals and EU migrants compared, by gender (%)

Marital status	Male national	Male EU	Female national	Female EU
Single	45%	38%	38%	34%
Married	50%	56%	47%	54%
Divorced	3%	3%	4%	4%
Widowed	3%	2%	12%	8%

Source: 1992 ELFS, Eurostat (1994) (based on specially commissioned tables)

[33] Lennon, M., McAdam, M. and O'Brien, J. (1988) *Across the water: Irish women's lives in Britain*, London: Virago.

[34] The higher rate of marriage among migrants is also likely to reflect the demographic structure of the EU migrant population.

cohabitation or separation, despite the fact that these women may have reduced Community rights.

While the aggregate statistics referred to above are useful in terms of assessing the legal status of migrants, they create a misleading impression of a migration dominated by married women and thus, by implication, of same-nationality couples nicely reinforcing the male breadwinning model. Our own research documents changes in marital status over the life-course and presents a somewhat different picture of a migration dominated by single women, many of whom subsequently marry nationals of the host Member State. While this latter pattern is quite prevalent, the findings also reveal the complex changes in marital status experienced by many women with important consequences for their citizenship status. Table 5.2 compares the marital status of respondents at the point of their migration with that at the time of interview. The overwhelming majority (some 65%) of the women interviewed migrated as single women with marriage very much a minority status (only 27% of the sample). At the time of interview the rate of marriage had increased to just over 60% (a figure broadly comparable with the Eurostat data), with increases also in the numbers divorced, separated and cohabiting. At the time of interview, some 8% of women were either separated or divorced and 11% were in cohabiting relationships.

Table 5.2: The marital status of migrant women at the point of migration and at the time of interview

Marital status	On migration	At interview
Single	222	61
Married	90	206
Cohabiting	18	38
Separated	2	10
Divorced	8	17
Widowed	1	9

Source: Survey of Migrant Women (1995)

A breakdown by country of residence shows an even greater prevalence of single female migration in some destinations: over 70% of women migrating to the UK and Greece, for example, were single, as shown in Table 5.3.

Table 5.3: The proportion of women who were single when they migrated, by nationality

Nationality	Number	Proportion
English	66	74%
Swedish	30	60%
Portuguese	32	43%
Greek	53	71%
Irish	31	60%
Italian	5	100%

Source: Survey of Migrant Women (1995)

More detailed analysis of the interviews indicates the inadequacy of even this comparison as a measure of 'family type' or citizenship status. Many of the women who married following migration spent extended periods (often several years) in cohabiting relationships prior to their marriage. In addition, some 45 respondents reported more complex changes in marital status during the period following migration. Some women who reported themselves to be married, both at the point of migration and at the time of interview (signifying no apparent change in status), had, in fact, been divorced in the interim period and then remarried. Others spent periods separated prior to divorce, then cohabited with a new partner. A proportion of these cohabitants were in same-sex relationships, although women were not specifically asked about their sexuality.

Forty-four women (13%) had been either separated or divorced and 65 women (19%) had lived in cohabiting relationships (in addition to those simply living together prior to marriage) *at some stage* since migrating. The following summaries give some indication of the sort of 'status shifts' women have experienced.

Case studies illustrating changes in marital status over time

Martine met her English husband in Spain while he was serving in the British navy there. She married in Spain and moved to England at the age of 18. They had two children and then separated and subsequently divorced. After a long period as a single parent she is now in a cohabiting relationship with a French man and plans to get married and move to France.

Louise moved to Sweden from Portugal to live with a Swedish man she had become acquainted with by letter. She lived with him in Sweden for 7 years and they had three children together although they never married. Following a period of separation she met another Swedish man and subsequently married.

Joanne migrated to Ireland from Holland as a single woman (to study and work). She then met and married an Irish man who subsequently committed suicide leaving her a widow. She now cohabits in a same-sex relationship.[35]

These case studies demonstrate the importance of considering the evolution of a woman's marital status over the life-course if we are to fully understand migration trajectories and the transitions experienced in terms of legal and social status.

The ELFS data referred to above suggest not only a migration of married women, but also, by implication, a migration of women married to males from the same country of emigration (in the typical male breadwinning model). The interviews challenged such traditional, gendered, assumptions about migration as the movement of same nationality couples. While this analysis *might* hold in some cases of international labour migration, it certainly does not appear to apply to intra-Community mobility. At the time of interview, some 58% of respondents had a partner who held the nationality of the host country. In the case of Greece, all but one of the women interviewed were married or cohabiting with a male Greek national at the time of the interview. The traditional model of same-national[36] migrating couples only applied to a relatively small proportion of the total sample (although it was slightly more prevalent in the case of women living in Portugal).

Among the 56 same-nationality couples identified (16% of the total sample), some women had met their partner after the initial migration, in the host State. So, although their profile would resemble that of the traditional migrant household in a cross-sectional survey, in practice, many of these women moved alone, prior to the marriage, and subsequently met their 'same-national' partner in the host State. This situation was

---

[35] Taken from interviews 008 (UK), 247 (Sweden) and 553 (Ireland) respectively.
[36] The reference to 'same-nationals' here is not to a concept of legal nationality, as many of the women interviewed had adopted the nationality of the host State, but rather to the country of origin.

quite common and reflects, to some extent, the geographical concentration of certain migrant groups (in London, for example, interviewees identified certain localities with relatively high concentrations of Spanish, Portuguese or Irish migrants). Other women had partners of another EU or third country nationality.

The evidence presented above does not support the idea of a male breadwinning family model but rather suggests a migration dominated by single women who then create a second home or family in the 'host' State. Motivations for migration are thus more complex, and gendered, than many mainstream models imply. In most cases, women do not migrate for one single reason but on the basis of a more complex evaluation; moreover, they often make more than one migration and may be constantly reviewing their decision in the light of circumstances. As one woman who moved between Portugal and Greece a number of times before deciding to settle in Greece put it, "my permanent establishment was done step-by-step"[37].

The following case is quite typical of women's migration histories:

Martha came to Greece on holidays with a friend in Rhodes. She returned to Sweden for a small time and then returned to Greece to establish permanently. Having found a job in Athens she then met and married her Greek husband. For the next six years she lived and worked in Athens during winter and in Rhodes during summer. In 1982 she and her husband went to Sweden for one year; the same thing happened in 1984 when they went there again for eight years. In 1992 they were again permanently established in Athens where they still stay.[38]

One of the limitations of ELFS data lies in its inability to identify the geography of migration over a period of time. Such cross-sectional surveys are typically based on a simple distinction between a person's nationality and their current country of residence and give the impression of unilateral migrations from a to b. In practice this is rarely the case, at least in relation to internal migration. Interview data illustrates the complex geography of the migration process. In 53% of cases, women had made a series of migrations at international level with women often 'yo-yoing' between two or more locations. Nine per cent of these women, together with

[37] Interviewee D441 (Greece).
[38] Interviewee D447 (Greece).

28% of the remaining women who had made only one international move, had subsequently migrated within the country of destination. In many cases, the subsequent interregional move (which was usually partner-determined) had a greater impact on the woman's autonomy (and employment status, in particular) than the initial international migration[39].

Understanding the migration of women: 'reasons for coming'

We have already seen the emphasis on economic determinants in much mainstream migration theorisation. Migration is conceptualised in highly gendered terms as primarily motivated by an informed evaluation of the economic benefits and employment opportunities. Underpinning such analyses is the notion that migrants move as families and that 'rational household decision making' ascribes a primacy to male economic roles. Women's roles in migration are thus obscured by the assumption of inferior labour market status and consensual household decision making processes. The adequacy of this approach has been questioned in the light of evidence of migration of single women, moving in their own right. The chapter now moves on to examine some of the literature on migration motives and to compare it with the reasons women gave for their migration and, of equal importance, for remaining in the host State.

Bogue's study of migrants living in Chicago specifically sought to determine whether factors, other than purely economic gains, figured in a migrant's decision to move[40]. He discovered that while economic factors were indeed instrumental, these were certainly not the only ones; family contacts, education benefits, dislike of place of previous residence and a desire to get away from family all featured as reasons influencing the decision to move. Bogue also refers to people migrating for marriage and for climate. The dangers of generalising about migration motives, and over-emphasising the role of economic factors, is similarly acknowledged by Peter Ackers in a biographical study of migrations from Wigan to Canada at the turn of the century[41]. While this study goes to lengths to uncover

---

[39] For more detail on the impact of migration on employment see Chapter Six.

[40] Bogue (1977), supra, note 18.

[41] Ackers, P.B.H. (1997) 'Exodus: labour emigration from the English curches of Christ to Canada during 1906 and 1907', *Journal of URC History Society*, vol 6, no 1, October, pp 34-46.

the complex web of factors precipitating migration, Ackers brings out the importance of a religious dimension in this particular migration context, both in terms of spreading the idea of migration and building religious communities in the host countries. Employment prospects were clearly an important factor in the decision to migrate but not in any narrow deterministic sense. Ackers cites the work of Thistlethwaite who suggests that, "it is a truism that nineteenth century emigration was predominantly economic in motivation [but] the actual determinants were very vaguely formulated", amounting to no more than a "laundry list of 'push' and 'pull' factors which were then left in the background"[42].

Thistlethwaite suggests that one explanation for the reliance on statistics (and economic determinism) in migration research is the colonisation of the latter by social scientists and the, "elusiveness of the usually anonymous individual migrant compared with other subjects of historical research"[43]. Perhaps social science could usefully learn from historians in this respect. In another interesting piece of historical research reviewed by Ackers we can see the complex interplay of economic and personal factors influencing nineteenth century migrants:

> **Sometimes, it is a mere spirit of adventure, a love of change. Very often the reasons are personal; sometimes they are involved and complicated, and however strongly felt, are but vaguely understood even by those who are under their influence. Whatever weakens the ties of home – bereavement, altered surroundings, domestic infelicity, social or political disappointment, economic difficulties, in short one of the many things which darken the current of life, urges men to a change of habitation.[44]**

The sentiments expressed in this paragraph are remarkably relevant to the current project: many women expressed a whole range of factors which

---

[42] Thistlethwaite, F. (1964) 'Migration from Europe overseas in the nineteenth and twentieth centuries', in H. Moller (ed) *Population movements in modern European history*, London: Macmillan, p 84.
[43] Thistlethwaite (1964, p 75), supra, note 42.
[44] Johnson, S.C. (1966, reprint of 1913) *Emigration from the United Kingdom to North America, 1763-1912*, London: RKP, pp 66-7.

---

together precipitated their decision to migrate[45]. The findings reported in the next section represent the explanations women have given for their *initial* migration. In many cases, women gave multiple reasons saying, for example, that they came to travel, to learn the language and to work as an au pair. In practice, it is often impossible to identify a primary motive. The data therefore simply enumerates the number of times in which specified reasons were given. The responses can be grouped into a number of 'clusters' as shown in Figure 5.14.

Figure 5.14: reasons for coming

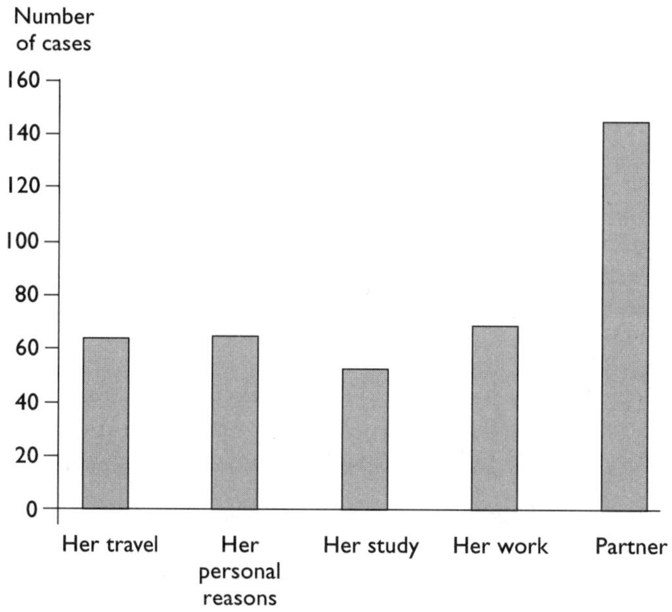

Source: Survey of Migrant Women (1995)

[45] While the project reported on in this book focuses specifically on women, this does not imply that mainstream migration theory has adequately understood male migration. Indeed, the words of Johnson suggest the remarkable similarity in the experiences of male migrants at the turn of the century to the women interviewed in this research.

1. Partner-related motives

One of the main issues addressed in the literature on women and migration, reflecting the preoccupation with economic determinants, is the relationship between migration and women's employment with most studies concluding that migration has a negative impact on women's job opportunities. Pahl and Pahl's study of interregional migration, for example, sought the opinions of wives who had migrated and revealed that the overwhelming majority of the women interviewed saw themselves primarily as wives and mothers, not workers. Reasons for migration were therefore attributed to the improved prospects of their husbands' careers (and their derived benefit) rather than their own. Their children's education needs and the area of relocation were other determining factors[46]. While the findings of this study would seem to concur with the economic models of migration described earlier, the labour market – and social attitudes – were very different in the 1960s from the 1990s as women's labour market participation increases. In view of this trend, Lichter suggests an increasing role for women in migration decision making, "... it seems axiomatic that women will acquire greater volition in the determination of job and geographic mobility"[47]. If women are having a greater say in migration decisions, as the authors claim, then this could have one of two conflicting outcomes. On one hand, it may hinder migration since it could be more difficult for both partners to find acceptable employment than just one. On the other hand, the fact that both partners are working may actually enhance migration, assuming that migration destinations tend to be to areas of employment growth, which might be of dual benefit[48]. If one partner of the couple wishes to move, the other may be willing to give up their job if they think they can get a similar or perhaps a better job in another area. Nevertheless, Markham[49] notes how dual-career couples encounter increased interpersonal conflict when deciding where to locate if the impetus to migrate is one-sided.

---

[46] Pahl, J.M. and Pahl R.E. (1971) *Managers and their wives*, London: Allen Lane.

[47] Lichter, D. (1983) 'Socio-economic returns to migration among married women', *Social Forces*, vol 62, no 2, pp 487-503 at p 488.

[48] Bonney, N. and Love, J. (1991) 'Gender and migration: geographical mobility and the wife's sacrifice', *The Sociological Review*, vol 39, no 2, pp 335-48.

[49] Markham, W.T. (1986) 'Sex, relocation and occupational advancement: the "real cruncher" for women', *Women and Work*, vol 22, pp 207-31.

A study which sought to investigate the influence of a wife's job upon residential mobility in the United States[50] suggested that working wives may inhibit long-distance inter-state movement but are amenable to short-distance movement between or within counties. On the other hand, households where the wife was not working were more likely to engage in long-distance migration than those where both partners were working. This study seems to support Markham's 'conflict' theory and may suggest that women who work are able to exercise more influence in the migration decision. Long arrived at the conclusion that, "marriage ties people to a given locality"[51]. He also observed that women who 'dropped out' of the labour market were often in households which had undertaken a long-distance move, illustrating the negative impact that such a move can have on a woman's career while increasing her husband's mobility.

Janet Finch's examination of the relationship between motives for migration and women's economic dependency on their husbands, found that couples who had moved nationally or internationally had done so because of the male partner's job priorities. The women felt strong economic and cultural pressure to accept the relocation and felt that migration had had a detrimental impact on their own job opportunities[52]. A further study by Bonney and Love substantiates Finch's findings that, "marriage transforms women from independent persons to ancillary supporters of male partners in their primary occupational roles"[53]. It is for this reason that women migrants have been referred to as 'tied-movers'[54]. If the perceived gains for migration outweigh the perceived losses, despite personal sacrifices on the woman's part, then the family/household generally decides to migrate[55]. Since women's careers are frequently inferior to that of men's in terms of salary and promotion prospects, then the decision to migrate becomes 'male or husband-centered'. Shihadeh's study of migration in Alberta, Canada, suggests that what appears on the surface

---

[50] Long, L.H. (1974) 'Women's labour force participation and the residential mobility of families', *Social Forces*, vol 52, pp 342-48 at p 344.

[51] Long (1974, p 344), supra, note 50.

[52] Finch, J. (1983) *Married to the job*, London: Allen and Unwin.

[53] Bonney and Love (1991, p 347) supra, note 48.

[54] Mincer, J. (1978) 'Family migration decisions', *Journal of Political Economy*, vol 86, pp 285-313.

[55] The word 'perceived' has been added here because potential migrants are never fully informed of all the facts and are making decisons based on presumptions.

to be a mutual decision, is actually one in which the husband assumes a more predominant role[56].

In the interviews with migrant women, 43% reported some partner-related reason for their initial migration (145 cases). Of these, 94 women suggested that their migration was driven by their partner's career. Figure 5.15 breaks this group of women down according to *where they met* their partner. The majority of this group (43 cases) involved partnerships with men of the same nationality migrating as a couple (although in eight cases the woman joined her partner at a later date).

It is important to stress that it is this 'form' of migration, of *migrating same-national couples,* which underpins most models of migration behaviour and yet in this sample it accounted for only 43 out of 341 cases (13%)[57].

Figure 5.15: Breakdown of cases in which 'partner' was cited as main reason for migration, by place of first acquaintance

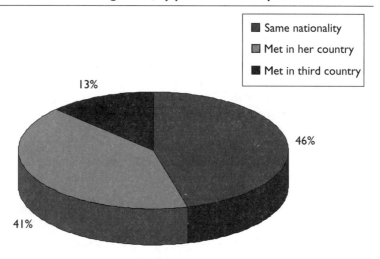

Source: Survey of Migrant Women (1995)

---

[56] Shihadeh, E.S. (1991) 'The prevalence of husband-centred migration: employment consequences for married mothers', *Journal of Marriage and the Family*, vol 53, pp 432-44.

[57] This pattern was, however, more prevalent in the Swedish and Portuguese sample where 24% and 17% of women, respectively, moved with their partner because of his work.

The other two categories of women moving because of their partner's career either met their partner in their country of origin (where he was studying or working) or in a third country, often while travelling or working abroad. They then relocated to the country of residence together. In some cases their partner worked for a subsidiary of a firm in their country of origin, in others they had been studying or returned to do military service. In other words, they met following some form of mobility on either their or their partner's side and the primary purpose of the migration was to be together, as a couple. In these cases the location decision becomes all-important. This decision was often determined by the male partner's employment prospects as the following cases indicate:

> **Julia came to the UK after marrying a British naval officer in Spain: "There was no discussion, no choice, his job was in England. At the time I was only 18."**[58]

> **"He went to Spain on holiday and met me. We fell in love and the following year he came back to Spain and we got married; that's why I came to England. I came here as Mrs Whatever. First we lived in London for some years, then we had to move to Birmingham, always owing to my husband's job, then to Southampton and then finally to Plymouth."**[59]

> **"I am what is called a love-immigrant. I met my Swedish husband-to-be in Ireland and moved back to Sweden because of his job."**[60]

This situation, of deciding which country to live in (and under pressure to relocate to Greece with her husband) caused one German woman some stress as she really wanted to live near to her family. However, her father encouraged her to go:

> **"My family helped me make my decision; my father told me, ... 'If your husband says so, you must do it!'."**[61]

---

[58] Interviewee D008 (UK).
[59] Interviewee D024 (UK).
[60] Interviewee D245 (Sweden).
[61] Interviewee D427 (Greece).

Indeed, this situation, in which a woman meets a partner in her country of origin, and subsequently migrates to return with him to his country of origin was surprisingly common in the Greek sample. We have already seen how all but one of the women interviewed in Greece was married to a Greek man. We also saw that 71% of the women in Greece were single when they migrated. Of those that were married when they moved to Greece, nearly all of them were married to a Greek man whom they had met in their home country. In other words, they were not same-national couples and the location decision was very much determined by the male partner's family and employment interests. In all, 27 women living in Greece (36% of the sample) met their Greek partner outside Greece and moved there with him.

In a number of cases the superior language skills of the woman actually supported the notion of returning to her partner's country on the grounds that his employment prospects would be adversely effected by his more limited language competency:

> "**Well I speak English and so I thought it might be easier for me. I didn't want him being dependent on me. I just didn't want that so I thought I'd make my way here. He really would have been dependent on me just even going shopping.**"[62]

> **They came to Portugal because it was easier for her husband to find a job, because he had family here, and the language would be easier too.**[63]

> "**I think that most of the reason I came here and my partner didn't come to Germany was really the language because I knew I could adapt much quicker than he could have done ... And to work in his job he needs communicative skills and he wouldn't be able to do that job in Germany. When I gave up my job I really felt that I needed a career change ... I think that this helped me to move because otherwise I would have found it difficult to stop working for a relationship. I don't think giving up everything for a relationship is a good thing.**"[64]

The examples above, albeit of women assuming a secondary labour market

---

[62] Interviewee D065 (UK).
[63] Interviewee D312 (Portugal).
[64] Interviewee D064 (UK).

role, nevertheless do not confirm a passive 'follower' mentality but rather a sophisticated evaluation of a range of factors influencing their overall quality of life and autonomy. While the woman in the last example gave up her job to be with her partner, his career needs were by no means the only factor in her decision to migrate; she evidently considered the move to be mutually beneficial despite the increased risk taken on her part. Sherri Grasmuck and Patricia Pessar's study of Dominican migration to the United States of America supports the argument that women attribute different meanings to migration (and even to work) than purely economic ones[65]. The authors observed a paradox in the experiences of Dominican men and women with regard to their employment situation in the USA. While women were receiving lower wages and had fewer opportunities for occupational mobility than their male counterparts, women were generally more satisfied with their jobs. Migration promised gains of personal autonomy which outweighed financial remuneration. An interesting finding of their study was that it was the women who on the whole had instigated settlement to the USA, as a mechanism to escape total dependence on their husbands; "women often cloaked their desire to migrate under the ideology of household economic maximisation"[66].

The remainder of women who moved because of their partner said they moved there because that was where he came from, where his family were or where he had property:

Helga had her own business in Germany and met her husband while he was in the Forces there. She gave up her business to move to the UK in spite of the fact that her husband was unemployed, "because he was homesick – he missed his mum and family here. I came back for a holiday and then I got stuck here – I don't know why."[67]

Marie moved from France to Portugal when she married: "I chose a Portuguese not the country ... In order to have her son back in Portugal, my mother-in-law bought a house. He decided to come back because of his friends, his family and his house."[68]

[65] Grasmuck, S. and Pessar, P. (1991) *Between two islands: Dominican international migration*, Berkeley, Los Angeles, CA and Oxford: University of California Press.
[66] Grasmuck and Pessar (1991, p 147) supra, note 65.
[67] Interviewee D007 (UK)
[68] Interviewee D309 (Portugal).

The first of these cases rather turns the 'rational household strategy' argument on its head, with the wife foregoing highly remunerative work because her unemployed husband missed his family!

2. Career: to work and/or study

A large number of the women in this research gave some career-related reason for their initial move[69]. Many of these women were single, although in some cases they were accompanied by their partners. This not only corresponds with Lichter's hypothesis (see footnote) but clearly challenges those models which assume that women only move for family reasons.

The concept of career is itself highly problematic and suggests a rational, linear, progression when, in practice, it might include a whole range of elements and discontinuities. In some cases it was clear enough, such as when a woman obtained a post with a multi-national company. In many others it is a question of interpretation when the consequences of a particular decision may only manifest themselves in career terms at a much later date. Many women said that a key reason for their migration was to develop their language skills. In some cases this involved a course of study (although full-time students were not included in the sample), in others it simply meant travelling to another country and obtaining a job (as a shop assistant or waitress, for example) to promote their fluency through daily exercise of language skills. In such cases it is difficult to know whether this was a 'career' decision as such, unless they were aiming at a particular occupation. The fact that many of them remained in the host State and developed a career on the basis of their linguistic ability might allow us to make that judgement retrospectively, even though it may not have been their original intent.

The following cases are quite typical:

Isabella came to England from Italy, on her own, after completing her degree in English and French, with the intention of returning home with good employment prospects; "[I came] to get a good job in Italy. Because of my studies I needed to have good English – that was the main reason for coming. To learn a language you have to spend some time – that was the

---

[69] More detailed consideration of the impact of migration on women's employment trajectories is the subject of Chapter Six.

> main point – and working here too – when I go back to Italy I
> can prove that I have good English."[70]

> Emma came alone to learn Portuguese in a Portuguese
> university. During her studies in her home country she had
> already studied Latin, Spanish and French and she wanted to
> learn another language studying abroad. She got a scholarship
> and she came to Portugal for one year ... And after she decided
> to stay.[71]

In practice, it is difficult to distinguish between educational motivations and work or career. Because we did not interview full-time students, however, where women said they came to study, this usually indicated that they remained for some other reason (work or a partner, for example). In all, 69 women (20%) gave work as one of the main reasons for their migration. This was particularly evident in the UK sample where some 28 women (34%) said they moved for their career. Education was given as a motive in 53 cases (15%) and, of these, 20 women migrated in order to study languages. Eighteen women said that they came over initially as au pairs. While being an au pair is clearly a form of paid work, many of these women used this type of work as an entry into the country in order to learn languages, or learn more generally about another country, and used it as a springboard to do other things. For others it was, as one woman put it, "the only form of employment a girl could find at the time"[72].

The variation in career-based reasons for moving which the women cited, suggests that using the term 'economic' as an explanation for migration is a rather broad-brush one. Some of the career reasons that were mentioned were:

- no work in country of origin
- to earn more money
- career change
- as a way of learning another language
- recommendation by other family members or friends
- secondment/work experience
- as a means of seeing relatives/friends
- to facilitate travelling.

---

[70] Interviewee D011 (UK).
[71] Interviewee D327 (Portugal).
[72] Interviewee D027 (UK).

3. Personal reasons: family and personal networks

Monica Boyd stresses how family and personal networks are important determinants of migration. Boyd argues that considering the role of such networks, "provides insight into the origins, composition, direction and persistence of migration flows"[73]. Decisions to migrate are determined as much by contact with people who have already migrated as economically-orientated decisions. King and Shuttleworth's investigation into the emigration of Irish graduates discovered the importance placed upon traditional family and ethnic networks in choosing their place of destination[74]. In their study, one respondent commented, "a major factor that made emigration substantially easier is the wholesale displacement of my network of friends from Dublin to London". The authors realised that in Ireland a 'migration culture' was prevalent to the extent that migration was regarded as a societal norm.

The role of family networks and friends was certainly an important feature of the migration stories of some of the women interviewed in this research. One Portuguese woman (Interviewee D087) explained how her mother had been responsible for the migration of firstly her husband, her sister and finally herself to London:

> **"At first I didn't want to come but then I decided why not? I was curious about England – I wanted to know why everyone in my family was talking about England. I was the last one to know what it was like so I decided to come."**

Her mother had other relatives already settled in London so she was able to stay with them and find work on behalf of her family.

4. The pursuit of personal autonomy

As with Bogue's study (see footnote 40), this research found that some of the women had migrated as a way of getting away from failed relationships, their parents (often fathers) or as a statement of their independence. Sixty-

---

[73] Boyd, M. (1989) 'Family and personal networks in migration', *International Migration Review*, 23, Fall, pp 638-70 at p 661.

[74] King, R. and Shuttleworth, I. (1995) 'The emigration and employment of Irish graduates: the export of high-quality labour from the periphery of Europe', *European Urban and Regional Studies*, vol 2, no 1, pp 21-40 at p 33.

five women gave some other 'personal reason'. One woman explained her decision to move as follows:

> "I thought it would be easier for me to start a new life because I was having a lot of pressure from my family and I thought life would be freer here."[75]

Another woman said that she migrated to escape from a relationship, "I was feeling claustrophobic and I wanted to get away"[76]. The personal reasons for moving indicate the importance of emotional determinants which rarely feature in migration theory. Indeed, for some women the desire to leave was a very powerful one. One woman moved to Britain from what was East Berlin when she lost her job as a result of reunification and was terribly depressed: "I came to rebuild my life"[77]. Another woman had moved to Portugal for similar reasons:

> Christine left Germany because after the first years of reunification her country of origin (GDR) was so different that she couldn't stand the changes. These changes and her personal problems (separation) helped in her decision to come to a southern country. She came to Oporto because there was a vacancy at the German school of Oporto.[78]

Others left countries which they felt to be oppressive to women:

> "Italy is a very male-dominated country – females in those days [1980s] had little chances to do a career – because most employers think that once you reach 24 you are going to get married and have children … And this is what I found."[79]

> "I couldn't stand the Italian machismo."[80]

Some women made a positive choice, moving to countries which they

---

[75] Interviewee D086 (UK).
[76] Interviewee D055 (UK).
[77] Interviewee D012 (UK).
[78] Interviewee D365 (Portugal).
[79] Interviewee D002 (UK).
[80] Interviewee D061 (UK).

felt supported a better quality of life:

> **"I wanted more space and less laws so we could do more as we wished. In Germany you always get told what you can't do. I wanted a child for sure and I wanted a good place to grow it up in and I think Ireland is a good place for kids to grow up."**[81]

> **"We came to Ireland for environmental and political reasons, [which coincided with health reasons on her husband's part]. He was under pressure with his job and wanted to give it up. He wanted to do farming. The land was too expensive to do this in Germany and there is too much pollution there ... [In terms of political reasons, this was prior to the reunification of Germany] ... we were always feeling like we were sitting on a bomb."**[82]

5. Travel and language

Migrating to travel and to learn a foreign language were frequently cited reasons. One woman said of her decision to migrate, "initially it was to have a six month trip to a European city and at the same time I wanted to learn a language"[83]. Another woman explained that she chose to migrate because, "I always actually wanted to go abroad. It was always a drive I had to go abroad. It's quite an adventure just to discover a different culture"[84].

Travel was a popular explanation for the initial migration with 66 women citing this as a key reason (19%). This category included women who simply went on a short holiday, those who wanted to travel for a longer period of their lives, to experience other cultures and those who travelled in order to learn a language. This latter category included 19 women all of whom had moved to the UK or Ireland to learn English. In these cases, the women said that they wanted to learn English in order to improve their career opportunities back home – although they did not return!

---

[81] Interviewee D516 (Ireland).
[82] Interviewee D517 (Ireland).
[83] Interviewee D073 (UK).
[84] Interviewee D075 (UK).

It became evident during the research that the reasons women gave for their initial migration often bore no relationship to their reasons for remaining. In many cases, women had simply 'drifted' into one country or another, on holiday or to work as an au pair, with no intention of staying. These cases highlight the problems of theories based upon models of 'rational decision making'. Lives evolve and circumstances change over time; what might be rational at a particular point in time may appear irrational at a later date. In practice, women's lives do not take the form of some ordered, mechanistic and linear response to objective external forces. Evaluation of migration behaviour must, therefore, take account of the context in which the migration took place. While the findings do not support mainstream migration theories, the male breadwinning family model is by no means redundant when it comes to analysing women's reasons for remaining in the host State.

Reasons for staying

Women were asked, in the course of the interviews, to explain their reasons for remaining in the host State *where these differed to their reasons for coming*. This was particularly the case for those women who saw their initial migration as a temporary stay but also figured in cases where, for example, a woman moved to accompany her husband and that relationship then broke down or he died.

In 93 cases (27%) women said that they remained in the country because they met their partner since migrating. Of these 93, 25 gave his career as the main determinant. The fact that women 'chose' to live in their partner's country – instead of relocating to their own country – was in many respects treated as a fact of life for many women. The alternative possibility of their partner moving back to their country was rarely considered at the time. This is less surprising than in the previous cases, where women met their partners in the partner's country of origin because the woman had already established herself in the host State, often with a job and highly developed language skills. More resentment was evident in those cases where their husband's job had resulted in multiple moves. One woman who moved from Spain to England in order to study and then met her partner and decided to stay, was subsequently required to relocate to another town due to his job and had to live with his family as a result:

> **"I did mind at the time. I had just got married and we couldn't sell our house so we had to live with my parents-in-law for**

eight months. I had to spend my pregnancy with them and come back from hospital to them. I wanted my own home but we couldn't sell for two years. Well, in a situation where you have to live with someone in a house who provides the money you have no choice."[85]

Thirty-two women (9%) said that they decided to stay on, even though the reasons for their initial migration had changed, because of their own career opportunities. In one case, a Spanish woman had 'followed' her partner in a number of moves and then decided to assert her independence and remain in Sweden without him:

Maria met her Swedish husband when he was on holiday in Spain and moved to France and subsequently on to Sweden because of his job. She is now living in Sweden with her two daughters while her husband has moved back to France with his job (and their son). She expressed her reasons for staying as follows: "I felt that I had gotten to the point where I couldn't go on just moving here and there but I had to do something for myself". She has begun studying in Sweden.[86]

Twenty other women said that they remained because their partner's family was there, because he had property or because his language skills made it difficult for him to move with her:

This French woman married a French man and moved with him to Switzerland for his job. They had a son and then divorced leaving her in Switzerland where she remained and then, because of concerns about her health and her son's education, moved back to live with her parents in France. She then came on a holiday to visit friends in England and met her English partner and subsequently joined him. Unusually, in this interview, her husband was present and they argued over the decision for her to stay (as opposed to him moving to France): "You never suggested the solution to go to France. You said, 'you come – end of story' – you never suggested to come to France".

---

[85] Interviewee D015 (UK).
[86] Interviewee D237 (Sweden).

[Husband replies]: "Well, I had a house". [Wife replies]: "Number 1, you don't speak the language, number 2, I do!"[87]

"I started to try to teach [him] French but it was difficult to know where to start – he wouldn't learn grammar and if you don't you can't speak proper French ... – he wouldn't mind moving back to France but he can only speak English. He wouldn't get a job; at least I had a chance here because I can speak English."[88]

"[We stayed here] because of the language problem – there would have been no possibility of him to find work in Germany – it would have taken too long to learn the language – and I thought I stood a better chance."[89]

The way these women represent the decision does not suggest passivity, or a sense of inadequacy, but rather an acknowledgement of their own, more highly developed, life skills and of their partner's limitations!

Another Spanish woman living in England had come initially to study and qualified as a teacher in England. She then met her partner who already had children in England. In explaining her reasons for staying, she refers to the language problem, her husband's children and also concerns about the transferability of her teaching qualifications[90]:

"It was clear because his children were here – it would be difficult for him to find a job without Spanish. The educational system is very different in Spain, to be a teacher you have to pass special exams. Speaking for myself now it would be difficult to get a job back in Spain because of my qualifications – this is one of the reasons why people don't tend to go back."[91]

Issues concerning children and their education were given as reasons for remaining in a number of cases. These cases reflected concerns about

---

[87] Interviewee D010 (UK).

[88] Interviewee D009 (UK).

[89] Interviewee D018 (UK).

[90] For more discussion of this issue see Chapter Six.

[91] Interviewee D014 (UK).

their children's careers (and the recognition of their qualifications), their identity and integration in society and also concerns about family policy[92]:

> **"I would like to move back to France – after [her son] has been to University in Britain. It's a project – we'll see how it goes – it's better he passes his A levels and goes to University in England."[93]**

> **"I don't think I will go back to Madeira. My son started school here. He came when he was five and started school. And now he doesn't think like a Portuguese boy. He thinks like a English boy in everything."[94]**

> **"I don't want to force my children to live in another country than the one they are living in – in a manner of speaking. I don't want to transmit a feeling of them living in the wrong place in the wrong country. I can live with this rootlessness that I feel but I don't want my children to have the same feeling. I think that if we stay here they are going to feel Swedish, and I don't see anything wrong with that."[95]**

> **"We thought about leaving during that period, not once we had children – that was when we decided that this was a pretty good, pretty safe environment for a start to rear our children."[96]**

Welfare tourism?

The development of substantive rights to social welfare under the free movement provisions has led to increasing concerns about 'welfare tourism'. Evans echoes this concern when he suggests the possibility that "persons will have an incentive to migrate to the more developed Member States

---

[92] The impact of migration on the children of EU migrants is the subject of a new project, currently underway and under the direction of Dr Ackers (the author).
[93] Interviewee D010 (UK).
[94] Interviewee D056 (UK).
[95] Interviewee D228 (Sweden).
[96] Interviewee D561 (Ireland).

primarily because of the comparatively high level of welfare provision available there"[97].

The inference here is that variations in welfare provision will influence both the decisions to move and where to locate. The evidence we have presented here, based upon the interviews with migrant women, does not support this assertion. Indeed, many of the women interviewed had moved away from countries with more 'progressive' family policies (such as Sweden or France) in the direction of the 'mother-daughter economies' of the Mediterranean Rim and the 'liberal' regimes of Britain and Ireland. Many women, it seems, have 'selected' locations which would appear to be to their detriment, at least in terms of their objective social status (or access to material social advantages). Indeed, a majority of our sample had effectively 'traded down'[98]. What this suggests is that, for this group of women at least, welfare tourism – or shopping around for gender-progressive social systems – does not appear to be a key factor determining migration destination. That this is the case is supported by the findings on location decision and reasons for migration. None of the women interviewed said that their move – or location decision – was primarily determined by considerations of comparative social status. In one case, the respondent, who moved herself to accompany her husband, suggested that other women were influenced by concerns about welfare and educational benefits but, even here, it is difficult to disentangle the issue of welfare status from that of employment prospects:

> **"My career opportunities were much better in England – no doubt whatsoever. In fact I know many Spanish girls who came to England because they couldn't get a job and in England they all have got jobs, places at the college, university and with a grant system and all the income support and welfare attached to it – it's paradise."[99]**

Indeed, when we asked women about the relative benefits in terms of welfare provision, many women really didn't know how the host State compared to their country of emigration. This can be largely explained by the fact that most women moved when they were quite young (and

---

[97] Evans,A. (1991) 'Nationality law and European integration', *European Law Review*, vol 16, no 3, pp 190-215 at p 201.

[98] For more discussion of the gender aspect see Chapter Seven.

[99] Interviewee D008 (UK).

single or childless) and had not had cause to familiarise themselves with social security and family rights. While such life-course factors help to explain the lack of interest in welfare status at the point of migration, this issue casts further doubt on explanations of migration behaviour based narrowly upon utility-maximisation and rational choice theory. We came across no women who had undertaken a comprehensive cost-benefit analysis of the pros and cons of moving either before they moved or indeed since![100]

Conclusion

This chapter has critiqued mainstream migration theory both in terms of the reliance upon secondary analysis and also the theoretical dominance of gendered models of family relationships and their impact on migration behaviour. Limitations in methodological approach are but one factor restricting the ability of migration theory to account for the behaviour of women who migrate. Data is readily available to interested researchers which evidences the presence (and in some cases dominance) of women – and single women – in EU migration flows. The fact is that most researchers have ignored it. We have also emphasised the problems of conflating theories of international migration with intra-Community migration; internal migration within the EU takes place within a specific legal framework and involves a different group of actors many, but by no means all, of whom come from relatively privileged backgrounds. As such, it must be distinguished from other forms of international or inter-regional migration. While statistics raise many questions about migration behaviour, they cannot begin to explain the complexity of migration or why people move. In this chapter we have presented findings from the qualitative interviews with migrant women which further challenge traditional theories of migration and, in particular, notions of rational and consensual household decision making and economic maximisation. Our research did not find much evidence to underwrite mainstream models of male breadwinning migration behaviour. On the contrary, many of the women expressed a high degree of volition in their decisions to migrate. In nearly all cases, there was more than one factor behind each of the

---

[100] The lack of specific reference to social welfare in women's explanations of migration, while raising serious doubts about the phenomenon of welfare tourism in the present EU context, did not imply that social status had a marginal impact on migrant women – a point picked up in Chapter Seven.

women's decision to migrate. Two other interesting themes emerged from this research: firstly, the migration routes the women had taken. Many women had made a series of moves at international and interregional level; any understanding of their migration trajectories needs to take each move into account. Secondly, many of the women had not originally intended to make their migration permanent and in many cases the women only planned to be away for a short while. The rationale behind prolonging their stay was often different from their original impetus to move. A number of the single women said that the reason why they stayed was because they had met a partner. In the words of an Italian woman, "It's a bit silly actually but I think it happens to a lot of people – I fell in love ... and I stayed here with him"[101]. While they had not conformed to traditional patterns of 'following' a male partner, life-course changes including marriage and family-building (and the increasing pre-eminence of male economic roles) frequently underpinned subsequent decisions about interregional migration and the prospect of returning 'home'.

---

[101] Interviewee D091 (UK).

SIX

Citizenship and paid work: the impact of migration on employment status

Introduction

The key to 'favoured' citizenship status is paid employment. We have already seen the importance of the concept of 'worker' in Community law and the qualifying criteria associated with it. It is this 'economic nexus' that gives rise to optimum, independent, social status. This chapter focuses on the impact of migration on the labour market status of European Union (EU) migrant women. It begins by examining some of the available secondary data, from the European Labour Force Survey (ELFS), and then moves on to consider the interview findings. There are no simple connections to be made here. What the interviews have revealed, most emphatically, is the complexity of interactions between employment status and other variables; it is difficult to disentangle the effect of migration, marriage, family formation and caring. In many cases it was not so much the initial migration (which may have been precipitated by a desire for career progression), as subsequent life-course events, such as meeting and marrying a partner in the host State or the evolution of caring responsibilities, which restricted career trajectories. Pre-migration employment status was a key factor determining post-migration experience; women in insecure, unskilled work could often pick up similar work in the host State. For women in high-level professional careers, on the other hand, two alternative scenarios were common; if their migration was motivated by concerns to develop their own employment trajectories, they may well have achieved career progression. If, on the other hand, as was very common, their migration was motivated primarily by their partner's career (or family circumstances) then they typically suffered a significant loss in status. The effect of this varied depending on the country of immigration, although it was quite profound in most cases.

The interviews also remind us of the need to maintain a life-course perspective. The effect of moving and family formation may take some time to unravel. In many cases the immediate post-migration experience was quite positive but subsequent events lead to a change in circumstances. In others, the apparent spiral of decline (in economic status) may be interrupted by a sudden shift in direction as a woman's life unfolds and new opportunities are seized.

The chapter identifies some of the key themes raised in the course of the interviews. It is written jointly with the partner responsible for the empirical work in Portugal. Many of the examples in this section are drawn from the Portuguese sample, carefully balanced with other interviews to ensure as fair a representation as possible.

The impact of migration on labour market activity: some indications from the European Labour Force Survey

The ELFS does not enable us to compare the labour market status of migrant women prior to and following migration. What it does provide, however, is some impression of how the activity rates of EU migrant women compare to those of female nationals (and to men) and the effect of child-bearing on economic activity. In making these comparisons we need to remember that the EU migrant population is, on the whole, younger than that of nationals[1].

Labour market activity rates for migrants are generally higher than those for nationals for both sexes, although female activity rates are considerably lower than those for men. Nevertheless, over 50% of migrant women are economically active compared to 44% of female nationals. Male activity rates remain at around 95% for all males aged 25-49, irrespective of the presence or number of children. For women, however, activity rates diminish in inverse relation to the number of children. This pattern is similar to that found in various Eurostat Reports[2]. Both the number and presence of young children affects women's relationship with

---

[1] Demographic details are given in the Interim Report to the European Commission: Ackers, H.L. (1995) 'Internal migration within the European Union: the presence of women in migration flows and the characteristics of female migrants'. Where there is a long history of migration, as in the case of Irish migration to the UK, the demographic structure of the migrant population mirrors that of the host State.

[2] CEC (1996) *Women in the European Community*, Eurostat Publications.

paid work. The presence of children under the age of five has the most marked impact on women's labour market activity, particularly in the population of migrant women where, in all countries apart from Luxembourg and the UK, this group of migrant women were less active than their national counterparts, as Figure 6.1 shows.

Figure 6.1: The activity rates of national and migrant women with children under 5 years of age

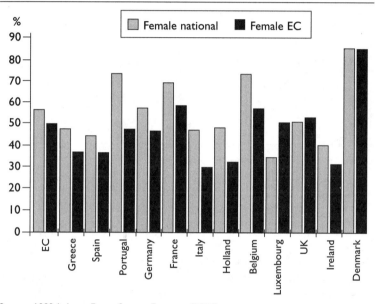

Source: 1992 Labour Force Survey, Eurostat (1994)

The presence and number of children also has considerable impact on the number of hours worked by women. Women with children are much more likely than men to be involved in part-time work restricting women's financial autonomy and entitlement to contributory benefits. The pattern for female EU migrants replicates that of female nationals but is more marked with a greater proportion of migrant women engaged in 'short' part-time work[3] as shown in Table 6.1.

---

[3] The impact of children on the labour market participation of EU migrant women may partially explain their generally lower levels of fertility despite their demographic structure.

Table 6.1: The impact of children on female working hours, by migration status

% Female nationals

Number of hours	No child	I child	2 children	3 or more children
I–I5	8%	9%	14%	21%
16–25	14%	19%	23%	24%
26–35	12%	13%	14%	33%
36–45	56%	52%	43%	33%
46 or more	9%	7%	6%	8%

% Female EU

Number of hours	No child	I child	2 children	3 or more children
I–I5	11%	12%	18%	29%
16–25	13%	24%	24%	22%
26–35	10%	11%	11%	14%
36–45	57%	46%	40%	26%
46 or more	9%	7%	8%	9%

Source: 1992 Labour Force Survey, Eurostat (1994)

The generally higher activity rates of female EU nationals (referred to above) exist alongside higher unemployment rates for this group, particularly in Belgium, Ireland and The Netherlands[4] as illustrated in Figure 6.2.

Only in the UK is female unemployment less than that of males and this probably reflects the definition of unemployment in the UK (which renders a significant proportion of women invisible due to their lack of entitlement to benefit) and higher levels of part-time working, as much as its incidence. These higher rates of unemployment among migrant women suggest both a strong commitment to paid work and higher levels of dependency upon male partners or the State as a result of their inability to find work. This also raises important questions about the citizenship status of these women in the light of the primacy attached to paid work as the basis of social entitlement and citizenship[5].

---

[4] Guarini, R., Di Palma, S. and Pennisi, A. (1994) 'The role of non-nationals on the EC labour market', Unpublished report, Eurostat, p 53.

[5] Matters discussed in detail in Chapter Four.

Figure 6.2: Unemployment rates in EU countries, by sex and broad nationality groups

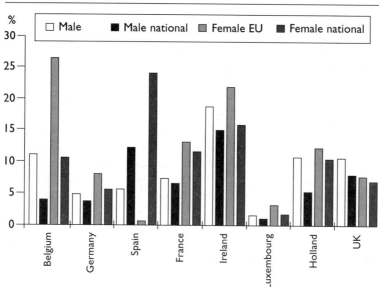

Note: No figures were available for Portugal, Italy or Denmark and data for Spain excludes EU females.

Source: Guarini et al (1994), supra, note 4, Table 2.2.3

The impact of migration on women's employment: evaluating women's experience

It is very difficult to generalise about the effect of migration on women's careers and financial autonomy, given the interaction of a whole range of life events. The motivations triggering the initial migration, together with women's employment and educational status prior to migration, have proved to be important determinants of the post-migration experience. Changes in marital status and family formation in the host State also have a substantial impact on women's labour market participation. The extent to which this reflects a lack of autonomy depends very much on domestic social policy and cultural attitudes around mothering[6].

Perhaps one of the most useful starting points in attempting to analyse

---

[6] These issues are discussed in more detail in Chapter Seven.

the impact of migration on women's employment trajectories is to consider their initial motivations or objectives, which constitute an important element colouring their perception of, and subjective reaction to, the situation. Chapter Five has already examined the reasons women gave for their initial migration. While many diverse reasons were cited, two groups are of particular interest here; those who said they moved in order to work or study and those who gave some partner-related explanation. The following discussion considers these two groups separately, although many of the experiences discussed were common to both groups (as well as to those women who gave other reasons). The impact of subsequent partner-generated migrations at either interregional or international level; of motherhood; problems of recognition of qualifications etc, together with the development of new opportunities and career trajectories were not exclusive to any one category. Nevertheless, they were commonly associated with one group more than another and will, for convenience, be dealt with under that heading.

Women who migrated in pursuit of employment

Where women have migrated with career objectives in mind, they are generally less likely to have suffered downward career mobility than in cases where women move in order to accompany or join their partners. This group includes women who left their country of origin for work, to study or to develop language competencies. In some cases, women who moved initially on a short-term basis in order to improve their language skills or simply to travel, subsequently secured employment and stayed. The following case was quite typical:

> **Hannah came alone to learn Portuguese. She got a scholarship and she came to Portugal for one year. After that she got another scholarship (to undertake post-graduate work) after which she decided to stay.**[7]

The nationality of the women and the economic situation of the sending and receiving countries also has an important effect. In general, Spanish and Portuguese women who migrated for employment-related reasons, perhaps because they were unemployed in their country of origin, benefited

---

[7] Interviewee D327 (Portugal).

---

from the move to an area where employment prospects were better. Factors such as better wages, new professional opportunities and the opportunity to develop language skills are referred to by these women as the positive consequences of their migration. In such cases, the decision to migrate was often influenced by the difficulties women encountered in realising their career aspirations (or simply finding work) in the labour market back 'home'. Several Italian respondents specifically referred to the level of sex discrimination in the Italian labour market as a key reason for their migration:

> "... the working situation (12 years ago) in Italy was very male dominated. Females in those days had little chances to do a career. The reasons why I came over is because I was made redundant by a very big company (I was a personnel manageress) and when the company went into receivership I had to go out and look for work and at 26 years old nobody would give me the chance. First I had too much experience so they had to pay me more and secondly, they thought that I was going to get married and have children and therefore I was going to be an expense ... And I always wanted to travel and this seemed the right time to do it. So I thought I'd come to England, learn the language, quickly, properly and then move around. I chose England because I wanted to learn English from the English and I was fascinated by London. I came over and really liked it so I stayed. And every job I applied for it didn't matter what age I was – in auxiliary nursing age actually helped me – I was more mature – in the meantime I was going to college as well – I worked for an agency so I could work when I needed it and carry on studying..."

> Marianne then got a permanent full-time job, which she loved, managing a small art gallery: "I personally think that I had a better professional career over here than I had in Italy. I could never have done something like run a small art gallery".[8]

Many other women were not so much influenced by 'push' factors encouraging them to leave their home State as the lure of new opportunities elsewhere, which often meant that they could utilise their skills to

---

[8] Interviewee D002 (UK).

maximum effect in the host labour market perhaps because they had a scarcity or novelty value or because they were related to language:

> Isabel came to Portugal four years ago with her sister with the objective of coming here to work. There was an opportunity for them to open a beauty centre and in France the market was completely full. "We couldn't buy there, we had to rent and we wanted to open a real big thing."[9]

> "[Leaving England] was very good because I teach English and in my country it is difficult to find a job of this kind. Here there are plenty of schools for English language."[10]

> Karen decided to emigrate because she didn't get a place at the London Dance Company .... She was invited by the director of the National Dance Company of Portugal to come to this country and so she came.[11]

Some women, as in the last example, secured an employment contract prior to their move, usually with a firm related to their country of origin or with a subsidiary company:

> "In Germany I had already worked with Portugal and Spain in the export/import business and I wanted to see my work from the other side ... they asked me if I wanted to come to Lisbon. It was an opportunity to know another culture, another language, another country ... coming here through the firm was important in professional terms..."[12]

Many women who moved in search of employment prospects had thus experienced a marked improvement in their economic or professional status and autonomy. In some cases, they had secured more highly remunerated work or greater professional responsibility, while in others they avoided unemployment and managed to work in areas they felt would

---

[9] Interviewee D315 (Portugal).
[10] Interviewee D325 (Portugal).
[11] Interviewee D373 (Portugal).
[12] Interviewee D374 (Portugal).

not have been open to them had they not moved. The following examples from Portugal are typical:

> "Maybe if I compare, today I have a better situation than some of my colleagues back in Belgium [...] I'm better off than those of my generation, I earn well."[13]

> "In professional terms, leaving Germany was an improvement, not in economic terms – in that aspect I went backwards – but in terms of career, in terms of responsibility."[14]

> "It's fine. I got my degree in a very bad economic period especially in Spain. I was lucky to be able to go to another European country and to get a job at once. Some colleagues of mine were unemployed when they finished their studies and they are still unemployed."[15]

> "I managed to work with programs I had dreamed of and that I would have never been able to in my own country."[16]

> "It was important for me to come to Portugal because of my profession. I could be earning more money than here but probably not in what I like to do: advertising. In Spain I could be working as a secretary or something else although my goal would always have been advertising. Here I like what I do."[17]

Nevertheless, it remains difficult to assess in any quantifiable way the impact of migration on career prospects. In one case, for example, a woman with legal qualifications and secretarial experience migrated because she was unable to find work in Spain and now works as a part-time waitress.

The interviews with women in Sweden similarly evidenced the problems of quantifying the effect of migration on women's careers. While the majority of these women had managed to secure paid work and while the general conditions for these women were quite beneficial (not least in

---

[13] Interviewee D320 (Portugal).
[14] Interviewee D367 (Portugal).
[15] Interviewee D326 (Portugal).
[16] Interviewee D313 (Portugal).
[17] Interviewee D344 (Portugal).

terms of their ability to combine paid work with caring) together with the educational opportunities open to them, the overwhelming majority of women had serious problems in getting permanent employment. Many of these interviewees referred to a sense of discrimination against foreigners in terms of employment contracts:

> **Clara moved to Sweden from Holland in order to study for a PhD. She then met her Swedish husband and had a child. Since then she has secured teaching work but has never held a permanent contract:**

> **"I'm not blind to the fact that foreigners have less privileged work conditions. It is a very strong hierarchy. Also European men have better opportunities than European women. If I compare my financial situation with those of my colleagues, mine have always been less secure."[18]**

It is clear from the discussion above that this group of women, who migrated primarily as single women, were not just 'drifting' into work as many non-migrant women might do, but had taken very positive and brave steps, involving international migrations, in order to achieve improved employment prospects. While the impact of the initial migration on their employment prospects was typically very positive, subsequent marriage and partner-determined migrations – either at international or interregional level – substantially restricted their financial autonomy. Meeting a partner in the period following the initial migration was one of the main reasons to turn an intended short stay into a longer, possibly permanent, one – a decision which often marks a significant shift in a women's employment trajectory. In some cases, women had intended to remain for a short period, often to improve their language skills with the intention of using these skills to achieve career advancement on their return. Where these women met partners and failed to return, their careers often suffered:

> **"The idea was to go away for two years [and then to return and continue her professional career] but that didn't happen because in the meantime I got married to a Portuguese."[19]**

---

[18] Interviewee D214 (Sweden).
[19] Interviewee D308 (Portugal).

The impact of marriage and family formation on women's labour market activity is well known and affects all women, irrespective of migration status. The degree to which labour market withdrawal, as a result of motherhood or wider caring roles, reflects the exercise of autonomy (and choice) on the part of women or the lack of opportunities to combine caring with paid work, depends on a number of factors. Chapter Seven considers some of these in more detail with a focus on the role of State welfare and the cultural climate of the country (affecting gender relations within the family and, in particular, the role of fathers in parenting). In the Swedish case, many women were supported by the State and by male partners, and therefore had more options open to them. The following two Greek cases reflect all too familiar experiences of the career dislocation brought about by caring:

> **This Portuguese woman had attended various courses in English before she moved to Greece where she worked as a secretary for a shipping company as well as teaching English on a private basis. She then married a Greek man and stopped working when she had her two children: "I stopped teaching because I got married, I had two children and I had no time". She also has caring responsibilities towards her mother-in-law who lives very close to their apartment: "We help her because she is old, she has kidney-illness and she needs our help very much".[20]**

> **Julia qualified as a secretary in Spain where she worked in her father's business. She then moved to France, initially, to study at University and then worked as an air hostess. In order to progress in this profession, she needed to improve her English and thus moved to the UK to study where she met her Greek husband, had two children and gave up work. They have since moved to Greece: "Now that my children grew up I wanted to do something. But if there is no-one, not even a mother-in-law [to take care of the children] it is difficult. I could work only part-time".[21]**

In some of these cases, it was not simply that women withdrew from the labour market in order to take on unpaid caring roles, but rather that

---

[20] Interviewee D437 (Greece).
[21] Interviewee D439 (Greece).

marriage brought with it the prospect of another move either at inter-regional or international level. The impact of such partner-determined moves depends on the availability of relevant employment in local labour markets. The desire to achieve a certain labour market status, on the part of this group of women, often meant that their initial location decision was very much determined by employment opportunities; many women in the UK, for example, moved to London in the first instance, attracted by its cosmopolitan nature and the availability of a wide variety of employment and educational resources, particularly for women with highly developed language skills. A subsequent move, to accompany a partner, to another part of the UK often restricted their ability to secure similar or equivalent employment.

In the case of the Italian woman (Marianne) already discussed above, who moved to London and managed to develop a career managing an art gallery, the effect of marriage and a subsequent move to be near her husband's family in a rural part of England, was to significantly reduce her ability to maintain this, or indeed any equivalent, career. In this case the woman had no children – it was the location decision that proved the key constraint:

> "For me I cannot have a career here – there is nothing for me in the job centre. To be able to do something I would have to go back to London – plus [her husband] earns more money than I ever did so we decided that I was going to have a little job – some two days a week or something and I was going to concentrate on looking after the house. I look after his books, make appointments for him – like a secretary. Sometimes I would like to do something more but what shall I do? So, at the moment, I am working two nights at a residential home and some hours in a café."[22]

Another example illustrates the problems of disentangling the effects of migration from subsequent marriage-related moves and caring:

> Anna qualified in France as a primary teacher and then moved to England, as a single woman, in order to learn English, intending to return to France to teach English at secondary level. Locating herself in London, she very soon established

---

[22] Interviewee D002 (UK).

herself in a career with a large French firm in the export department, using her language skills. She then married an English man and continued to work in this job for five years until her children were born. They then moved to an isolated rural area, "every move has been for his job, it was for his security, his personal satisfaction; he became difficult to live with". Anna's children both have health problems with the younger child quite severely disabled. As a consequence, she has been unable to work and now describes herself as, "a mother at home and a wife". She is currently thinking about returning to work but feels that her French teaching qualifications may not be recognised in the UK.[23]

Anna's career has suffered a number of 'blows', the first of which reflected a degree of choice. Anna felt very strongly that women should stay at home when their children are young, continually asserting her view that babies should not be left in nurseries for reasons other than financial imperative. The subsequent migration to an isolated, rural, area where she had no family support and few employment opportunities close by, further restricted the opportunities available to her. Finally, the consequences of having children with disabilities effectively prolonged the period of dependency, making it virtually impossible for her to return to work.

'Tied movers': women whose migration was 'partner-determined'

This migration pattern is more prevalent in the Portuguese case than elsewhere, which may reveal a certain specificity of the EU migration to Portugal, being more in accordance with a 'traditional' model of family migration, and dominated by partner-related employment reasons. In many cases, the decision to move to Portugal was determined by a husband's career (or in some cases their family circumstances). Some 45 women in this sample (60%) said that they came to Portugal because of their partner. Of these, 19 (25%) referred to their partner's career and the employment opportunities the move presented for him:

Tania's husband works as an hotel director and every time he wants to progress in his career he has to move to a greater

---

[23] Interviewee D001 (UK).

hotel in another town or in another country but always belonging to the same French economic group, "That's why we came to Portugal: here there was a job opportunity for my husband".[24]

Mary came to Portugal, "because my husband was sent here by his firm to direct the Portuguese branch".[25]

In 18 cases couples moved to Portugal because the husband was Portuguese or had family there:

Esther came to Portugal two years ago with her companion who is of Portuguese origin. They were already living together in France where they met: "He came to Portugal because he wanted to know the country since he had always lived in France .... The choice to come was his".[26]

Mikaela was born in Italy and met her husband in Paris. He was a teacher at the University and she was about to finish her graduation thesis. Her husband is Portuguese which is the reason she came to Portugal.[27]

Some of these women, whose migration was primarily partner-determined, managed to secure equivalent employment status post-migration:

"I usually follow him, but he always asks me if I want to go." This time she would only come if she could keep on working. Since the bank where she was working in France had a co-operation agreement with a Portuguese bank she, "was lucky to come to work in Portugal".[28]

Anne came to Portugal eight years ago with her ex-husband and two children when he came to teach at the French Institute. Now she stays here because of her work: "I like the country

---

[24] Interviewee D337 (Portugal).
[25] Interviewee D356 (Portugal).
[26] Interviewee D342 (Portugal).
[27] Interviewee D361 (Portugal).
[28] Interviewee D306 (Portugal).

very much and there is a lot of opportunities in the field where I'm working. I will make a new life here, now". She works as a painter for several museums.[29]

A woman's employment status and educational experience in the period prior to migration has an important effect on the impact of the move itself. Women in lower level, unskilled, areas of work can often resume this type of work on a casual basis in the host State:

Clare left school at 14 to work in a factory. She then met her partner, migrated with him and worked part-time in a restaurant until her children were born when she gave this up. When they started school she went back to similar part-time work. She is now working full-time and has a second part-time cleaning job.[30]

Mary did unpaid work in the family shop and at home prior to migration. After moving to be with her partner she worked part-time in a shop and is now a full-time housewife.[31]

While we have noted in the section above that country of emigration (and particularly the local labour market) is an important factor in predicting the impact of migration on that group of women who move for employment reasons, it is important not to make generalisations about countries' employment markets. In cases where women have highly developed professional careers, a move from the Mediterranean countries may actually prove detrimental both in terms of salary and status, perhaps reflecting the market value of their skills in the different employment markets. A number of professional women in Sweden, for example, noted the impact of high taxation and lower salaries:

"We can probably live better in Spain since it is not that expensive and I would have had a very good salary, but that depends on which social class you come from. In Sweden the differences between social classes are much smaller than in Spain."[32]

---

[29] Interviewee D343 (Portugal).
[30] Interviewee D079 (UK).
[31] Interviewee D093 (UK).
[32] Interviewee D232 (Sweden).

The most severe consequences of migration for women's financial autonomy can be seen in such cases – of women with professional qualifications and well-developed careers moving because of their partners. The following examples reflect an all too common trend identified in the interviews.

Simona worked as a lawyer in Italy and had also commenced studying at post-graduate level. She left the course in order to join her partner in Sweden. She had been working on a full-time permanent basis in Italy for a law firm (and noted the shorter working hours in Italy) and was given a period of unpaid leave:

"I want to hang on to this employment. We might go back to Italy in two years or something, but my husband cannot do it right now because of his work. I could keep my job, but he cannot, so he has to think hard before quitting his job. I've applied for jobs since I came to Sweden, but without any success. If I would find a job in Sweden I would quit my job in Italy."[33]

Emily had a well paid permanent University position, as a lecturer and researcher, in Belgium before coming to the UK to accompany her husband who had the opportunity to join a research project. She came on the understanding that her job would be kept open in Belgium for a year (unpaid leave) and that she would be able to get work in the same University as him. In practice, she was unable to get work at this level or in teaching and is currently working in unskilled, part-time, temporary office work for which she gets very low pay. Her husband then decided to prolong his stay and her unpaid leave expired. She is beginning to think about having children but has lost her entitlement to maternity leave:

"I came here for my husband's job and to learn the language but it wasn't too much of an issue at the time because they kept my job open. For me it was not too hard because I thought I would go back and have my job. Now it's more difficult. I'm glad to do it because as a labour economist I'm

---

[33] Interviewee D205 (Sweden).

interested to see how it is. I'm a receptionist and work part-time, but I do 35 hours a week. It's strange conditions because we don't know our timetables the week before – I don't know next week what I do. I am paid hourly and what surprises me is I have no right to bank holidays (or extra time off). I quite often work weekends but this is not too bad as I then get a day off during the week and can go the University. If I work nights it's OK – I work 4.00pm to 11.30pm and go to the University in the morning. I can then use the computer and go on the Internet."[34]

Helena had a full-time permanent position as a doctor in a Finnish hospital, with very good chances of having a fantastic career, which she had to give up in order to follow her husband. "It is me that has given up the things that I've wanted to do in order to go with my husband where his job has taken him."[35]

Many women, as in the examples given above, suffer a serious loss to their personal financial status as a result of the prioritisation attached to the male partner's career. The economic consequences of migration are nevertheless quite complex: in many cases the move has increased the financial status of the family as a whole through its impact on the partner's status and earning capacity. The decision of a household to migrate may thus appear to be 'rational' in any narrow cost–benefit analysis of aggregate family income, but at the cost of increased levels of dependency and loss of personal autonomy for female partners. Where the pursuit of this 'rational household strategy'[36] justifies an international move for the family, the consequences for the female partner's career are quite severe. This situation was particularly evident in some of the Swedish interviews where the majority of women had experienced serious problems securing permanent employment.

Veronica worked full-time as a secretary prior to the migration but has been unable to find equivalent employment in the host state (after three years searching).

---

[34] Interviewee D019 (UK).
[35] Interviewee D228 (Sweden).
[36] Taylor-Gooby, P. (1991) 'Welfare state regimes and citizenship', *Journal of European Social Policy*, vol 1, no 1, p 101.

"In terms of job and career the migration to Sweden was a success to my husband, but more or less a disaster for me. Because I really want to work. Before I came to Sweden I was independent and I don't want to stay at home anymore ... I become so depressed and frustrated. And also as a woman, if I don't work I will not qualify myself for receiving any pension/retirement subsidy."[37]

Martha has a post-graduate degree and worked as a biology teacher and freelance landscape gardener before the migration but was unable to find a satisfactory job in Sweden: "I didn't get any job. I looked and applied for so many jobs that it is unbelievable. The only thing I could get was teaching Dutch for children from Holland. That's what I was offered. But I'm not a language-teacher .... This was a very difficult period in my life, and I didn't want to tell my husband of my unhappiness because he was really happy here".[38]

"For my husband and for the family I think that the migration has been positive. I mean my husband has a very good job now and he is well paid. I don't think he would have the same opportunities in Finland. But to me and my career the migration has been a disaster .... I've talked to my husband about this, especially in the beginning, but I don't think that he understands how I feel. Also I think if you are very happy with your situation and your job it is very difficult to understand someone who doesn't feel the same."[39]

Anne gave up her degree course in order to marry and move with her husband to Switzerland, for his career. They subsequently had a son and then divorced (her husband returning to France). Anne was forced to take a factory job, for fear of deportation: "the hours were long and it was hard physical work". Concerns over her son's and her own health precipitated a return to France to work in her father's business. She then had to find work again, "because my brother took the

---

[37] Interviewee D204 (Sweden).
[38] Interviewee D221 (Sweden).
[39] Interviewee D227 (Sweden).

**business – my father didn't want two children working together".
Anne visited England and met and married an English man.
She was unemployed for a year, got a clerical post, was made
redundant after eight months and then secured some part-
time shift-work with a French travel company. Anne has since
progressed within this company and is now working on the
development of a new computer reservations system – a job
which requires liaison with colleagues in France.**[40]

In quite a few cases, women's inability to 'hold down' careers was a result
of repeated international moves as a result of their partners. This was
particularly the case where the husband worked for a subsidiary of a large
company:

**After the marriage she lost any job prospects. Her husband
stays so shortly in the same country that, "I stay like this; I pass
my time and do nothing ... I'm waiting for being able to have
a normal rhythm of labour".**[41]

**She never got a job mostly due to the frequent need to move
because of her husband's professional career.**[42]

The impact of migration on women's careers, particularly in cases where
they are 'following' or 'joining' male partners, evidently depends not only
on the employment situation in the host country but also on the extent
to which their skills are recognised. A specific problem facing many women
concerned the recognition of their qualifications ranging from school
examinations to degrees and professional qualifications. Of the 40 women
who specifically referred to this problem, almost half were migrants in
Ireland. In some cases, women were unable to gain suitable employment
in the host State while in other cases, where women had taken advantage
of educational opportunities in the host State, problems of recognition
restricted their ability to return to their home country. Serious concerns
about the recognition and transferability of their children's qualifications
influenced post-migration decisions, perhaps resulting in a longer stay
than anticipated (often until children completed compulsory education

---

[40] Interviewee D008 (UK).
[41] Interviewee D301 (Portugal).
[42] Interviewee D332 (Portugal).

and progressed into higher education) or complex manoeuvres to ensure continuity in their children's education. The following examples from Sweden indicate the sort of problems women were having:

> "I went to the Swedish employment agency to get some help to find me a job and also to get some advice about how to register my qualifications, but they were not that helpful. I believe that the migration has had a positive impact on my opportunities in the future, because I've gotten a very good education here. At the same time I'm a bit worried because I think that the better opportunities will foremost be located in Sweden, because to go back to Germany presenting a Swedish Degree will also present problems, because they don't know really what kind of an education I have."[43]

> When it comes to work, Julia has had some problems in getting jobs, especially permanent positions, and she thinks that this partly is due to her being an immigrant. When Julia came to Sweden she could not get any position in equivalence with her education, partially because Swedish employers do not know anything about what her education is worth or what it involves in practice: "many times I felt that my knowledge was wasted by the Swedish system".[44]

> "Well I would move back if I could ... there was one thing that annoyed me in Sweden, that my British qualifications were not recognised for anything. To teach English on a regular basis I would have to go through it all again, and get a degree in English here. But I got a job because I can talk myself into anything, you need contacts though, and I got them ... I was not good enough to teach English in classes, but I was good enough to teach at University. You cannot teach English because you went to an English University!"[45]

---

[43] Interviewee D229 (Sweden).
[44] Interviewee D202 (Sweden).
[45] Interviewee D208 (Sweden).

This problem was by no means restricted to Sweden but was also common in the UK and Portugal, although no cases were cited in the Greek sample:

"There was something pretty shocking – my demand for a degree equivalence. I had to ask in France for documents proving all the levels, all the years I had done and when I got to the University they wanted me to pay 100,000 Escudos, because in every year I had to pay more. And it would take me one year to get the equivalence. I gave up. And then I asked for the baccalaureate equivalence and they wanted me to do the 12th year exam (last year of secondary education). It's an abuse."[46]

"It is almost impossible to have our foreign certificates to be recognised here in Portugal."[47]

"I thought possibilities here would be the same. The first thing I did was learning the language, a thing Spanish people never do when they come here. Then I started to send my curriculum. As I didn't have any equivalence, things started to close down for me."[48]

One woman reported that she had never practised her nursing in Cork. She said that she is not allowed to work as a nurse in Ireland because her qualifications are not recognised. "There is no body for recognition of my degree".[49]

This French woman reported problems in registering her degree in Ireland: "Actually it was very lengthy. I had to get my degree approved here so that I could teach and they went into every minute detail and I had to pay as well which I resented a little bit at the time, I think it was over £100."[50]

In addition to the general difficulties women experienced in having their qualifications assessed and recognised by authorities and employers in the

---

[46] Interviewee D313 (Portugal).
[47] Interviewee D347 (Portugal).
[48] Interviewee D357 (Portugal).
[49] Interviewee D514 (Ireland).
[50] Interviewee D516 (Ireland).

host State, many women had more specific barriers in relation to linguistic competencies. In the following case, a young French woman who came to the UK as a single parent with a two-year-old child has experienced considerable problems securing not only appropriate employment but any employment. She came to the UK with two HNDs in economics and marketing and also undertook a course in European Marketing which involved a work placement with a British newspaper. Nevertheless, despite her qualifications and her excellent English, she relates her experience as follows:

> "It took me eight months to find work ... I think some people who cannot speak any languages are scared of the language barrier, they cannot really understand what is your level. If you have an accent it scares them to death. I had someone say to me, 'you're incompetent because you have got an accent' .... Anyway I got a job in reservations at [...] and I've given them my CV. It's a step inside the company so I can do something else – apparently its the kind of company where you can expect to climb up ... English people won't believe in French qualifications. If I had the time to take an English exam in marketing it would help me to find a job in my field. I went for a few interviews and the language barrier always ... I have never been taken seriously. First it's my qualifications, they don't know what it means, the different names. It's not the same at all [as an English degree]. That's why I'm working in reservations because I couldn't find anything and I would have done anything [in preference to this job]. I work shifts – one weekend in five off and I start at 5.30 in the morning – I hardly see my daughter, my neighbour takes her to school and picks her up."[51]

In this case, the difficulty in securing appropriate employment has resulted in the acceptance of a post for which she is not only over-qualified, but which also presents particular difficulties for a single parent attempting to combine work with parenting.

In addition to these kinds of problems, reflecting prejudice on the part of employers and indicating the sorts of problems in enforcement of policies in this area, the Irish cases stand out as clear examples of the material

---

[51] Interviewee D009 (UK).

consequences of policy decisions (and, in particular, the implications of the ECJ's ruling on 'linguistic knowledge' in *Groener*[52]). This case involved a Dutch national who was refused an appointment to a permanent teaching position in an art college because she had failed to pass an examination in Gaelic, despite the fact that Gaelic was not essential to the post. The Court found that this did not amount to discrimination as it was imposed as part of a policy to protect the national language. The following cases give some impression of the impact of this ruling on migrant women in Ireland:

> "I am trained as a primary school teacher and had I stayed in England I would have done it but because of Irish language complications I cannot teach, I cannot carry on with my career so I have switched to voluntary work in adult literacy ... so I am part-time teaching 25 hours per week. I had a career path teaching at primary level and then I was thinking in terms of teacher training myself, being a lecturer. None of that could happen so I have built a career in adult education instead. There is no barrier to working in the voluntary and private sector but there is in the state system."[53]

> Mary married an Irish man in England and moved with him to Ireland with the intention of continuing her career in primary teaching. When she got to Ireland she found that her teaching qualifications were not accepted because she could not speak Irish. She did a whole variety of jobs including teaching art in secondary schools and teaching in the private sector where the Gaelic requirement did not hold: "The job I came for an interview for, I didn't get. When I got here I found that my qualifications were not valid here because I didn't speak Irish".

> Another English woman qualified with a music degree and teaching qualification, left her job to join her husband in Ireland, unaware of the problem: "I hadn't realised I needed to speak Irish to get a job in a school. I trained as a music teacher and presumed that I might get a job in a secondary school". She was unable to teach in a school and works instead as a musician.[54]

---

[52] *Groener*, Case C-379/87 [1989] ECR 3967.

[53] Interviewee D551 (Ireland).

[54] Interviewee D563 (Ireland).

Ms Groener (who took the case to the ECJ) was interviewed in the Irish sample and spoke of the effect of the ECJ ruling on her career:

> **"I was back to being part time – I lost the job. It also means that if you don't have the Irish, you don't get any increments in your job so I felt for years I had been on the bottom scale of the job that I do well, while my colleagues would get each year a higher income doing the same work."**

The decision of the ECJ in *Groener* has thus caused serious problems for many migrant women living in Ireland, particularly those qualified and wishing to work as teachers. As a consequence, many qualified teachers are unable to secure permanent employment in the State sector but have, instead, managed to obtain part-time work in the voluntary and private sectors where the linguistic requirement does not apply. This work is, of course, often less well paid and less secure. This specific problem in Ireland, coupled with more general concerns about the recognition of teaching and nursing qualifications across all Member States leads us to question the relevance of Bonney and Love's assessment of the impact of migration on the careers of 'tied movers'[55]. This research, concerned solely with the impact of interregional migrations, suggested that the impact was less serious than anticipated as wives typically assume a 'secondary labour market role' (prior to migration) and often take up occupations (such as teaching and nursing) which, "positively facilitate discontinuous careers". Long and Spitze present similar views about the 'receptiveness' of certain occupations (nursing, teaching and clerical work) to discontinuous career trajectories. Spitze concludes that, "it may be that the geographical transferability of these occupations has played a part in their perpetuation as favourite career choices of women"[56]. In a European context, at least, this argument evidently does not hold as these careers, particularly teaching and nursing, prove especially difficult for migrant women to enter. One might also wish to unpack the concept of career implicit in this work, as research on 'dual career' households is increasingly showing that while

---

[55] Bonney, N. and Love, J. (1991) 'Gender and migration: geographical mobility and the wife's sacrifice', *Sociological Review*, vol 39, no 2, pp 335-48.

[56] Long, L.H. (1974) 'Women's labour force participation and the residential mobility of families', *Social Forces*, vol 52, pp 342-8; Spitze, G. (1984) 'The effect of family migration on wives' employment: how long does it last?', *Social Science Quarterly*, vol 70, pp 231-4.

both partners might be said to maintain a 'career', in many cases the progression of one partner (typically the male) takes place at the expense of the career profile of the other partner (typically the woman) who is simply,'treading water'. The following case is quite typical. Louisa continues to teach but on a very different professional basis.

Louisa gave up a teaching post in France to accompany her partner to Portugal and has since only been able to get teaching jobs in private schools: "It was the end of the possibility of having a career in my teaching profession. Here it's completely impossible to have a career. I have no career".[57]

In addition to the specific issues concerning the recognition of language competencies (and qualifications) raised in the section above, many other women who had moved to accompany partners (and in that sense were less well prepared for life and work in a foreign country) simply lacked the language skills to commence work in the host State – partly explaining the high levels of unemployment detailed above. In some cases, the period of unemployment was quite short but in many others it extended over a longer period, impacting significantly on women's quality of life in the host State:

"When I came to Portugal, it was impossible to get a job in journalism since I didn't speak Portuguese".[58]

Since she is in Portugal she never had a paid job: "It would be difficult for me to get a job because of the language problems".[59]

She got a job a month ago, after a whole year in unemployment. For her it was very important to get a job because "after spending a whole year at home, for me who have been working since I was 18, it was driving me mad".[60]

In some cases a woman's downward career trajectory reflected not so much a failure to recognise qualifications, but more substantial differences

---

[57] Interviewee D347 (Portugal).
[58] Interviewee D309 (Portugal).
[59] Interviewee D340 (Portugal).
[60] Interviewee D311 (Portugal).

in the nature of professions. The equivalent professions simply did not exist or were not so highly developed:

She used to work as a specialised nurse in the UK. She had to stop working when she came to Portugal, "because that job is not available here".[61]

Maria had many problems getting her qualifications as a speech therapist recognised and to be able to exercise her profession in Portugal.[62]

The implications of unemployment for women's status as independent citizens are clearly quite serious and result in high levels of personal dependency on breadwinning partners. To escape the consequences of unemployment, many of the women interviewed took jobs well below their previous or expected employment status, experiencing high levels of de-skilling and over-qualification and a decline in their financial autonomy. As such, migration often implies a significant shift in their professional lives involving employment in a position well below their real skills.

Julia is a psychologist. After being unemployed for one year, she got a job a month ago, in a tourism agency that belongs to the Spanish Tourism Bureau in Lisbon, which has nothing to do with her profession.[63]

Emma moved to Portugal following her degree to study for a post-graduate qualification in European Law, intending to return to Belgium. She then met her Brazilian partner and stayed. She was unemployed for a period and now has three part-time, short-term jobs doing secretarial work, some translation and works as a tour guide:

"I do a lot of things because we have to survive. These are activities which are below my skills and I suffer with that .... So I must content myself with the under-employment or with jobs which I would never take in Belgium .... I'm also a victim

---

[61] Interviewee D307 (Portugal).
[62] Interviewee D317 (Portugal).
[63] Interviewee D311 (Portugal).

of my education: I have a degree, several courses and good skills. But those skills are not appreciated here ... well perhaps in Belgium they also weren't ...."[64]

"When I first came to England I wanted to work in a museum ... I haven't been able to find a job in a museum so I have done restaurant work because I need the money."[65]

Tanita moved from Spain, where she had worked for her father as a manageress of one of his shoe shops, to get away from family pressures and learn English. While acknowledging the fact that she is working well below her previous level, she partially accepts this as the price of moving to another country and of acquiring language skills: "Well in a way my status changed a little bit because I had to learn the language for about two or three years you know. And I worked in hotels as well as a chambermaid and doing cleaning jobs. And I was also ... well sometimes I was unemployed you know for some periods and ... you know ... and basically I just had in mind that I wanted to learn English and to improve it. And I did all the examinations for students like the first certificate and the proficiency. I've been poorer here. I mean my status is a different one you know ... I mean here I am below working class. Working class, I don't know whether that is right but I am talking about income you know. It's not that my family is well off or anything but my status is completely different. There are things that I do here that I wouldn't do there. I mean like cleaning, I wouldn't do that there because I come from a middle class family and you know it's a small place and if someone knew that I was doing something like that ... it wouldn't occur to me. But that's the good thing of being here or going somewhere else where you can do a lot of things, learn about a lot of things, I don't know ... be a waitress. It makes you learn as well".[66]

The interviews thus revealed widespread evidence of de-skilling, or the

---

[64] Interviewee D327 (Portugal).
[65] Interviewee D080 (UK).
[66] Interviewee D086 (UK).

employment of migrant women in areas of work for which they were substantially 'over' or inappropriately qualified. This particularly affected women qualified as teachers and nurses but also chemists and academics. This comes as no surprise and affects all women in the labour market. A specific manifestation of this was, however, apparent in relation to the abuse of women's language skills – or particular links with their country of origin. Many of the women interviewed were working, often on a part-time, casual or low paid basis in various forms of language teaching or translation work or as secretaries for firms with European connections (such as the travel industry) often on poor wages and with poor conditions. Almost one third of the women interviewed in Portugal were involved in some form of teaching – mostly as language teachers. In that sense it seems that the language skills of these women are often treated by employers as simply an added bonus – an extra secretarial or public relations skill – attracting no more status or remuneration, in much the same way as women's caring skills are abused in the labour market. Some examples are given below:

> **Jane has a degree in design and worked for two years in a museum of German history, in what was East Berlin, with responsibility for historical exhibitions developing design concepts, "it was very interesting, very good, then the wall came down – it was given to the West as a present – all the people in the East German museum were made redundant. It was the biggest arms collection of Europe and they just got it as a gift". Following a period of unemployment and depression, she secured a full-time post working as a journalist. Jane then decided to pursue her chosen career in advertising and travelled to England to improve her English intending to return. After a very difficult relationship she decided to stay, undertook some training in computing, a diploma in management and a certificate in English and attempted to get work. At first she could only get clerical work in a shop but then she got a job working full-time as a business analyst in the German department of an international company which sells business data around the world. Jane finds this work very interesting and enjoyable but has a temporary, part-time, contract for which she is paid only £4.50 per hour.[67]**

---

[67] Interviewee D012 (UK).

This French woman is a qualified social worker with a degree in sociology and experience of research work. Since her migration to Greece she worked as a hotel secretary and then got a fixed-term research contract and now works as a translator in a government department.[68]

Another woman with a degree and nursing qualification migrated to Greece and subsequently worked as a child-minder, then spent two years working in the tourist industry. Since having her children she has stopped paid work.[69]

A Dutch woman comments "I did the traditional thing, I accompanied my husband". In Holland she qualified as a biology teacher and taught for eight years and then she freelanced as a landscape gardener:

"After the migration I tried to get a job in this area, but I didn't get any job. I looked and applied for so many jobs that it is unbelievable. The only thing I could get was teaching Dutch for children from Holland. That's what I was offered. But I'm not a language teacher. Since that was the only thing I could get I did that for the first three years. But otherwise the employment agency offered me a job as a shop-hand. I was so disappointed and depressed that I stopped looking for jobs. This was a very difficult period in my life, and I didn't want to tell my husband of my unhappiness because he was really happy here." She says that if she had known how difficult it would be she would never have accompanied her husband and advises all women that, before moving to Sweden, "see to it that you have a job waiting for you".[70]

This Spanish woman had made two migrations, first to Argentina, then back to Spain and latterly to Portugal. She describes the impact on her career as follows:

"It was quite a disaster, because I'm a psychologist. In Argentina

---

[68] Interviewee D457 (Greece).
[69] Interviewee D460 (Greece).
[70] Interviewee D221 (Sweden).

I couldn't live from my profession alone. I had to do other jobs and be a psychologist as a hobby. I worked for free at the hospital and for a living I had to do translations and teach English." In Spain she managed to live from her profession. She had an office and a network of patients and colleagues. She left this work in order to accompany her husband to Portugal for his career: "I stopped doing that. It had been a great effort and it was very important for me to have achieved that. And that was one of the reasons why I had so many doubts about moving to Portugal. All that, I lost here". Since then she has been unemployed for a year and started a Masters degree by correspondence. She now works in a Spanish tourist office.[71]

A German woman was working full-time as a law lecturer and judge prior to her move. She moved in order to accompany her Greek husband to Greece. She was unable to secure similar employment in Greece and spent over a year unemployed. She now teaches German to lawyers.[72]

The examples given here reflect one of the most prevalent scenarios identified in the course of the research, with a large proportion of women working in areas connected with language and tourism, irrespective of their previous employment or qualifications.

We have already discussed the impact of marriage and family formation on the careers of women who moved for work purposes. Marriage and family life are some of the most influential factors in terms of female professional histories for both migrant and non-migrant women. The situation for the migrant carer is, however, particularly stark given the unevenness and limited awareness of welfare provision together with the lack of informal support and the complicated web of caring obligations across space (issues discussed in more detail in Chapters Seven and Eight). The following cases represent typical examples of the relationship between migration, family formation and career in the lives of women whose moves were partner-determined.

Clarissa met her English partner in Germany and then returned with him to the UK because he was homesick. Her husband is

---

[71] Interviewee D311 (Sweden).
[72] Interviewee D450 (Greece).

unemployed. Prior to migration Clara had her own hairdressing salon which she sold. After coming she worked full-time in a hairdressing salon: "I wasn't very happy – the pay was very low. It is much better in Germany. I had a higher income. Here my earnings were as high as an apprentice in Germany – down rock bottom – so after seven months I went self-employed – mobile – and went to people's houses to do their hair". [She got an allowance from the Enterprise Scheme to start the business and had to attend a course on business management.] She then had two daughters:

"I could have continued but what would I do with the child – all the chemicals and sprays – it wouldn't have been fair. Now, I'm a mum – I'm pretty involved in the school and toddler groups. I have also been doing some evening classes in French and Italian and took an A level in biology last year – and trying to keep fit as well". Her children are now aged three and five and she has begun to get eczema from the chemicals, "... so I told myself, I'm 35 now and I don't want to be a hairdresser in my 40s – I'm not in the mood to stand all day – and I got accepted on the European Society and Policy degree course at the University and I have got Sue into nursery."[73]

Claudia qualified and practised as a nurse in Holland. Since coming to Greece she worked as a child-minder for a short time. Then one year in a tourist agency, and one year in a souvenir shop. She doesn't work now, because she doesn't have anyone to leave her children with.[74]

She did a secretarial course and worked as an 'attaché de direction' for five years in an engineering business. She stopped working when she was 26 because her husband asked her to and because she had her children[75]. She had a breakdown in her professional activity, because she decided not to work during her pregnancy and while her child was a small baby.[76]

---

[73] Interviewee D007 (UK).
[74] Interviewee D460 (Greece).
[75] Interviewee D300 (Portugal).
[76] Interviewee D337 (Portugal).

"When the husband has a profession, it's usually the woman who sees her profession sacrificed. There are times when women revolt because it seems that all there is are diapers and children and one cannot fulfil herself."[77]

In several cases (as in D007 [UK] above) when children grow older, women go back to work or return to education, usually on a part-time basis, enabling them to combine work with family responsibilities:

In 1972 her daughter was born and she stopped working. In 1976 she went back to work part-time as a health visitor.[78]

"I've put my children before my career. I like my work [she is a mathematics teacher] and my career never developed a lot because it demanded more availability than the one I could give because I had my children rather late and adopting a child demands a lot of energy, a lot of time. We decided I would be working part-time and be more available for the children, someone had to be around and I don't feel like it has been a sacrifice."[79]

The impact of migration on women's careers and its evaluation by women thus varies a lot according to different factors. Some women do not share this feeling of 'sacrifice', referred to above. For them, giving up work in order to care for children is considered to be the right option to make, at least when children are in their early years.

Having left her country had a big impact because she stopped working. "I had worked in banks for 10 years ... I was leaving my job because I was getting married. For me the professional career is not very important."[80]

"Having quit my job to stay with my children was the right decision to make."[81]

---

[77] Interviewee D305 (Portugal).
[78] Interviewee D307 (Portugal).
[79] Interviewee D345 (Portugal).
[80] Interviewee D318 (Portugal).
[81] Interviewee D304 (Portugal).

Of course these same women may present a different perspective if we re-interviewed them in several year's time when their children are more independent.

> **"When children grow up and go to school, if the mother hasn't got any job outside the home, she is bound to feel lonely and get depressed. When my second child started going to school, I remember sitting on the sofa and feeling useless and hopeless, with just the housework to do and nothing else. I was glad to go back to work."**[82]

We have seen, in the section on de-skilling above, that many women refer to the problems not only of lack of status or remuneration, but also to the impact migration has had on working conditions in general, and in particular to the problems of insecure contracts, part-time and shift work. These problems faced by migrant women need to be understood in the context of general changes in the labour market across Europe – of increasing precarisation and 'flexibilisation', phenomena that disproportionately affect the female labour force. The following examples give a general impression of some of the conditions women were working under following their migration:

> **She was unemployed for four months. She is now working as an architect-urbanist at a private atelier. She has no contract.**[83]

> **She has been doing some temporary jobs painting T-shirts, decorating discos and especially making interpretation. These are jobs which are not declared for taxes nor social security.**[84]

> **She worked for two years at the English school, "more than 48 hours a week, there was always work to be done".**[85]

> **"It is not a safe job and I feel my wage is very low."**[86]

---

[82] Interviewee D032 (UK).
[83] Interviewee D330 (Portugal).
[84] Interviewee D339 (Portugal).
[85] Interviewee D308 (Portugal).
[86] Interviewee D349 (Portugal).

"My working time reduced from 16 to eight hours a week. So I have to live with half of the money. There is no stability."[87]

"I also miss holidays. I only have 22 days of holidays and in Germany we have 30, 31 days."[88]

"It was horrendous because at the beginning I worked weekends, shifts, until midnight, up at six in the morning ... I was not getting a lot financially but I desperately wanted to work."[89]

"It's horrible, in every way; they want people to do three people's work and one person to do it."[90]

Other women had suffered from forms of racism, often associated with language and accents (as in the examples given earlier). In one case a German woman living in Plymouth had experienced quite explicit racism at work:

"It was the same as in Germany when we had Turkish girls working in the hairdressers and they had problems exactly the same as I have had here ... They [the other staff] were younger than me and made jokes about the war, Jews, Germans, just to whack you one over and they did because I thought, 'why?'. They have never been in the war – neither was I. In the end you think they are just silly and keep away from them. I had one customer that was Jewish and she did let me know it and every time I tried not to see her she rang back and asked me to do her hair – and she got so much satisfaction out of it – she told me about Israel etc – I think she wanted to mentally torment me. With every hairdo I got a lecture as well."[91]

We saw above how, for many women and particularly those who 'followed' partners, the migration precipitated a fundamental shift in employment status. For some this was very much a case of de-skilling. Although the

---

[87] Interviewee D359 (Portugal).
[88] Interviewee D374 (Portugal).
[89] Interviewee D008 (UK).
[90] Interviewee D054 (UK).
[91] Interviewee D007 (UK).

overwhelming impression from the interviews was one of career dislocation and downward career mobility, for other women this sudden change of circumstances spawned new opportunities, enabling women to develop new career trajectories, perhaps capitalising on their language skills and connections and developing their own businesses. This increasing self-confidence may partially explain the relatively high numbers of women, particularly in Portugal and Ireland, who are self-employed (around 15% of the women interviewed in Portugal, for example). Self-employment was, in some cases, an answer to the difficulties found in getting a good job as an employee:

> "Because of the language [I had problems] when I tried to get normal jobs in normal firms ... But when I decided to go into business by myself I think it was easy. I easily reached firm's managers, marketing managers. I spoke Portuguese very badly and I think people were very open."[92]

> She began working as a stylist when she was 20. Neither her or her husband had much money and she decided to create clothes and to try to sell them to Portuguese factories. She worked as an independent for several factories until she managed to open her own shop. Now she has three outlets and employs several women.[93]

> A physiotherapist had problems obtaining work in Irish hospitals even though she is chartered in Ireland and now runs her own private practice.[94]

> Leanne has a law degree from Germany where she met her Portuguese husband. She moved with him to Angola and then on to Portugal. She wanted to go on studying but, as she puts it, "it's that problem with women: a woman is supposed to stay home". In Angola she was a housewife: "Women were not supposed to be working but it was me who did all the mailing with other countries. For many years I did contracts with Germany and Italy". After arriving in Portugal she stayed as a

---

[92] Interviewee D309 (Portugal).
[93] Interviewee D338 (Portugal).
[94] Interviewee D555 (Ireland).

housewife until 1992 when she opened an antiques shop where she works every afternoon. It is her first job but "I get no salary. It all goes to the house, to the lot". In the mornings she paints, "it's both a job and a hobby".[95]

Many other women, whose employment was adversely affected by the migration, subsequently managed to establish themselves in good careers:

Catherine met and married an English serviceman in Spain and returned with him to England. They had two children and subsequently divorced. She had not worked prior to migration and had no post-school qualifications. She obtained some part-time office work which she had to give up when the children were born as she worked shifts and she had not worked there long enough to qualify for maternity leave. She was then offered her post back and progressed through the company to the point at which she is now a full-time business analyst with the company.

Maria has made a series of moves primarily motivated by her husband's career. She first gave up a full-time post as a decorator in Spain to move to Sweden where she secured part-time work and then returned to Spain where she returned to full-time work. They subsequently moved to France where she was unable to work in her profession as her qualifications were not recognised and she was unable to return to study as she had three young children. Eventually Maria re-trained for work as a framer. When her children grew up she returned alone to Sweden (although they have not separated as such) where she is now training to be a nurse. Maria makes the following evaluation:

"Well the migration was important to my husband's career, that is for sure. But I have always felt that it has been important for me to take care of my children and to be with them and I have been very happy taking care of them so I haven't considered this to be a problem until now. But now when they are grown up I feel that I need something for myself to do for the next 20 years."

---

[95] Interviewee D302 (Portugal).

"My partner couldn't speak any German so I took the plunge and came here. Originally I tried to apply for jobs that were linked to what I had been doing (chemistry) in laboratories but I got no response at all – they wouldn't recognise any of the qualifications – not even the A levels". She eventually found a part-time office job and moved from part-time to full-time work and eventually to section leader and finally to manager. Since coming to Britain her husband has had to give up work due to illness so she is now the main breadwinner."[96]

The last case is quite interesting as it indicates a quite common phenomenon, previously discussed in Chapter Five, concerning the impact of women's superior language skills on the household decision-making process. Somewhat ironically, the more highly developed language skills of the female partner often appear to underline the justification of the male breadwinning strategy. Rather than being seen as a marketable skill in its own right, the under-valuing of women's language competencies (and the evaluation of them more as a general life-skill) re-affirms the prioritisation of male careers. In other words, it makes rational sense to locate in his country of origin as his lack of linguistic competency would restrict his economic potential in another Member State.

Conclusions

The research findings presented in this chapter evidence the difficulties many migrant women have reported in securing commensurate employment. The fracturing of women's careers, as a result of migration, marriage and caring, leaves many women on the margins of employment. Some have experienced long periods of unemployment while others have been forced to accept forms of work not recognised in Community (or indeed national) law, working in the black economy (particularly in areas concerned with tourism and language tuition) or in family businesses. The inability of these women to qualify as Community workers denies them independent access to social protection in the host State, resulting in high levels of dependency on partners.

For a much larger group of women, the consequences of partner-determined migrations and family formation are a decline in economic status and financial autonomy. Problems in gaining acceptance of

---

[96] Interviewee D018 (UK).

qualifications and language competencies, together with access to appropriate opportunities in local labour markets and the lack of informal support with caring roles, result in high levels of de-skilling and vulnerability to insecure and part-time contracts. These processes particularly affect women who had well-developed professional careers or qualifications prior to the move. Included in this group are those women who had qualified as teachers and nurses, careers which are generally considered to, 'facilitate discontinuous careers' but which, in a migration context, prove especially difficult to recover. The research thus found a very high proportion of women working in areas for which they are substantially over or inappropriately qualified, in jobs they have secured by virtue of their language competencies and yet for which they are rudely rewarded. A significant number of this group are women whose partners make repeated moves, often working under contract for large multi-national companies. In these cases it becomes very difficult for women to maintain careers.

For that group of women who moved to accompany partners, the effects of migration are felt quite keenly in their post-migration employment experience, which not only impacts significantly on their financial autonomy and quality of life in the medium term, but also restricts their access to contributory benefits (such as maternity and sick leave) and pensions.

The consequences of migration were generally less serious in the group of women whose migration was motivated by concerns for personal career advancement and financial independence. The consequences, in the medium term, following the initial period of language acquisition and general dislocation, were often quite beneficial, with many women taking full advantage of training and educational opportunities in the host State and utilising their skills to best effect in the domestic labour market. Although many women in this group experienced similar problems to the previous groups (in terms of recognition of qualifications etc), migration generally presented new opportunities. Career dislocation and downward mobility often accompanied changes in post-migration personal status, with marriage, family formation and the evolution of caring obligations. In many cases, these women subsequently experienced the kind of problems associated with the previous group, as partner-determined interregional or international migrations took place resulting in difficulties in using their skills in local labour markets.

To conclude, on a more positive note, this chapter has evidenced not only the devastation of many women's professional lives, but also significant periods of re-building. The display of courage and the pioneering qualities exhibited by the women interviewed, irrespective of migration motive, often results in a period of re-construction in which the sheer tenacity and entrepreneurship of migrant women encourages them to create for themselves new opportunities, either through the grasping of educational and training opportunities or through self-employment. The degree to which this was evident in the interviews suggests that the LFS data significantly under-estimates the incidence of self-employment, undeclared and unpaid family work among this group of women. Migrant women are not simply the passive victims of labour market discrimination and gender-role stereotyping; they have proved themselves to be capable of utilising their skills in innovative ways, greatly enhancing their financial autonomy and quality of life.

SEVEN

Facilitating mobility? Migrant women's experiences of living in different welfare systems

Chapter Four traced the evolution of social entitlement under the free movement provisions from its somewhat narrow foundations, in measures to reduce discrimination in access to employment, to a wider recognition of the migrant worker as a member of a household with family responsibilities. This lead to the extension of entitlement to members of the worker's family in order to, as Kirsten Scheiwe suggests, "augment the male migrant's mobility"[1]. The focus on measures to facilitate labour mobility is not only reflected in the institutionalisation of a dependent status in Community law for the spouses of migrant workers; it is also evidenced by the, "wide lack of special provisions or structural policies that could augment female worker's mobility through the improvement of childcare facilities or other infrastructures which would reduce obstacles to the free movement of the female workforce"[2].

The broadening of the personal scope of entitlement to families and wives, in the absence of measures to promote a more genuine and pro-active extension in material entitlement (which recognises the specific difficulties facing women as migrants and employees), thus amounts to a somewhat hollow 'family policy'. This lack of specific concern, at Community level, to identify or respond to the issues facing migrant women renders them vulnerable to disparities in domestic social policy. What this means, in practice, is that, for some women, the decision of whether or where to move may be heavily influenced by their evaluation of the impact of migration on their citizenship status and reproductive rights. In that sense, divergence in women's social status across European

---

[1] Scheiwe, K. (1994) 'EC law's unequal treatment of the family: the case law of the European Court of Justice on rules prohibiting discrimination on grounds of sex and nationality', *Social and Legal Studies*, vol 3, no 2, pp 243-65 at p 251.

[2] Scheiwe, K. (1994, p 251), supra, note 1.

welfare regimes may constitute a barrier to mobility as Linda Hantrais suggests:

> ... the cumulative effect of differences in the ways in which a family is conceptualised and the associated institutional arrangements a migrant worker can expect to find in another EU Member State may be important factors in encouraging or deterring intra-European family migration.[3]

We have already seen that, in the majority of cases[4], female European Union (EU) migrants move of their own volition, displaying high levels of determination and autonomy. Given the 'voluntary' nature of this migration, one could predict a movement of women, as individual actors, towards those Member States which offer them the widest opportunities; a movement, that is, away from those countries identified as 'woman-hostile' and towards those identified, in the typologies, as 'woman-friendly'.

The development of social entitlement under the free movement provisions, particularly through the Court's broad and expansive interpretation of 'social advantages'[5] and the concept of worker, theoretically opens up domestic welfare systems to exploitation by an EU-precipitated wave of welfare tourism (already referred to in Chapter Five). Concerns over the unleashing of this new migratory phenomenon, based again on presumptions of materialistic, economic-maximising behaviour, coupled with the predictions of feminist comparative social policy, might suggest that 'welfare tourism' is itself a gendered process. In other words, prospective female migrants might be expected to move towards the magnet of Northern Europe, turning their backs on the high levels of dependency that characterise Southern European 'welfare societies' and the 'liberal' or 'strong male breadwinning' economies of the UK and Ireland.

In practice, the interviews do not suggest such a high level of awareness of, or interest in, social policy or gender relations at the point of migration (when many of the women were young and single and less concerned

---

[3] Hantrais, L. (1997) 'What is family or family life in the European Union?', Paper to the Immigration Law Practitioners' Association and the Centre of European Law, King's College London Conference, 'The legal framework and social consequences of free movement of persons in the European Union', 27-28 November.

[4] See Chapter Five.

[5] See Chapter Four for detailed discussion of the legal framework.

with matters of family policy) and if they were, there is little accessible information available to them to assist in such an evaluation. The lack of evidence of 'welfare tourism' (or migrations motivated by concerns to maximise social status) does not, however, imply that social status is an irrelevance to women. The specific meaning of 'social advantages' in any given domestic welfare context, while perhaps only one of many considerations affecting the migration decision (and frequently not the deciding factor), nevertheless impacts significantly on the post-migration experience, shaping the infrastructure of opportunities and constraints which the woman migrant must then negotiate as her life and circumstances evolve in the host State[6].

This chapter begins to address the sort of questions Scheiwe and Hantrais have raised through an examination of the experiences of migrant women. In the context of 'facilitating mobility' then, what is it about the quality and nature of different social arrangements and support systems that would promote or impede the mobility of women, influence the selection of destinations and improve or restrict their quality of life once they have moved? How do women interpret different forms of dependency and which configuration of policies and provisions promotes their sense of autonomy?

These questions take us away from a legalistic evaluation of rights into the realms of comparative social policy, raising complex questions about method and approach; how, for example, do we begin to assess the relative attractiveness or impact of different social systems? The chapter explores some of these issues of migration and social welfare through an analysis of women's unique experiences of living in at least two welfare systems[7] and the means by which they negotiated the constraints that faced them.

I have already emphasised the importance of understanding the complexity of the citizenship concept as a mechanism for evaluating women's quality of life and autonomy. In particular, the limitations of measures of 'formal equality' as statements of theoretical entitlement and labour market participation, as a proxy for outcome, were referred to in

---

[6] In highlighting the importance of wider considerations of social policy and family life to the citizenship experience of migrant women, I do not intend to suggest that this applies only to women. I hope that, in the process of addressing concerns raised by women in this research, we can also begin to widen our understanding of the experience of migration for all citizens.

[7] Many of the women interviewed had, in fact, made more than one international migration and would therefore have experience of two or more welfare systems.

Chapter Two and, in the context of feminist methodology, in Chapter Three. In practice, formal social policy provision is often compared, in academic literature, with some prescribed feminist 'ideal' which, in the past, often took the form of normative modelling, but with the development of comparative method has increasingly been a particular 'regime type'. In this way, Scandinavian 'social-democratic' welfare states are typically presented at the 'woman-friendly' end of a hierarchically-defined, linear, continuum ranking the status of women in the countries concerned. This kind of approach, which was quite influential in early feminist comparative work, has been criticised for the following reasons[8]. Firstly, it presumes a strong correlation between theoretical entitlement and outcome (that women and men are aware of and exercise their rights). There is also a universalising tendency within this approach, presuming a common aspiration, or desired outcome, on the part of European women as a group. Secondly, there is a tendency to characterise women's status in 'material' terms as recipients of welfare services or benefits rather than to see these as vehicles for the achievement of broader quality of life objectives (reflecting autonomy and empowerment). In so doing, it encourages an approach to both theorising and methodology which emphasises passivity rather than agency.

Given the nature of life-history interviews, and our research focus on issues connected with migration, women were not asked a series of standard questions inviting them to compare welfare policies and their interaction with culture and popular attitudes. Rather, they were encouraged to talk generally about their experiences, as women, of living in different societies. The responses therefore reflect the priority respondents attached to certain issues and their interpretation of what the researcher wanted to hear. In that respect the 'findings' are difficult to compare in any systematic way, with some women referring to issues about image, femininity and dress and others to paid work and state support for working mothers, the role of the family or the attitudes of men.

It would be possible to group the interviews by the national origin of the respondent, thus gaining some impression of the effect of nationality on women's responses. The text of the interviews, however, suggests that the country of residence (in which the interview took place) was more significant, with women typically talking about that (and their immediate experience) first and then reflecting on the differences they have experienced, either prior to migration or through subsequent contact

---

[8] See Chapter Three for more discussion of these points.

with the country of emigration. It is important to bear in mind, as many women suggested, that both the societies from which they came (in terms of provision and culture) and their own life circumstances had often changed since the initial migration. In that sense, women were comparing their current experience, as a mother and wife, for example, with their perception (or second-hand knowledge) of the situation in another country. Of course many had sisters and friends with whom they compared experiences.

Before turning to examine the differences women identified between European welfare systems, it is important to note first the extent to which women spoke of convergence. This was particularly noteworthy in the interviews with Finnish women living in Sweden. Here, in every case, before discussing the distinctiveness of the two systems, women made reference to their broad, and increasing, similarity. This was also common among women from Germany, Ireland and Spain who often referred to changes taking place in their 'home' State. In most cases, women referred either to 'progressive' developments in national law or policy improving the *formal* status of women or to the impact of welfare retrenchment, the levelling down of social infrastructures and fears about the future of welfare[9]. As we shall see later, this convergence in formal status does not, however, always imply increasing convergence in women's experiences.

I have focused attention on two subsections of the sample, namely the women living in Sweden and Ireland, bringing in other cases for comparison. My justification for focusing on these two groups is partly pragmatic, given the size of the sample and the quantity of qualitative material available, but also reflects the distinctive nature of the national context and their relevance to the discussion in this chapter.

Sweden forms an interesting case because it is typically held up as the yardstick against which to compare other welfare regimes; almost a model of gender equality. Ireland, on the other hand, receives less praise, representing an example of a liberal welfare system dominated by Catholic public policy and with some of the most restrictive social rights in the EU. It is interesting to witness, through the interviews, how women who have moved to these two countries have responded to the relative freedoms and constraints of the host State.

---

[9] Concerns about care for elderly people were quite common and are reported in Chapter Eight.

Migrant women's experiences of living in a 'woman-friendly' welfare system: the case of Sweden[10]

The following section considers the experiences of those women who moved to live in Sweden, as this group of interviews illustrate particularly effectively the strengths and weaknesses, and the contradictions, inherent in contemporary 'social democratic' societies, from the perspectives of migrant women. In many ways, their narratives under-write the work of feminist comparativists, based largely on secondary analysis and policy evaluation. On the other hand, they emphasise the poignancy of the tensions and conflicts, the dangers of determinism and the status of women as individuals, interpreting and negotiating the framework of opportunities and pressures to shape their own lives.

Rather than turning immediately to a breakdown of the interviews thematically, I have first presented five case studies. The advantage of presenting some of the material in this way is that it demonstrates the way in which women weigh up the checks and balances and prioritise issues and reduces the distortion inherent in 'cut-and-paste' qualitative work.

Case 1: Helen is a Belgian woman who married a Swedish man, subsequently divorced and now lives with her Swedish partner:

"I find Swedish women to be very paradoxical. There is a wider freedom in terms of behaviour but at the same time they are very tied to their homes. In Sweden women could be said to be one social class. In Belgium there are strong hierarchies between women. There it is very common to have a housekeeper, a maid or a cleaner, which is not common at all in Sweden, so the social difference in Belgium is bigger than here in Sweden. In Sweden all women face the same demands and the same rights. You are to have a career, a family and your house shall be well looked after. So I believe that Swedish women are living under enormous demands and expectations. They are a sort of working class you could say; everyone is cleaning their own toilets.

---

[10] I would like to acknowledge the contribution of Kristina Eriksson, who conducted all the interviews in Sweden and did such an excellent job not only in interviewing but also in transcribing and translating the material.

Also, in Belgium we have inherited the Catholic values where women are to be subordinate to men. But in Sweden normally men and women are quite equal ... At the same time I find the gender-equality to be a problem in Sweden because they have misunderstood the meaning of gender equality. It is not the same as equality. I believe that you shouldn't demand things from a woman that she is incapable of doing. They are living under such demands and expectations to be able to have a successful career, a family and a home, all at the same time, which means that they are stressed out. To me, equality is that you are to have the same rights and obligations, without having to become a man to get it. You are a woman before anything .... Another thing is the sexual. In Belgium there is a lot more secrets involved with the bodies and the sexual. In Sweden you go naked and have saunas, which is really nice, but I was really shocked. I thought that you were only supposed to show your hands and then let the man fantasise about the rest! Let him become passionate. I miss the passion in the Swedish love life.

So, I believe that Swedish women are very tough with a lot of potentials and knowledge about food, health and so on. She is also often very self-reliant and secure in herself. If we talk about women there is also of course the work opportunities. In Sweden you work as a woman, which is not at all that common in Belgium. Belgian women often stay home but have maids and housekeepers so they don't have to work in the home either."[11]

Case 2: Anna is a German woman married to a Swede:

"My husband has always been very helpful. He is an example in that respect. When I had my first child, I started working after six months and then my husband worked close by and he arranged his working hours so that he could be home when I had to work and went to work himself when I came home. We were privileged. Today he is working full time. But it is always he who puts the children in bed, and he really loves kids. Actually it was he who wanted and longed for children in the first place.

---

[11] Interviewee D210 (Sweden).

Most of my friends in Germany have also shared the responsibility for the children with their husbands. Swedes seem to think that German women are only standing in the kitchen, taking care of the children. And of course it is much more of this family arrangements in Germany than here. Most mothers stay at home with their children. My mother was at home during the whole of my childhood. But still ... Also, today it's become almost impossible to be able to support a family on one person's salary, so lots of women are working now, they cannot afford staying at home to take care of their children, even when they want to. But Swedish women are, I would say, hysterical about the job. It is a groundrule, 'I have to work', otherwise I'm not emancipated. They put their children in day-care centres – I would never do that for as long as I can manage. But I mean it is different if you are single then, of course, you have to do it ... When I bring this up with my Swedish friends they cannot understand what I'm saying when I tell them that I want to be home with my children. They tell me that I will get all frustrated and miserable and that my children will feel that too. But I mean they don't even see their children enough for them to be able to know or feel anything of what their parents feel or are going through ... Swedish women are striving and making career. I've also always felt that Swedish women, especially, seem very sure of themselves. They are almost radiant, almost too much for me." [12]

Case 3: Carol is a Dutch woman married to a Swede:

"I'm not blind to the fact that foreigners have less privileged work conditions. It's a very strong hierarchy. Also, European men have better opportunities than European women. If I compare my financial situation with those of my colleagues, mine have always been less secure. I was very disappointed when I first came here because I had expected the Swedish women to be very strong and forward also when it comes to their jobs and so on. But my experience is that they often are very timid and quiet. If we have important meetings where

---

[12] Interviewee D209 (Sweden).

there is a decision that has to be made, the women are always very quiet and don't say what they believe. But afterwards, drinking coffee they can tell you that they thought the decision made was a mistake. I don't understand it! In Holland I was listened to much more than I've been in Sweden, which I think had to do with me being the only woman. So maybe the many women working in Sweden might not be all good. I thought you would have done more and come further thanks to the long tradition of women working. In Holland my generation is the first generation of women taking work for granted. But still most women stay home after they have their children.

Another thing is that the work within the home has much more status in Holland than here, due to the tradition to look upon men and women, public/private, as different but equally important. It's more valued ....

Also I think that women expect themselves to have a cultivation, garden, a clean home, a career and so on. They want to do everything at the same time. But I think that these aspects have become easier since I had my son, because you get a new perspective on life and what is important in life. Also, the job is more fun today, because sometimes you get fed up with being a mother, but at the same time having a job it is more fun to come home. So today I'm more satisfied with my life and the quality of life, I'm also more sure of and in myself, than I was before, even though I probably have more things to do today."[13]

Case 4: Susan is a Dutch woman married to a Dutch man:

"I'm very grateful that I didn't have very young children when I came to Sweden, because if that would have been the case I wouldn't have stayed. The life is in many ways so much easier in Holland when you have babies and young children, because in Holland you can support a family on one person's salary. But that is impossible here. So if you have young children it is

---

[13] Interviewee D214 (Sweden).

much more difficult to cope in Sweden. Therefore, Dutch mothers have a much better situation than Swedish ones. Here they are running to the day- care centre even when the children are sick! No, I wouldn't like to have young children here. But in Holland women working is becoming more and more common, but it is a different atmosphere; it is not as much constraint. You are not forced to work. At the same time you have maternity leave and maternity benefits that are so much better than the Dutch ones but I don't know that much about this since I came here when my children were grown up. Another thing is that while husband and wife share everything in Holland, [in Sweden] you are more individual, which is reflected in, for example, the bank-system. In Holland we shared one banking account. Here when we went to the bank to organise our finances they automatically assumed that we were to have separate banking accounts. That felt very strange."[14]

Case 5: Isabella is Portuguese, lives with her Portuguese partner and was expecting their first child:

"I think that Swedish women (or may be it is the society) that is more open. In Portugal there are still a lot of traditional and religious things ... and it is not very well seen – like two girls going out at nights alone. You should never live with your boyfriend if you are not married [loud laughter] ... My parents were quite strict ... it was very difficult for them because on the one hand they were very happy of course [about her pregnancy] but on the other hand they were very worried because it is very different in Portugal. You don't have any laws to protect you being an unmarried mother. It is like you are a bad girl ....

Also, women in Sweden have more liberty to do what they want and to behave as they please. In Portugal you have to suppress a lot more being a woman. If you have children there is really no alternative for the mother than to stay home looking after the child and if the child becomes ill it is always the woman who does it because the father doesn't have the right

---

[14] Interviewee D221 (Sweden).

to stay at home because of the child's illness. This law is about to be changed now, though. And you can see the result from this politics, because it is always the men who qualify themselves for really high and powerful positions, while women get to work with what is left over. You are always 'punished' for the time that you have spent at home with children ... Also the maternity benefits are much better in Sweden ... 12 months isn't it? It really enables you to have a career and have children at the same time, I think. In Portugal you have four months paid maternity leave and then you have to go back to work, and leave your four months old baby in a kindergarten. It is also very common that the grandparents or a hired maid [looks after your child]. It is easier to do that in Portugal because it doesn't cost that much ... Well, I'm not sure whether it is more difficult to have children in Portugal but you get more benefits here and more time to spend with your child."[15]

Taken together, these five cases identify a whole series of issues repeatedly referred to by migrant women living in Sweden. A particularly strong theme running through the interviews, largely independent of nationality, concerned the quality of state welfare and the relative 'generosity' of Swedish maternity and parental leave provision and nursery care and the importance of this infrastructure of state support for their ability to combine paid work with motherhood – a point made by Isabella and Susan (above). Other women made similar comments.

Reconciliation of work and family life

"Working part-time is much more common in Sweden than in France and it is very difficult to have a career and children at the same time in France. In Sweden you can have a family and combine that with a successful career. And the maternity (parental) benefits are so much better in Sweden and the leave is a lot longer. I think it is eight weeks in France in comparison to 12 in Sweden...."[16]

"One difference though is women's opportunities in the labour

---

[15] Interviewee D230 (Sweden).
[16] Interviewee D224 (Sweden).

market which is so much better in Sweden. And being able to have children and at the same time a career, that is a big difference from Spain. The problem in Spain is that when you have children you don't have any parental leave or parental benefits, so when you have a child you often lose your job. In Spain the consequence is that less and less women choose to have children. If you want to be at home with your child you can have an intermission for one or two years, but without any benefits or financial support. It is very sad especially if the husband wants to take care of the child, because he is still often the one with the better salary, so that is virtually impossible."[17]

"As to maternal benefits I think that the Swedish system is very generous. It has enabled me to stay home with my children during the most important period, when they've really needed me, and also the Swedish childcare system with day care centres is a really good thing. What would I have done without it? And during the period that I've been studying everyone has really tried to help me out making it possible for me to manage both having four children, my finances and school." (Finnish female lone parent with four children)[18]

A number of women referred, as in the second example above, to the decline in fertility and the increasing age of first-time mothers as an indicator of the problems of combining work and motherhood in Southern Europe and Ireland. Rather than indicating greater emancipation and a greater degree of economic development, as much of the academic literature suggests, women interpreted this as reflecting constraints and financial pressures on women to forego having more children. Christine expresses this in the following sentiments:

"Irish women don't have the pressure that [Swedish women] have to work full-time. It is more or less taken that she can be home taking care of the family ...You've been able to support a family on one salary, but the younger people say that you can't do that anymore, because the prices have gone up so

---

[17] Interviewee D220 (Sweden).
[18] Interviewee D239 (Sweden).

much. And as a result of more women working, the number of children women have is now two and it used to be four."[19]

It is interesting to compare this perspective (that reduced fertility may suggest a reduction in, rather than an expression of, choice) with the reaction of migrant women resident in the UK to their observation of a high proportion of very young, unmarried, mothers which they interpreted as a reflection of social polarisation and welfare dependency.[20]

The relationship between public policy and gender roles

The most significant and welcomed aspect of Swedish social provision, however, was not simply the provision of services for mothers, enabling women to share their responsibilities with the state, but rather the impact that such provision had on their relationships with male partners, effectively enabling them to negotiate arrangements between themselves, their partners, and welfare services.

The Spanish woman's comments[21] emphasise the consequences, in Spain, of the interaction of poor State provision with labour market discrimination, not only for women's autonomy but also for men's ability to share care. It was the length of Swedish parental leave arrangements and the extension of entitlement to fathers, together with more flexible labour market practices enabling part-time and homeworking, which were most remarked upon by women as maximising their ability to combine the public and private aspects of their lives (and therefore to achieve full independent citizenship status). As one woman put it, comparing her life in Sweden with a Swedish partner with what she might have experienced in Austria:

> "Life is totally different! My husband and I share equally the responsibility to raise and look after our son. My husband has taken half time off from his job in order to look after Martin ... But we want to take care of our children together, and this is a big difference from Austria. My personal belief is that one of the parents should be home taking care of the child for at least two or three years before going back to work ... and if we were living in Austria we wouldn't have quite the same possibilities.

---

[19] Interviewee D245 (Sweden).
[20] Interviewees D025 and D007 (both UK).
[21] Interviewee D220 (Sweden).

> There is a well functioning parents-leave and a special fathers-
> leave, in Austria as well, but very few uses it. The fathers do
> not stay at home. Here it is totally accepted that parents share
> the responsibility for the children."[22]

This woman is making a very similar point to that made by Anna (case study 2 above). Her comments on the support she has received from her Swedish partner with parenting reflect the extension of parental entitlement to fathers but also the apparent relationship between formal equality in Sweden, in terms of social welfare and legal entitlement and the social attitudes of men and women. In other words, rather than have formal equality imposed, by the state, on a structure of private patriarchal control (a situation often reported by French women as existing in France), it seems that the Swedish system reflects and shapes gender roles and attitudes and that men are, in practice, beginning to combine paid work with childcare. This situation did not go unnoticed by interviewees. Simona, an Italian woman, made the following comments:

> "I must say that I often see young fathers as well sharing the
> caring responsibility for the children, ... it seems as if the Swedish
> husbands help out more and take a bigger interest in the up-
> bringing of their children than Italian men. Well the money is
> really important and you get a lot of money and financial
> support for your children. You have much more help from the
> state and from organisations and more day care centres. And
> since people have three and more children and still the women
> are working a lot I think that the system must be working
> pretty well here in Sweden. It is very nice that you can work
> part-time, which a lot of mothers seem to do, because that
> allows you to have time to take care of your children as well,
> without making you totally financially dependent on your
> husband. This is not common in Italy, either you work full-
> time or you don't work outside of the home at all. And in
> Sweden it is okay for a man to stay home with his children at
> least for a couple of months, but that is done very seldom in
> Italy. *Legally you do have the possibility but the mentality in Italy is
> that there has to be something wrong with the men who choose to stay
> home with their children.* It is still very traditional and the gender-

---

[22] Interviewee D206 (Sweden).

roles are very strong in Italy, stronger than in Sweden I'd say."[23]
(author's emphasis)

Another Italian woman makes a very similar point about the relationship
between formal equality and social reality:

"**Legally the jurisdiction in Italy and in Sweden are very similar
... The difference is that in Italy the mentality of the Italian
people have not changed.**"[24]

It was thus not only the differential status of women in the countries
concerned that was remarked upon; many women placed more emphasis
on cultural differences affecting the usage or take-up of rights which, in
some cases, appeared to exist only at the level of policy.

While longer periods of maternity leave, more formalised entitlement
to shorter working hours and a greater involvement of fathers in parenting
was widely welcomed by women, another key element of the Swedish
social system appeared to receive less support[25]. The infrastructure of
institutionalised pre-school provision, often applauded by feminist
comparativists as a key factor facilitating women's labour market
participation and financial autonomy, was interpreted in a very different
way by many of the women interviewed, often as reflecting the limitations
of Swedish social policy, the lack of family care and cultural pressures on
women to undertake paid work. These views were very often bound up
with ideas about motherhood and what constituted good parenting and
suggest carefully circumscribed support for the principle of socialised care
within a broader welfare and working environment, enabling couples to
share care more effectively. Women appeared to favour an equality strategy
which is less interventionist in terms of service provision (or benefits in
kind) and more facilitative, in the sense of promoting individual choice;
not so much a transfer from private to public (or socialised) responsibility
but rather for a public policy which maximises the scope for negotiation
of responsibility within private relationships. Where private relationships
had broken down, women were quick to distinguish the needs of lone
parents; an infrastructure of pre-school childcare was clearly identified as

---

[23] Interviewee D248 (Sweden).

[24] Interviewee D249 (Sweden).

[25] A point not without relevance in the context of recent developments in childcare
provision in the UK.

an important resource and entitlement in these cases. The interviews suggest that, while tampering with the delicate balance between statutory service provision and labour market integration might promote a framework of formal equality (at least to the extent that women's profiles begin to resemble those of their male counterparts), this did not necessarily promote autonomy and may indeed restrict freedom of choice. The following section examines these issues in more detail, focusing on women's views of the impact of Swedish social policy on the framework of choices and constraints available to them.

Labour market participation: choice or constraint?

Higher levels of labour market participation in social-democratic regimes are typically presented as indicative of gender equality – a testimony to the successful socialisation of caring, thus freeing women to take their position alongside men and gain financial autonomy. The costs of maintaining Swedish social policy were, however, seen by some women as creating a situation which actually reduced the possibility of exercising choice. A large proportion of interviewees described the Swedish situation in the language of constraint rather than opportunity, for a number of reasons. One popular view reflects an appreciation of the fiscal costs of social-democratic welfare policies both to the state and to individual families. One woman simply said, "the Swedish system with parental benefits is very good for the individual parents but not for the state, since it is a very expensive system"[26]. Many others were less concerned with the fiscal burden on the state than with the implications for their ability to exercise choice through purchasing power, given the high levels of individual taxation. Anna (case study 2) emphasises the impact of taxation on an individual mother's decision making, echoing the comments of a majority of interviewees when she says, "It's become almost impossible to be able to support a family on one person's salary ... [women] cannot afford to stay at home to take care of their children even if they want to"[27]. Susan (case study 4) articulates this sentiment in the language of constraint, expressing her belief that many Swedish women are, "forced to work" because of the high levels of taxation. This view was not restricted to the women from high wage economies but was also expressed by Portuguese and Irish women. Maria makes a similar observation that

---

[26] Interviewee D231 (Sweden).
[27] Interviewee D209 (Sweden).

---

women in Sweden are pressurised into taking paid work, contrasting her experience there with life in Portugal:

"I had a tendency to think that Swedish women don't want to have more time with their children. Their priorities are different, that they want to have a career more than staying at home looking after the children. But I've met many women now that really would like to have more time and that would prefer staying home longer periods looking after their children but they feel that they can't do that because of financial reasons. I feel that Sweden is a rather hard society and that people very often are afraid of being themselves, that they hide behind their profession. They don't put themselves forward as they really are, but they are what they are working with. As to the standard of living I think that the Swedes are too materialistic. People worry too much about owning things and looking in a certain way instead of spending time with their children which I think is so important. I don't understand women who don't hesitate to leave their children to someone else when they are still very small. I'm going to have to do that and I hate it. It is like a nightmare, but many women feel that it is a relief. I can't understand that and those values are very important because they are the basis of the society and our children and how we raise them is so important for the whole society ... I really don't find the Swedish society to be a society where the children's interests are looked after. I think the opposite, but in Portugal it is even worse, because there you have to leave your children after four-and-a-half months which is ridiculous. In this aspect, the Swedish system is much better even though I think that things could be improved here as well ... About Sweden I think that you say that this is a democracy, but I don't believe in democracy, because people don't have any chance of getting to know the truth and thereafter form their opinions ... I know that there are a lot of women who want to stay home with their children and if this society was democratic and for the children, then the possibility to choose to be home with your children should exist, but it doesn't ... But in Portugal it is usually the grandmothers who look after your children, the family is more stressed and you have stronger bonds in Portugal than here. Here it is quite unusual for a grandmother to take care of her grandchildren while her daughter is at work. Also I feel that this society is segregating people a lot. I think that the older, the children and the working people are kept apart in separate groups and that is not good. What kind of society is that?"[28]

Maria refers not only to the financial pressures on women to work, but also suggests something about the acquisition of status and identity, referring to the materialism endemic within Swedish society, as she sees it, and the extent to which people are defined by their employment status. She also suggests that women's voices are not adequately heard or acknowledged in the Swedish political system, perhaps because of the primacy attached to labour market issues and the nature of political group formation and representation. The final point she makes about family structure and informal care in Sweden is interesting, not least the reference to segregation, and will be revisited shortly.

The valuing of unpaid work in a society preoccupied with labour market integration and regulation as the principle vehicles for the achievement of gender equality, was referred to in many interviews as reinforcing the cultural pressure to work. This view is expressed by Carol (case study 3, above) when she talks about the importance of valuing work within the home. The following women make a very similar point.

Valuing paid work

"In Sweden there is a totally different set of expectations and acceptance towards working women. Maybe it has to do with the fact that being a housewife in Sweden is a very low status thing to do, while it is quite accepted and to some extent respected in German."[29]

"Another thing is the role of housewives. It is much more common in Germany and also *more respected*. But here it is totally different. For a short period I worked part-time and then people told me 'oh, but it is your husband who has to support you now'; as if I was at home just being lazy, doing nothing. But we'd just bought a new house and we were

---

[28] Interviewee D247 (Sweden).
[29] Interviewee D229 (Sweden).

renovating it so I definitely didn't do nothing. But that is typical Sweden, everyone has to do their share especially when it comes to work. You are supposed to work until you die from it and preferably you should get several heart attacks before you turn 40 ... I'd say that in Sweden there is in a way an illusion of the individual free choice. There is no real choice but to become someone through your work, and it is very important that you have a certain position."[30] (author's emphasis)

"I think that the situation of women in Holland and Sweden is becoming more and more alike. But it is still much more common that women here are working and being financially independent of their husbands or fathers. This difference has effects on and shows in the division of labour, where Dutch women still are holding the caring responsibilities for the children and for the whole family situation I would say. But I don't know, if you look upon the Swedish factual situation I'd say that Swedish women are still carrying the major burden of family responsibilities. But Swedish women are still more independent even if this is done to a very high cost, where they have to work and have to take care of the family so they have like a double burden ... In Sweden it is practically impossible to stay home for more than a year to take care of your child and of course being able to do that gives you the opportunity of leading a pretty free life and I wouldn't mind doing that. I don't care that much by whom I get paid for the work that I do."[31]

The Dutch woman in the last example clearly feels that the source of her income is less of an issue to her status or autonomy than her freedom of choice as a mother. While many women referred to the cultural climate in Sweden and the dominance of the work ethic as denying women the choice of caring for their children, other women welcomed the 'freedom' from cultural pressures, dominant within other societies, to combine paid work with motherhood in the absence of stigma:

[30] Interviewee D244 (Sweden).
[31] Interviewee D235 (Sweden).

"In Holland ... many believe that it is the most natural thing that it is the woman who quits her job to stay at home looking after the baby. And if she would choose to work she'd have to have a part-time job because the children cannot be sent off to a day care centre for a whole day, because that makes you a bad mother ... the mother is still the main caregiver. Here in Sweden these things are much better. You can have a job if you want to without being stigmatised."[32]

The Dutch woman in the case above evidently felt less pressure to justify her public role (as paid worker) in Sweden compared to Holland.

Many of the migrant women in Sweden voiced quite strong feelings about mothering, and the costs to children, as they perceived them, of the priority which Swedish women and society in general attached to paid work. The Austrian woman referred to above[33], for example, expressed her preference for (shared) parental care within the home at least until the child is aged three. The woman in the following example, draws out the tension she perceives between the needs of children and mothers and the disjunction between the daily routine of schooling in Germany with employment policies:

"Well, in Germany people look at you if you are a single mother taking your children out to eat at McDonalds. In Germany it is a sort of tradition to get together and have your dinner with your family at home. Most schools, for example, don't have any cafeteria or restaurant for the children to eat in. Instead they are expected to go home during the break to have their dinner, which is expected to be fixed by their mother. I think that it is good for the children. They get a healthy meal and get out of school for an hour, but at the same time it makes the mother's situation very difficult. It is very rare that she can find a job that allows her to leave in the middle of the day just to be able to go home and fix dinner for her children. So, as to where women's job possibilities are concerned this is not a good arrangement. The Swedish system is better in this aspect, where the children have their dinner or lunch at school ... When you have small kids in Germany it is more taken for granted

---

[32] Interviewee D222 (Sweden).
[33] Interviewee D206 (Sweden).

that the woman will stay at home taking care of the children. And it is not that common that you leave the child to be taken care of by someone else at the age of one year in Germany. Personally I feel that it is too early. I wouldn't want to leave my baby while she's still that young. Here I can feel my German background and the German values being of importance. I think that it is a good thing that this solution exists in Sweden, but at the same time I cannot see myself using it."[34]

The following Spanish woman expresses similar views about what constitutes 'good parenting' and the respective roles of mothers and fathers, almost inferring negligence on the part of Swedish women. Interestingly, she states that women in Sweden play a greater public role than women in Spain, suggesting that their access to paid employment – and the public world of paid work – has influenced Swedish society in a much deeper sense:

"I think that Swedish and Spanish women differ in a lot of ways. Swedish women are much more interested in and are more responsible when it comes to social issues. They take responsibility for what is happening in their surroundings, it can be issues within the family but also and foremost they are concerned about the state of the world, like the question of equality between the classes as well as the sexes, environmental issues and things like that. They participate a lot more in the discussion of the state of the world than do the Spanish women. So she doesn't only take on the responsibility of the children ... maybe the Swedish woman even takes this responsibility a bit too lightly ... A Spanish woman is responsible for her job and for her children but doesn't care that much about the rest ... I feel that Swedish women sometime get their priorities wrong when they put work and career before taking care of their children."[35]

Another Finnish woman relates her own anxieties and sense of guilt, both at work and at home, at combining mothering with paid work. It is when you hear women talking in these terms, irrespective of their cultural

[34] Interviewee D242 (Sweden).
[35] Interviewee D237 (Sweden).

or national background, that the broad commonality of interest and sense of shared experience is most profound. While she evidently appreciates the advantages of the Swedish system, and her ability to work, it nevertheless causes her emotional stress:

> **"I feel really bad and have a bad conscience because of the fact that our youngest son is almost always the first to come to the day care centre in the morning and the last one to be picked up in the evenings. Now he's started to react himself and when he wakes up in the mornings he often asks me if I really have to go to work today, and couldn't I stay home just this one day? It really tears my heart apart. I like it here but at the same time I'm constantly having this bad conscience towards my children when I'm working and towards my job and my colleagues when I'm with my family."[36]**

This concern, about cultural pressure on women to undertake paid work and the devaluing of unpaid caring work, was also common in the interviews undertaken in the UK. In the following examples, two migrant women in the UK welcomed what they saw as the greater 'choice' available to them to work or to stay at home and look after children, the result, not of public policy, but rather in spite of it[37]:

> **"In Holland women are more career-oriented. Most women in Holland, if you had a good job and then had children, they go back – its a norm – maybe because that's what most of my friends have done and I'm very pleased I'm not doing that because for me that time is so short. I think had I stayed in Holland I would have[gone along with it]."[38]**

The German woman in the following case had moved to England to accompany her husband whom she met when he was serving in the army in Germany. She gave up her own hairdressing business to move, despite the fact that her husband was unemployed. While clearly aware of the

---

[36] Interviewee D228 (Sweden).

[37] It is interesting to note the apparent contradiction between what the Dutch and German women living in Sweden say, compared to those living in the UK; it seems their attitudes depend very much on the point of reference!

[38] Interviewee D004 (UK).

benefits of German public policy, she suggests that this has contributed to an environment of constraint and evidently feels that she has been able to exercise more conscious choice in the UK. Nevertheless, now her daughters are a bit older and she wants to return to study, she regrets the lack of good, affordable, childcare in the UK. This interview illustrates the importance of understanding how women's perspectives may change over her life-course in response to family circumstances:

> "Most women in Germany are more independent, more self-confident, more confident to tackle their surroundings. There are better maternity leave provisions, crèches etc, definitely. My sister has three children and worked before she had the first child and she gets over 90% of her wage for three years and 10 years credited on her pensions with each child. She has three children now so if you count out the years you get a good wage income for years to come. When I started Krispien in the nursery, what I pay in a week for fees she pays in a month. But, I'm sorry to say, if I had stayed in Germany, I don't think I would have two beautiful little children now. I probably would have lots of money and be working hard ... I don't think I would have found the time with my own salon, I would have had to give it up or found a partner. You want the money, success – to be up there and to show everyone that you are capable and can get there."[39]

It was evident from the interviews that many women in Sweden were opposed to the replacement of 'family' care with institutional day care, particularly for babies and young children and over extended periods of time. The appeal was not so much for informal support from the extended family (and grandmothers), but rather for a more effective sharing of responsibility within the nuclear family; an insistence not so much on the value of 'mothering' but on 'parenting'. Birte Siim[40], referring to the problematic use of atypical work as an indicator of gender inequality, notes the shifting demands of women in Denmark, from the provision of socialised childcare to demands for a shorter working week, suggesting

---

[39] Interviewee D007 (UK).

[40] Siim, B. (1991) 'Welfare states, gender politics and equality policies: women's citizenship in the Scandinavian welfare states', in E. Meehan and S. Sevenhuysen (eds) *Equality politics and gender*, London: Sage.

that some Danish women may prefer to work shorter hours in order to spend more time with their children.

These findings demonstrate the problem of using terms such as 'family' loosely when, in practice, family policy or family support can mean very different things to different people. Women may talk, for example, about the strength of the family and the emphasis on family values and care in liberal or Southern European societies while, at the same time, saying that the role of the family was more supported in Sweden. This raises questions not only about what constitutes 'family policy' in different countries (which may, indeed amount to non-decision) but also about what people mean when they talk about families. We may, on the one hand, be referring to inter-generational relations or, on the other, quite narrowly about relations between partners. Christine's observations illustrate this point quite well:

> "Irish women don't have the pressure that [Swedish women] have to work full-time. It is more or less taken that she can be home taking care of the family ... Life is more relaxed in Ireland. Here it is hectic, dropping your children off at the day care centre. In Ireland it is usually the mother or the mother-in-law who takes care of the children ... Sweden is more family oriented in that they allow both parents to be at home with the children. And then they want you to get back into the system, whereas in Ireland I think that they view that the woman should be home at least until the children are in primary school."[41]

On the one hand Christine suggests that Sweden is, 'more family oriented' while, in the same breath, saying that women in Ireland are under less pressure (financially or culturally) to work full-time and, when mothers do work, life is less stressful due to the greater reliance upon family support for childcare. Maria's comments[42] similarly illustrate the difficulties in comparing Portugal with Sweden, for although she accepts that parental leave arrangements are better in Sweden, she also refers to the extent to which women's choices (to stay at home and care for their children) are restricted by a lack of extended family support and cultural pressure to work which she sees as reinforced by the political system – to the detriment of children. While, on the one hand, Swedish public policy assumes a more interventionist role, effectively socialising key aspects of caring and

---

[41] Interviewee D245 (Sweden).
[42] Interviewee D247 (Sweden).

freeing women from dependency relations within the family, it is important to recognise that the family is not only the source of obligations and dependency but also of support and interdependence, or reciprocity. One consequence of Swedish family policy would seem to be a reduction in the availability and acceptability of grandmothers (and other relatives) as key providers of childcare[43].

Evaluation of family policy depends not only on how we define families (what sort of unit we are talking about), but also recognition that there exist competing interests within that institution and prioritisation of a particular dynamic (say, gender relations) may create tensions elsewhere. Increased autonomy for adults may reduce the quality of life of children. One casualty of the greater level of 'privatisation' of family life in Sweden may be, as Maria states, a higher level of inter-generational segregation with less communication and contact taking place over three generations within a family. Interestingly, none of the women who referred in the interviews to the greater reliance on unpaid informal systems of support in other countries actually commented on the 'gender' implications of this type of 'family' care. The continued availability and quality of unpaid care, principally by grandmothers, was apparently uncontested. While women were clearly aware of gender imbalances within their own nuclear family unit, they did not immediately identify the 'fact' that the availability of family care itself reflects the gender relations within their parent's families, their mother's own experience of paid and unpaid work and their exercise of autonomy. In that sense, women may be reinforcing gender role stereotyping that has shaped their own mother's lives. Quite simply put, why is it any better for a daughter to rely on the unpaid support of her mother than it was for her father to rely on that same support in the past?

One Portuguese respondent, alluding not so much to emotive 'quality of care' issues, but to economic factors, refers to the greater reliance in Portugal on grandparents and private arrangements (the use of maids etc) as a cheaper, and more flexible, source of care. Similar reference is made to the more limited use of private sector help in Sweden, by Helen (case study 1). Helen draws out some very interesting differences between women, as a group, suggesting a greater universality of experience and less hierarchical social structure in Sweden than in Belgium. In contrast with

---

[43] Although we could perhaps postulate that the breakdown of extended family structures pre-dated more recent shifts in public policy and that, for many households, particularly those which have migrated, access to informal care is simply not possible.

the sophisticated language of contemporary social theorists, Helen sums up her perception of the situation succinctly with the statement, "everyone is cleaning their own toilets". Rather than celebrating the apparently greater level of equality between women and bemoaning social polarisation in Belgium, however, Helen reflects that even this position raises contradictions for women, particularly in terms of workload and stress. Although one may disagree with her analysis of social change as a form of 'proletarianisation' suggesting an overall reduction in the quality of life, she nevertheless raises an interesting point, highlighting the much narrower articulation of dependency in Sweden with more limited reliance on either informal care or privately-purchased assistance in the home and exposing, more starkly, the relationship between the State and private patriarchy.

Some of these complex issues, rarely raised in feminist comparative social policy, concerning forms of interdependency (and exploitation) between different groups of women[44], were evident in the interviews in other countries. In the following discussion, a French woman who had spent a lot of time in Spain and is now teaching in the UK refers to what she sees as the 'brainwashing' of British schoolgirls into accepting labour market withdrawal as a natural consequence of motherhood. It is interesting, given this acceptance, that the young women themselves consider the employment of paid domestic work, common in Spain, not only as 'bad mothering' but also as a form of exploitation of women, by women:

> "What shocks me is the expectation men, or society, has of married women in this country when they get children. It's horrendous ... the facilities, I mean! The women themselves are brought up in such a way! I have been trying to change my sixth form girls' attitudes. They just say I am inhuman, heartless and so on. I consider that women who have children should be able to work full-time and have a nanny or something as far as the child is well looked after obviously. There should be a crèche (free or cheap) so women can work if they want to. Here women are expected to stay at home with the child. In Spain I know lots of people my age, girls in France too, who have babies and small children and they work full-time and their husbands work full-time and they have in Spain what they call 'chica' – someone who looks after the children during

---

[44] An issue I discuss in more detail in Chapter Eight.

school time – and they cook and prepare the dinner and clean the house and do everything so the people go home and just look after the children. They have got to pay for it – those people who are very career-minded can do that and still spend time with the children. [When some] English girls went to Spain on a school trip and saw that my friend had a 'chica', they said, 'this is horrendous – it's slavery of women by women'. I said, 'it's not, because my friend works, she's got her independence and the other woman has her independence too because she has money'."[45]

The response of the English girls to this issue is very interesting to me and does not simply suggest a form of 'brainwashing' by the system as the respondent intimates, but rather calls for a much more detailed consideration of the multiplicity of highly complex relationships of exploitation and reciprocity that characterise most women's lives.

The price of Swedish equality: dual burden and time poverty?

Reservations about the meaning or impact of a formally more egalitarian social system on women, raised questions about the quality of mothering and cultural and financial pressures to undertake paid work. Perhaps the most powerful criticism of Swedish society, from the perspective of migrant women, can be seen in what they viewed as the costs of this dual burden. The following narratives illustrate the strength of feeling on this issue.

'The woman's trap'[46]

"Finnish women seem to be stronger than Swedish women in a way. They are more in charge of what is happening at home and I think that they are not as stressed out as Swedish women are. Swedish women try to do everything. I mean they have a career, a husband, a family, a house, a garden and so on and everything has to be taken care of splendidly. They put a lot of demands on themselves and therefore they are stressed out in my opinion at least."[47]

---

[45] Interviewee D021 (UK).
[46] Interviewee D228 (Sweden).
[47] Interviewee D235 (Sweden).

"I think that life might be easier in Germany, because life is more traditional there. Children are still the women's responsibility ... one salary is still enough to support a whole family ... the sex roles are not as 'confused' or as mixed ... that is a better word for it ... as they are here. At the same time I think that for women, life in Sweden offers a more full life, where you get to try a lot of different things, getting a lot of life experiences, both within the family and in your job. This sound great, doesn't it? [Laughter] But I think that this also can be a danger to Swedish women, because to me it seems like they are – excuse me for the expression – working their a-s off. They are really being stressed out, because they try to do everything at the same time."[48]

"There is so much talk about gender equality in Sweden, but I still feel that in behaviour Swedish women are no different than other women ... there is a big difference between theory and practice. Swedish women work a lot without letting go of their traditional female role, which means that they have to work double. They are often still responsible for the home and the children. At the same time I think that Swedish men do help out more than German men. But it's not at all a 50-50 arrangement. Also the roles are very gender-bound ...There is a lot of talk about men participating in the chores at home, but the women do not demand that they share equally."[49]

The views expressed in these and many more interviews certainly support Jane Lewis' contention (1992) that women in social-democratic or weak male breadwinning systems are, 'particularly time-poor'[50]. In that context, increasing feminist interest in research on the gendered use of time is to be welcomed. Contrary to the dominant view reflected in the interviews, of Swedish policy responding to and breaking down traditional gender roles, some women felt that Swedish social arrangements, specifically designed to reduce this dual burden, were actually reinforcing labour market segregation. This point resurrects the age-old dilemma of how to respond to the specific needs of women with gender-sensitive policies without

[48] Interviewee D242 (Sweden).
[49] Interviewee D216 (Sweden).
[50] For more discussion on the question of time-poverty see Chapter One.

reinforcing gender roles in the process. A Finnish woman who had experienced living in both Germany and Sweden made the following observations about combining paid work and caring and the disadvantages of the Swedish 'part-time' solution:

> "I think that being a full-time working mother it is actually easier to be in Finland because the Swedish system is based on the fact that one of the parents do not work full-time. People like us therefore have a problematic situation to manage ... women's double working-load [is reduced by the policy of] normalising part-time jobs especially for women. By doing this there is a sort of acceptance that there is the women who are supposed to take care of the things that have to be done in the private family life, like taking care of the children, and that is scary.
>
> And in Germany they have this system that one of the parents, almost always the mother, stays at home while the children are young. It is what we would call a sort of 'women's trap'. But I think that this is not always the case if you think of it. I think that I'm trapped as well in a sort of women's myth where I get worn out before I'm 50, because I have to do so much, and I never have time to catch my breath. German women could have an intermission for about 10 to 15 years, but then you have to remember that in Germany normally a family can get by on one person's salary. There are also some differences within the jurisdiction that guarantees women financial situation when they are retired even when they have been home taking care of their children. I'm not sure how it works really. But I think that in Sweden it is very hard on the woman that she has to build her safety and financial security all on her own, to be sure that she will manage when she's retired. I believe that you should look upon the family as one entity not as different individuals, because in order for the family life to function someone have to take care of the children every now and then for the other to be able to work. So we do just as important job looking after the children as the husbands who financially support us. So in this respect maybe the German system offers a better quality of life for women."[51]

---

[51] Interviewee D228 (Sweden).

In this case the interviewee clearly felt that the 'option' of reduced working hours to facilitate 'private' caring solutions, as an alternative to more extended socialisation of caring, actually reinforced gender roles. Moreover, she questions the benefits to women, of the individualisation of financial arrangements so central to feminist strategy. Clearly the presumption of dependency within marriage and consensual and fair allocation of household resources that has underpinned so many social security policies is highly problematic, not least when relationships break down. Nevertheless, the development of policies of individual taxation and pension entitlement, when based narrowly on forms of economic contribution, do little to advance the financial status of women. Other women remarked on the persistence of labour market segregation, suggesting that important symbols of inequality remained in the Swedish system:

> "Sometimes I feel as I'm an anthropologist looking around to see what this exotic people are doing and how they are behaving, so yes I have some reflections. I can only say what I've seen on the surface of the Swedish society and of course I have noticed that the cashiers in shops are always women as are the nurses in hospitals and the teachers and things like that, so the working situation doesn't seem to differ that much from the one in Italy."[52]

These last two women, in common with many of the previous respondents previously referred to, suggest that there may be a considerable gap between the rhetoric of Swedish equality[53] (as expressed in formal policies) and the reality of everyday life for women in Sweden. There did seem to be a general acceptance that the environment was genuinely more egalitarian but that this did not necessarily facilitate more freedom of choice for women. The fact remains that women retain the primary responsibility for childcare and domestic work. One woman expressed the reality behind the veneer of formal equality, in the context of her own relationship, in the following poignant statement, "I feel that I am the necessity person and my husband is the possibility person and we are both needed for our child"[54].

---

[52] Interviewee D248 (Sweden).

[53] See, for example, the comments made by Helen (case study 1, Interviewees D210 and D244 [Sweden]) where they talk about the 'illusion of choice'.

[54] Interviewee D248 (Sweden).

Another interesting, culturally specific, 'contradiction' observed by interviewees can be seen in what some women viewed as symbols of Swedish conservatism – namely, the dominance of heterosexual marriage. Many women remarked upon the fact that progressive family policies and relations between men and women did not go hand-in-hand with liberal attitudes towards same-sex relationships and, although social provision itself did not penalise cohabitation or stigmatise lone parenting, the tradition of marriage remained surprisingly influential. One Dutch woman expressed herself in the following way:

> **"I sometimes feel that Swedish women often appear to be very emancipated and independent, but beneath they are actually quite often rather traditional. To a lot of Swedish women it seems to be okay that the man is dominant in the relationship and she might not even notice it. Also, marriage is more common in Sweden than in Holland. We are used to just living together. And speaking of relations and marriage, I think that homosexuals are much more accepted in Holland. In Sweden you sweep them under the mat, pretending that they don't exist, but the laws in this area are rather progressive in Holland."**[55]

In a couple of cases, women referred to the interaction of gender with migration status, suggesting that their status as immigrants had an important influence on their experience as citizens. Carol (case study 3) illustrates this point well when she says that, "I'm not blind to the fact that foreigners have less privileged work conditions. It's a very strong hierarchy". This situation was only referred to in the context of employment status and women's abilities to secure employment of a permanent nature[56].

The material presented above and taken from the in-depth interviews with migrant women, emphasises the impact of social status on women's lives. The general impression was one of support for the Swedish social

---

[55] Interviewee D222 (Sweden).

[56] Interviewees' awareness of the impact of migration status on their experience, as women, was more evident when they were talking about their employment. Of the 50 women interviewed in Sweden, very few had permanent employment contracts and many women attributed this to their status as migrants with some specifically stating that progressive gender policies in Sweden did not extend to the migrant population. These issues are taken up further in Chapter Six.

system and the translation of statutory policy into a more genuine equality between men and women. On the other hand, the interviews evidenced a great diversity in women's attitudes, underlining the dangers of generalising about women's experiences and feminist goals. They also emphasised the importance of taking a life-course approach: women's perspectives were not static but rather evolved over time in response to changing personal circumstances and social conditions.

While we found little evidence in the research to suggest that social advantages constituted an important determinant in the migration or location decision, migrant women were evidently aware of the long-term impact of the move on their citizenship status. Rather than seeing this primarily in terms of material gains or losses, their evaluations were more commonly concerned with the effect on their freedom of choice. Statutory welfare provision clearly has a big impact on the choice framework available to women, and women were generally welcoming of infrastructures which offered a continuum of options, including private sector and informal support. The interaction of formal provision and popular culture, however, had a more profound impact on women's ability to exercise choice. In some societies there appeared to be little relationship between formal or legal status and outcome; in these cases pressures, either to undertake paid work or to stay at home to care, restricted independence. In order to understand citizenship, we must evaluate the impact of any formal entitlement on women's autonomy at any given point in time. The comments of the women interviewed here very much support Julia O'Connor's central focus on, "independence as the key to citizenship and in the services and on activities that foster the achievement of independence for those with social care needs as well as those involved in care-giving work"[57].

The second part of this chapter now turns to consider the quite distinct experiences of the group of women interviewed in Ireland. They are introduced here, not so much to facilitate direct comparison with the Swedish sample, but rather to consider the different set of issues fundamental to women's citizenship status which migrant women identified in Ireland. While the study of family policy is central to an understanding of women's citizenship status, it must extend beyond the detailed study of the plethora of material rewards and sanctions, mediated through statutory welfare to draw into the analysis, "issues of sexual and reproductive rights, including

---

[57] O'Connor, J. (1996) 'From women in the welfare state to gendering welfare state regimes', Trend Report, *Current Sociology*, vol 44, no 2, pp 1-25.

---

abortion, [which] are fundamental to women's citizenship"[58]. While this contention clearly holds across all European societies, none of which grant unconditional, unstigmatised or universal reproductive rights to women[59], the uniqueness of the Irish situation merits attention.

Internal migration and the negotiation of citizenship: the struggle for reproductive self-determination in Ireland[60]

Characterised in welfare typologies as an example of a 'liberal' welfare regime[61], a 'strong' male breadwinning state[62] and a 'private patriarchy'[63], it would be reasonable to expect systems of social entitlement in Ireland to be based narrowly on notions of economic contribution and for married women to derive entitlement via male breadwinning partners[64]. Despite the lowest marriage rate in the EU (apart from Spain); one of the highest proportions of births outside marriage (20%); a very dramatic decline in fertility and the highest mean age at first marriage of 26.6 years[65], Ireland continues to see itself as, "the last bastion of moral and sexual purity and of the traditional family in the Western World – a beacon and haven for traditional Catholic values – appeal[ing] to a need for status, presence and self-importance in the collective Irish psyche"[66].

---

[58] Smyth, A. (1996) 'The women themselves, they just don't come into it – Ireland, abortion and European Union citizenship', Paper to the DIOTIMA Conference, 'The gender of rights, power and citizenship', Athens 9-10 February, p 17.

[59] Rolston, B. and Eggert, A. (1994) *Abortion in the new Europe: A comparative handbook*, Westport: Greenwood Press.

[60] This section is based on the article Ackers, H.L. (1996) 'Internal migration and the negotiation of citizenship: the struggle for reproductive self-determination in Ireland', *Journal of Social Welfare and Family Law*, vol 18, no 4, pp 397-413.

[61] Esping-Andersen, G. (1990) *The three worlds of welfare capitalism*, Oxford: Polity Press.

[62] Lewis, J. (1992) 'Gender and the development of welfare regimes', *Journal of European Social Policy*, vol 2, no 3, pp 159-73.

[63] Mahon, E. (1994) 'Ireland: a private patriarchy', *Environment and Planning A*, vol 26, pp 1277-96.

[64] cf Mulcahy, M. and Sapouna, L. (1995) 'A study of European migrant women's lives: the Irish experience', Interim Report from the Irish Partners.

[65] Eurostat Demographic Statistics (1997)

[66] Smyth (1996, p 8), supra, note 58.

In addition to the unearthing of 'implicit' pro-family policies embedded within welfare systems, the interviews highlighted the impact of explicit attempts by the Irish State to control women, through its policy of denial of fundamental reproductive and marital rights operating at both institutional and cultural level. The next section maps out the formal framework of constraint which structures the citizenship experience of all women in Ireland, before proceeding to examine the response of migrant women exercising their right to free movement within the EU.

The control of fertility and marriage in Ireland

Finbarr Murphy[67] notes how the ratification of the Maastricht Treaty in Ireland was dominated, not by issues of sovereignty or fears of economic and monetary union, but by abortion – a subject not directly referred to in any of the Treaties. The context for this debate in the Irish ratification process stems from the Eighth Amendment to the Irish constitution in which, "The State acknowledges the right to life of the unborn and, with due regard to the right of life of the mother, guarantees in its laws to defend and vindicate that right".

Concern to protect the Eighth Amendment arose following an access to information case brought by the Society For The Protection Of The Unborn Child (SPUC) against student's union officers in *SPUC v Grogan*[68] in the year before the ratification of the Maastricht Treaty. SPUC sought an injunction to prevent the distribution of information about abortion services in other Member States, by student organisations in Ireland, on the grounds that the provision of such information was in breach of the Irish constitution. The defendants argued that Irish law was in breach of the freedom to provide services contained in Article 59 of the EC Treaty. The Court found that while the provision of abortion services did fall within the scope of Community law (it was an economic service), because the distributor of information was not linked commercially to the service itself (the student's union was effectively a third party), the link was 'too tenuous' and there was, therefore, no breach of Community law. Following this case, and in order to insulate the Irish constitution from any further threat from the EU, a protocol was annexed to the Maastricht Treaty providing that, "Nothing in the TEU [Treaty on the European Union], or

---

[67] Murphy, F. (1994) 'Maastricht: implementation in Ireland', *European Law Review*, vol 19, pp 94-104.

[68] *SPUC v Grogan*, Case C159/90 [1991] ECR 1-4685.

in the Treaty establishing the European communities ... shall effect the application in Ireland of Article 40.3.3 of the Constitution of Ireland"[69]. The purpose of this protocol was thus to prevent the free movement provisions, especially the right to travel to receive services and the right to information about services, from undermining this fundamental *national* interest. Just three days after signing the Treaty, the whole issue blew up in the light of the *X* case involving a 14-year-old girl who became pregnant after being raped and who was prevented from travelling to England with her parents for an abortion[70]. The defendants contested the restrictions, arguing that they had a right to travel to obtain a service legally available in another Member State and that the life of the girl was at risk because she threatened to commit suicide. The Court held that abortion *was* an economic service within the meaning of Articles 59 and 60 EEC but that the freedom to receive services was subject to the aforementioned public policy derogation. The risk to the defendant's own life from suicide was much less and of a different order of magnitude than the certainty that the life of the unborn would be terminated. Following growing international criticism, the Supreme Court allowed the appeal and found that, on true interpretation of Article 40.3.3, where there was a "real and substantial risk to the life of the mother" which can only be avoided by termination, then termination was permissible.

Following the *X* case, the Irish Government sought deletion of the protocol. Member States were reluctant to agree to this for fear of re-opening a Maastricht 'can of worms'. As a compromise, in May 1992 a Solemn Declaration (of uncertain legal status) was made which seeks to give a legal interpretation to the protocol at variance with its original intent. The constitutional ban on abortion was then changed again in the second referendum of November 1992 which asked people to vote on three separate amendments:

- The 12th amendment: The Right To Life, permitting abortion in very limited circumstances where there is a threat to the mother's life (excluding suicide).
- The 13th amendment: The Right to Travel.
- The 14th amendment: The Right to Obtain/Make Available Information in Ireland about services in other member States.

---

[69] OJ 1992 C224/130.

[70] *AG v X and others* [1992] IRI, ILRM 401.

On the day, 60% voted 'Yes' to the right to travel and information and 65% voted 'No' to the right to life amendment. The latter group included both the hard line anti-abortion lobby opposed to any abortion whatsoever and those who argued that abortion should be available in cases where a woman's health was at risk and in cases of rape or incest. The legal situation remains unclear.

At present the only right to abortion in Ireland rests on the Supreme Court judgment in the X case, providing a limited right to abortion where there is a real and substantial risk to the life, as opposed to the health, of a woman. With not one abortion known to have taken place in Ireland, this leads Smyth to refer to the policy as one encouraging 'abortion tourism'. Indeed, available figures from the British Pregnancy Advisory Service (BPAS) point to around 13,000 *known* cases of Irish women (from both the North and the South) going to England every year for abortion. This is probably the tip of an iceberg and certainly excludes all those women giving English addresses. Smyth concludes her assessment of the Irish situation, and the response of the EU, in pessimistic tone:

> **The sorry state of abortion affairs in Ireland ... raises complex questions about the modus operandi of the EU and its relations with Member States and, crucially and urgently, about the meaning of European citizenship. Europe has failed to provide any solutions, in a concrete way, for women trapped in second class citizenship.[71]**

She is referring specifically here to the status of Irish women and the failure of EU law to protect them. It is also important to consider the impact of Irish domestic law – and the EU's response – on EU migrant women in Ireland who are similarly forced into forms of 'tourism'[72]. Despite a significant decline in fertility in recent years, Ireland still has the highest fertility rate in the EU. The dramatic decline in fertility has been 'explained' by demographers as a response to modernisation processes reflecting increased levels of education. This type of explanation, however, "ignores how and why women are exercising their reproductive rights,

---

[71] Smyth (1996, p 15), supra, note 58.

[72] While the term 'tourism' implies the exercise of autonomy – or voluntarism – it is increasingly used in a generic way to identify all forms of migration motivated by other than purely employment-based interests. In practice, many of these migrations represent a negation of choice.

and thus denies women personal agency"[73]. Murphy-Lawless documents women's campaigns to gain legal access to contraception during the 1970s noting the McGee case in 1973 in which a 29-year-old mother of four took a constitutional case against the government ban on contraception on the grounds that another pregnancy would pose a risk to her own life (she had a serious heart condition). As a result, in 1973 the Supreme Court lifted the ban. Access to contraception then gradually increased. Despite the formal legal situation, however:

> **Information, decision-making and access to appropriate contraceptive methods are not guaranteed even now. Access is unequal for women of different social classes, backgrounds and in different regions of the country. Furthermore all women have to negotiate access to contraception through the medical profession ... The availability of all forms of contraception was restricted to married couples over the age of 18 who had obtained a doctor's prescription.**[74]

Local doctors and pharmacists were permitted to 'opt out' of providing family planning under the 1979 Family Planning Act, leading to unevenness in service provision. Furthermore, women must still pay for contraceptives. It was not until 1993 that legal restrictions on the sale of condoms were removed, "not because the state finally recognised women's rights to control their fertility, but because of the spread of AIDS"[75].

Another important restriction on women's freedom of choice in Ireland, which further controls their reproductive autonomy and structures gender relations, concerns the prohibition on divorce. As recently as 1986 some 63.5% of the Irish population vote, against the introduction of limited divorce rights. The most recent referendum held in November 1995 was carried by a very slight majority[76]. At the time of the interviews, Ireland remained the only country in the EU in which divorce was illegal. This did not, however, mean that there are no divorced or separated women in Ireland.

---

[73] Murphy-Lawless, J. (1993) 'Fertility, bodies and politics: the Irish case', *Reproductive Health Matters*, no 2, p 54.

[74] Murphy-Lawless (1993, p 60), supra, note 73.

[75] Smyth (1996, p 11), supra, note 58.

[76] 50.6:49.4%

Citizenship and personal agency: migrant women's response

I have already referred to the tendency, in much of the citizenship literature, to define citizenship in terms of formal legal or political status and to view women as passive victims of patriarchal legal and social structures. Notwithstanding the profound impact of the Irish State and private patriarchal control on women's formal citizenship status in Ireland, the Irish interviews illustrate some of these tensions and contradictions; between choices and constraints, between citizenship as formal rights and citizenship as agency, in a very immediate and interesting way.

Marital status and citizenship

The following excerpts from the interviews give some indication of how EU migrant women have interpreted and responded to the Irish context and its impact on their decisions about marriage. Some women felt compelled to marry in order to avoid stigma for themselves and their children and to promote their integration in Ireland. One Dutch woman married her Irish husband in Holland before they moved to Ireland because they felt that, "not being married would have been disastrous for his job"[77]. Another German couple who had cohabited for over 15 years, married several days before migrating because, "we felt it would be better for the child if we were married when we came to Ireland"[78]. In one case, a woman's decision *not* to marry was based on the divorce situation, "I think the absence of divorce is a very bad thing and I'm glad I'm not married here. And if when my children decide to get married there's still no divorce, I will advise them not to get married"[79].

Another group of women who did not marry on migration had experienced a variety of problems and stigmas in Ireland which lead them to conceal their status. One woman in a cohabiting relationship said that she, "pretended to be married because people here were very Catholic and it would have been disgraceful not to be married and live together"[80].

Others reported problems in finding accommodation and being accepted by relatives:

---

[77] Interviewee D514 (Ireland).
[78] Interviewee D516 (Ireland).
[79] Interviewee D534 (Ireland).
[80] Interviewee D506 (Ireland).

"Many foreigners still have to hide their partners from the landlords."[81]

"He never actually openly told his family that I was coming over to live together ... and even now we are not totally regarded by his family as a couple."[82]

Two women who moved to Ireland as divorcees had similar problems:

"It is seen as bad to be divorced, so I haven't told many people."[83]

"For me the down side [of moving to Ireland] would be that issues like abortion and divorce are just ignored and I find it shocking, it startles me every time that I have to fill in a form that there is no box for the divorced women; and I have either to make a box or ask how to fill it in."[84]

Although we did not specifically ask a question about *where* women were married, nor indeed anticipated its relevance, the issue was raised by respondents in 12 of the interviews (all of whom married Irish men). It became clear how important the location of marriage was for women's autonomy and the opportunity to escape an unsatisfactory marriage while still retaining a right to re-marry. The lack of an 'option' to divorce, for those who marry in Ireland, while clearly not preventing marital breakdown, removes the right to re-marry and provides no right of maintenance to estranged partners. Awareness of this situation had an important bearing on many women's decisions about where to marry. Nine of the women interviewed made a point of saying that they returned to marry in their country of origin in order to safeguard their rights to divorce:

Negotiating citizenship: location of marriage

"I actually wanted to get married here but ... just in case we did decide to get divorced we decided to get married in Scotland. It did influence our decision."[85]

---

[81] Interviewee D501 (Ireland).
[82] Interviewee D518 (Ireland).
[83] Interviewee D524 (Ireland).
[84] Interviewee D529 (Ireland).
[85] Interviewee D561 (Ireland).

"Divorce – that was one of the reasons I got married in Holland – my [Irish] husband was divorced before. Luckily he had married in England. We took the advice of an international lawyer in Holland who said we would not able to get a divorce in Ireland if we married there. He was older than me so we stepped into it rationally. I know about six Dutch women here, married to Irish men – who had tremendous trouble [when their relationships broke down] with maintenance and children. They've all gone back to Holland; they have a better chance at home."[86]

"I was married in France for that reason. Not that when you get married you think of divorce but at the same time it's a consideration, and actually I was talking to another French friend of mine and she said the same because we have a common friend who is French who got married here and whose marriage has broken down and she can't get divorced."[87]

"The divorce situation was a very important consideration [affecting her decision to marry her Irish partner in France] I'm afraid to say, because that is the way I suppose a French woman would think."[88]

Another woman had made several migrations solely in order to establish her marital status:

"My [Irish] husband was married and divorced in England and we went back to England for a long time and did all the things right and established the right residency and so forth for his divorce. As soon as he got his divorce he wanted to come back. We tried to apply to get married but they said no, you came back too soon, you can't have it and they wouldn't let us get married again. So a year later, we had to establish residence in England for a length of time in order to get married there. Since then we have spoken numerous times to our solicitor [who] still thinks we wouldn't be allowed to be married

[86] Interviewee D514 (Ireland).
[87] Interviewee D562 (Ireland).
[88] Interviewee D550 (Ireland).

here. My situation of being a semi-married woman or whatever title has coloured a lot of my time here."[89]

Recognition of the importance of marriage (and the right to divorce) as a key determinant of social status affecting women's personal lives has evidently influenced the decision making of migrant women in Ireland, resulting in previously unrecognised forms of mobility[90]. In addition to taking practical steps to maximise their own freedom of choice, many respondents expressed outrage at the Irish divorce laws:

> **"Nowadays we should be able to do what we want with our body and our conscience."**[91]

> **"I think the main problem is religion – the choice to have an abortion, the choice to get divorce. In Greece we have the choice. In Ireland I do not. Obviously I would like to be given the same. It's right to have choice in such private matters."**[92]

Strong resentment to the situation and to their inability to influence domestic policy through the electoral process (by voting in the Referenda) had lead many women to express dissatisfaction with their political rights as 'citizens':

> **"I have very few rights and on all the major issues I have been subject to, I have no rights to vote ... Now the divorce issue comes out. I certainly feel at the receiving end of it and have no right to make an impact on it so, yes, I find it a very important issue."**[93]

> **"Initially when I was in the situation where I really needed and wanted a divorce, I was really very upset about it and wanted to vote in the referendum."**[94]

---

[89] Interviewee D555 (Ireland).

[90] Although the notion of moving between Member States in order to negotiate the benefits and constraints of different legal orders has begun to be discussed in the context of recognition of same-sex partnerships.

[91] Interviewee D518 (Ireland).

[92] Interviewee D508 (Ireland).

[93] Interviewee D553 (Ireland).

[94] Interviewee D555 (Ireland).

Reproductive rights

In addition to concerns about marriage, and the impact of national law on their citizenship status, interviewees expressed concern about the constraints on their right to control their own fertility in Ireland (compared to their country of origin). Many women were acutely aware of the impact of this situation on women in Ireland and the links with mobility as women in Ireland are forced into 'abortion tourism', "I just feel it is very sad ... So it seems OK if you're Irish and you go and have your abortion in Britain but don't have it here – it's pretty shameful actually"[95]. Others were conscious of retaining their own citizenship rights in their country of origin:

> **"My Irish friends feel my life is easier because if I want an abortion I can just hop on a boat to Germany and get it – I need my choice."[96]**

> **"We all know that women are going for abortion [but] people don't seem to want it on their doorstep and that worries me as I said, not for myself because I am still French and maybe that's one part why I keep my French citizenship. But for my children, I don't want them to grow up in Society like that."[97]**

This form of 'tourism' was also evident in migrant women's attempts to control their fertility[98]:

> **"When we first came over ... when it was time to get the pill, I didn't know what to do, I wasn't very old. I went back to England in the end and got it but you know that type of thing is very hard."[99]**

---

[95] Interviewee D561 (Ireland).
[96] Interviewee D502 (Ireland).
[97] Interviewee D562 (Ireland).
[98] It is important to remember that some of these women migrated some time ago and their experiences reflect the situation at that point, before contraception became more widely available and acceptable.
[99] Interviewee D563 (Ireland).

"In some ways I have to say I am pleased to be Dutch ... when I came in 1983 it was an unholy era for the contraceptive pill and I remember going for the pill to the local chemist and he would want to know what the reason was and I said I don't want any children. He was appalled – a good healthy young woman like myself should have them."[100]

"I have been practising contraception for centuries! That is my personal choice. I have come from a country [England] where those sort of issues, a women's right to choose, is on the cards, whichever way I would personally choose, politically I would believe in that. Because of the close ties between State and Church, those choices are not allowed. Then there is a thing where it is just stupid, a couple of times when I have needed a morning-after pill ... I haven't gone to a doctor here, I have arranged to get one from [Northern Ireland]."[101]

"I had a friend who was given the pill for one month only so she 'phoned her father in Holland and he sent her some."[102]

"Things like contraception, abortion are serious issues. I have managed by living in Dublin and having access to England too – we used to bring condoms in. Had we lived somewhere else and had we not been as equipped for dealing with things like that it could have been difficult."[103]

Other women reported that, while not having to return home for contraception, access in Ireland was uneven and largely depended on personal contacts:

"Things are still a big problem here. It's more concealed, more at a cultural level. It depends on your family doctor – you can see it in their body language. Some will give contraception – others won't, it depends on the doctor."[104]

---

[100] Interviewee D553 (Ireland).
[101] Interviewee D557 (Ireland).
[102] Interviewee D514 (Ireland).
[103] Interviewee D551 (Ireland).
[104] Interviewee D509 (Ireland).

> "It depends on who you know. If my husband was not Irish it
> may be difficult. You have to travel a bit."[105]

These responses indicate some of the difficulties women experienced in gaining adequate contraceptive services in Ireland and the influence of religious values, resulting in problems of territorial justice and access in general, restricting women's ability to control their fertility. These women are not passive victims of Irish policy, however, but have determined to safeguard their reproductive autonomy through the retention of important rights in their country of origin. They have also shown themselves to be highly interested in the domestic political situation.

Another specific denial of an assumed right in many other Member States, was raised by two respondents denied amniocentesis. While clearly another example of fertility control, this denial has serious long-term consequences for women's caring responsibilities. Amniocentesis has never been routinely offered in Ireland to women at risk of having abnormal foetuses, as it is in the UK (to all women over 35). Information from the Family Planning Association suggests that the only option for women concerned about this risk is, "to go up North – they get very little help here"[106]. Two of the respondents referred to the lack of availability of amniocentesis (as a result of the abortion policy):

> "I think women put up with an awful lot here, which I wouldn't
> put up with. In a way now it doesn't affect me because when
> I came I knew where to get contraception; if my daughter got
> pregnant I would know where to go for termination. But,
> interesting enough, I did get pregnant here when I was 42 and
> in England I would have immediately been offered an
> amniocentesis to see if the baby had Downs Syndrome, and I
> would have automatically been offered termination and I
> understand because of the Catholic influence that wasn't an
> option here, and it did sort of bring me up against politics in
> my personal life and I lost the baby through a miscarriage. I
> was actually told by a doctor in hospital that if I got pregnant
> again she would give me the address of a clinic in Belfast where
> I could go, but I wasn't to tell anyone because if I did she
> would lose her job; and this kind of things just seemed so

---

[105] Interviewee D520 (Ireland).
[106] Citation from a telephone interview.

---

crazy and so unreal, when all we would need is access to better information."[107]

Another woman reported the effect of restrictive abortion laws on her professional work as a teacher as she was unable to give any advice on pregnancy. She had recently had an English student who, on discovering that she was pregnant:

> **"... got on the next boat home because she went into such a panic ... she wanted to have proper advice. She decided to have the child in the end but got on the boat home to get that advice, to think it through, to talk it through. It's not that you are looking for an abortion, you are looking for advice that treats you seriously as a woman who could make choices."**[108]

Women's reproductive and family law rights are central to the citizenship question both as matters in their own right but also as central elements affecting women's relationship, with paid work and their financial autonomy. The EU's response, in permitting Ireland's 'opt-out', severely restricts the status of Irish women and their ability to exercise their freedom of movement throughout the Community. The research also highlights the problems of designating such matters ones of 'national interest' or wholly internal to the Member State: the framework of constraint impinges not only on Irish women but also underpins the experience and behaviour of EU migrant women exercising their right of free movement. Many of these women are pressurised into forms of social relations and dependency which severely restrict their autonomy. Notwithstanding, the evidence presented demonstrates the importance of seeing women as actors or agents in the citizenship process, not simply as passive victims of patriarchal institutional and cultural practices. Women were clearly aware of the effect of migration on their rights and, in some cases, managed to make decisions (such as marrying outside the Irish jurisdiction or obtaining contraceptive or abortion services 'back home' or in a third country) which maximised their autonomy, albeit within a framework of severe constraint. Women's response, to restrictions on their political efficacy similarly demonstrated a recognition of the importance of the issues to them, their

---

[107] Interviewee D533 (Ireland).
[108] Interviewee D557 (Ireland).

equivocal status as Community citizens and a desire to actively influence Irish domestic policy.

The material presented in this chapter and extracted from discussions with migrant women about their experience, as women, of living in different social systems, supports the call for the development of a theory of citizenship which is less grand, less abstract, and more grounded in the day-to-day reality of women's lives. There is no evidence here to support a theory of 'welfare tourism'; European women do not appear to be 'shopping around' for the optimum bundle of social advantages. In practice, women are more likely to move for employment reasons, in a period of their lives prior to family formation. Once established in the host State, however, the complex interaction of formal social status with popular culture has an important influence on their autonomy. In some cases, post-migration mobility is taking place as women move in order to maximise their access to social resources and to exercise fundamental human rights.

It is interesting to note the difference in issues identified in Sweden and Ireland, given that similar, general, questions were asked in both countries and no specific questions about divorce or abortion were asked in Ireland. In Sweden the preoccupation at the time of interview was with attempts to reconcile public 'work' roles with private 'caring' roles whereas, in Ireland, perhaps because of the pending referendum, women spoke almost exclusively about their reproductive and marital rights and relatively little about employment and financial autonomy.

If it is possible to begin to answer the age-old question of 'what women want', or what measures might attract or impede mobility, on the basis of the findings presented here, we must conclude that women are looking for a system that affords them maximum choice in their attempt to reconcile, on an individual level, and with their partners and family, the balance between their public and private roles. As such, statutory provision is not a panacea, enabling women to shift from dependency on male breadwinning partners to the state, but rather a mechanism increasing the infrastructure of potential support which women may contract into or out of as their lives evolve; more facilitative than interventionist in nature.

It was very evident from the interviews that women recognised the fact that 'the state' is by no means a neutral agency simply setting out its stall and inviting citizens to select goods from a range of options (like soap powders on a supermarket shelf). Rather, the specific basket of social goods on offer in any system reflects and reinforces often covert, ideologically-driven, motives or political expedients, which may have little to do with gender equality or empowerment. This baggage of cultural expectations and pressures to conform, sanctioned via social entitlement was experienced as oppressive by women in all the countries concerned to a greater or lesser degree, whether presented in a 'marriage-forcing', 'work-forcing' or 'care-forcing' guise. Women wanted to be genuinely 'free' to negotiate their own, individual arrangements, drawing on a whole network of support whether of a public, private or informal nature.

Moving from one social system to another introduces new and different sources of opportunity and control. These were interpreted by women in a variety of ways depending on their own perspectives, no doubt coloured by their past and their socialisation within the family and society in the country of origin, but also on their relationships with others. These relationships included not only male partners but also 'other' women, as mothers, sisters, friends and employees. It is this last issue, of women's relationships with each other, that poses one of the most critical questions in feminist citizenship theory at the present time – a point we shall return to in the course of the next chapter.

EIGHT

Caring at a distance

Introduction

We have seen, in Chapter Four, how 'citizenship of the Union', for the present at least, does not confer a broad equality of entitlement on the basis of membership, but rather a hierarchy of status dependent upon forms of social contribution and marital status[1]. Within that hierarchy, full independent social entitlement accrues only to economically-active migrants: persons involved in unpaid care-giving gain a derived benefit by virtue of their marriage to a breadwinning partner. We have also argued that this type of benefit, conditional as it is upon marriage, presumes and reinforces high levels of dependency within families. Chapter Six focused on the impact of migration, and marriage, on women's employment trajectories and Chapter Seven on women's experiences of statutory support in their ability to juggle their public and private lives. This chapter develops our understanding of the lives of migrant women, and the limitations of Community law, still further through a more detailed focus on aspects of informal care and women's responses to family obligations, rarely considered in comparative research.

Caring over the life-course

This chapter focuses on the relationship between caring and autonomy, both in terms of the impact of migration on carers' support networks in the host Member State and in terms of persistent (and developing) caring obligations in their country of origin. Despite clear differences between Member States in terms of the provision of support services and the degree of socialisation of care, the 'mother-daughter' relationship continues to characterise the welfare systems of not only Southern European countries

---

[1] Reinforcing forms of status differentiation operating within domestic welfare systems.

but all countries to a greater or lesser degree[2]. The support provided by women's mothers during their own period of early motherhood has been shown to be an important determinant of women's labour market participation. Daughters, on the other hand, have played a key role in the provision of care and support for elderly and disabled family members. Until recently at least, however, the literature and research on issues concerned with caring has tended to polarise the debate.

On the one hand, the debate about citizenship, particularly at European Union (EU) level, has been dominated by concerns about the impact of motherhood on women's labour market participation (and particularly issues of maternity rights and pre-school provision). In this context, women are not defined as 'carers' as such, but in terms of their biological relationship with their children. The key determinant of women's autonomy is generally understood to lie at the axes of paid work and motherhood, leading to a focus on labour market participation as the principal source of financial autonomy and on the latter as the key to inclusive citizenship for women. The absence of a life-course perspective on gender inequality in this literature is highlighted by Geraldine Pratt and Susan Hanson:

> **The family, and particularly the young family, has played a key role in feminist explanations for women's marginal position in the labour force ... While marriage and children have a non-trivial impact on many women's (and men's) lives, one that reverberates throughout them, a description that highlights a single period in one type of life-course is clearly partial. This description has played an important role within feminist critical (as well as human capital theorists', male trade unionists' and employers') rhetorical performances, but its partiality now seems more obvious and increasingly problematic.[3]**

Issues concerning the development of social rights and services designed to modify the relationship between paid work and motherhood, to facilitate

---

[2] This phrase was first used by Langan and Ostner to describe the gendered nature of the 'welfare societies' concept in Southern European countries; Langan, M. and Ostner, I. (1991) 'Gender and welfare', in G. Room (ed) *Towards a European welfare state?*, Bristol: SAUS Publications.

[3] Pratt, G. and Hanson, S. (1993) 'Women and work across the life-course: moving beyond essentialism', in C. Katz and J. Monk (eds) *Full circles: Geographies of women over the life-course*, London: Routledge, p 28.

---

the labour market participation of young mothers, have thus dominated the EU policy agenda. Moreover, the discussion about private patriarchal control – and gender dynamics within the family – has, in the main, similarly focused on the parenting role of men, as fathers, in this delimited, biologically-defined period. As a result, the political and policy agenda focuses attention on a limited span of women's lives (mainly women aged 25-45), and on issues of motherhood, parenting and childcare, particularly of pre-school, able-bodied children. In other words, on children that are themselves passing through a predictable chronology from high levels of initial dependency to eventual independence with a concomitant evolving disengagement for parents.

Another growing body of literature, again framed in the context of citizenship rights, is concerned with the implications of demographic change and welfare retrenchment on the State's ability to support an ageing and increasingly dependent elderly population. In this debate, concern is typically couched in terms of the citizenship status of the 'victims' of institutionalisation – of dependent individuals as opposed to carers[4] (in response to the critique of 'total' institutions and the perceived moral superiority of 'community care').

Concern over the implications of increased dependency ratios, particularly the increasing number of dependent elderly persons in European societies (and the need to secure a supply of unpaid caring labour) at a time of fiscal crisis and welfare retrenchment, has lead policy makers and feminist scholars to draw attention to the relationship between caring and citizenship. Now defined in a more functional sense as 'carers', the locus of concern has shifted from a narrow correlation with labour market participation (and financial autonomy as the source of all autonomy) to the relationship between women and welfare or, more specifically, between carers and services. The function of welfare, in this context, is less commonly seen in terms of enabling women to undertake paid work, but of securing the continuation of interdependency (between carer and

---

[4] The distinction between carers and dependants in analyses of women's experiences of giving and receiving care has been criticised as 'unhelpful' (Tester, S. [1996] 'Women and community care', in C. Hallett [ed] *Women and social policy: An introduction*, Hemel Hempstead: Harvester Wheatsheaf, p 145), particularly in the context of disabled people, elderly people and childcarers. Indeed, the evolving nature of relationships of reciprocity and interdependence was clearly evident in the interviews (reported below). The distinction has, however, dominated much research and played an important role in shaping policy.

the person cared for) in contexts of increasing dependency, through the provision of domiciliary/support services. Welfare intervention is thus less concerned with the autonomy of carers, as facilitating decarceration and preventing or delaying the institutionalisation of dependants. The rights of carers are thus 'derivative' in that they stem from the individual rights of dependants.

Various policy initiatives have developed to promote the progressive commodification of care and thus secure the requisite volume of caring labour. One increasingly dominant feature of many European systems has been the institution of systems of payment of benefits directly to care-recipients with the expectation that they will then use the monies to purchase their own 'care packages'[5]. While such schemes have been actively pursued by sections of the disability rights movement and represent important demands for disabled people to be treated as individual citizens and consumers of services, they conceal the conflict of interest present in many caring relationships, which fundamentally restricts the personal autonomy of carers as individuals. Citizenship, in this context, defined, in the rhetoric of market individualism, in terms of the consumer status of persons requiring care, places carers as a somewhat impotent third party in the relationship between the State and the dependent person. There is thus a real risk that developments in the commodification of care will shift the balance of power from care-giver to care-recipient[6]. The 1986

---

[5] For a discussion of developments in the payments for informal care see Ungerson, C. (1995) 'Gender, cash and informal care: European perspectives and dilemmas', *Journal of Social Policy*, vol 24, no 1, pp 31-52; Ungerson, C. (1996) 'The "commodification of care" and the new generational contracts', Paper for the EC programme, 'Gender and citizenship: Social integration and social exclusion in European welfare states', Netherlands Institute for Advanced Studies, Wassenaar, July 3-4; Glendinning, C. and McLaughlin, E. (1993) 'Paying for informal care: Lessons from Finland', *Journal of European Social Policy*, vol 3, no 4, pp 239-53; Daly, M. (1996) 'Recent changes in cash transfers in European welfare states and their implications for women', Paper to the Conference, 'Engendering citizenship: Work and care', Wassenaar, 3-5 July.

[6] The payment of cash benefits to care-recipients can be contrasted to benefits for children which are typically paid to carers. Indeed, the campaign to retain the payment of universal child benefit has a special symbolic importance for the British women's movement as the only benefit paid directly to mothers in recognition of their caring role.

Disabled Persons Act[7], for example, has been applauded for being the first piece of UK legislation to explicitly recognise carers' rights. In practice, however, the relevant section of the legislation places a duty on local authorities, when assessing the needs of disabled people for services, to "take account of the abilities of the carer" (Section 8). Carers do not, therefore, have any independent rights to services (to enable them to undertake paid work or choose not to continue in their present caring role) but simply a notional right to have their abilities to care assessed (and for service support to enable them to continue to care)[8]. Carers' status is thus manifest not only in the type of services provided but also in the *timing* of service intervention (or entitlement). In an overview of community care policy in Europe, Susan Tester notes,

> ... formal services are only offered when the carer is unable to care alone or needs support to continue to do so. In effect the principle of subsidiarity is applied, although not explicitly, as in Germany, where family members are required, in certain situations, to provide care [or to finance it].[9]

In this new context, citizenship becomes articulated in terms of the relationship between carers and services; carers are not accorded the status of paid workers, but of secondary consumers of publicly provided services and benefits, and services do not exist to promote the autonomy of carers (or reduce the 'restrictedness' of caring[10]), but instead to ensure the continued supply of unpaid work (and interdependency). Indeed, where carers' needs *have* been recognised in community care policy, intervention has focused on supporting and, in some cases, compensating them for loss of earnings (through the development of carers' pensions and payments for informal care[11]). Such policies do not seek to promote the 'option' of

---

[7] The 1986 Disabled Persons (Services, Consultation and Representation) Act.

[8] Although, in practice, the implementation of even this 'right' was delayed and, in the absence of additional funding, is likely to remain more of a formality than a reality (for more details see Ackers, H.L. [1989] 'The social construction of disability and its research implications', Paper to the British Sociological Association Conference, University of Plymouth, July 1989).

[9] Tester (1996, p 141) supra, note 4.

[10] Twigg, J. and Atkin, K. (1994) *Carers perceived: Policy and practice in informal care*, Buckingham: Open University Press, p 39.

[11] Ungerson (1995; 1996); Glendinning and McLaughlin (1993), supra, note 5.

labour market participation for carers, but to provide (weak) incentives for labour market withdrawal and to foster the continuation of dependency.

The importance of labour market participation is apparently less of a concern in relation to this group of carers, partly because of a presumption of a fairly rigid chronology which characterises them as 'mid-life' or 'older' women and therefore less likely to be active in the labour market (or to positively wish to undertake paid work). Financial autonomy is thus considered to be less of an issue. As Fincher notes, in the context of support for carers in Australia:

> ... the focus [of state resources and concern] suggests, first, that caring women, when they are combining caring with paid employment, are generally envisaged as young mothers with small children ... not much attention is presently paid to women in their 'middle years' as labour force participants who require assistance with their caring responsibilities ... everyone assumes that such carers will give up paid work.[12]

The tendency to polarise the debate over caring and citizenship (and to disaggregate aspects of family policy – and women's lives) has been exacerbated by the development of the policy agenda at EU level. Circumscribed by legal limits on its competency to act in the social field (and the interpretation of the subsidiarity principle), the evolving 'gender debate' has prioritised those social issues directly connected with employment policy[13]. To some extent this reflects not simply limited competency, but also a received wisdom on what constitutes women's 'core' interests – or the optimum feminist strategy, reflecting a strong belief within Commission circles in labour market integration as the panacea to all forms of marginalisation and in financial autonomy, via paid work, as

---

[12] Fincher, R. (1993) 'Women, the state and the life-course in urban Australia', in Katz and Monk (1993, pp 255-6), supra, note 3.

[13] This focus on the employment/childcare issue is evident in much of the recent feminist literature dealing with the impact of the EU on gender dynamics. See, for example, the important new book, L. Hantrais and M.T. Letablier's (1996) *Families and family policies in Europe*, London: Longman, where, to all intents and purposes, the concept of family policy is used restrictively to refer to aspects of parenting/motherhood. Similar 'presumptions' are evident in C. Hoskyns (1996) *Integrating gender*, London:Verso, and J. Pillinger (1992) *Feminising the market*, London: Macmillan.

the principal determinant of citizenship. Even within this labour market focus, however, explanations based upon a particular life-course (and the tensions between motherhood and paid work) are likely to be partial and inadequate:

> **While feminists are unlikely to reproduce this particular biological essentialism (that of collapsing the category 'woman' within a temporally constrained set of biological conditions that may not even be relevant to every woman of child-bearing age (eg, those who choose not to bear children [or cannot have children]), we have tended to over-generalise the links between sex and a specific set of household relationships in our explanations of occupational segregation.[14]**

While we might expect the gender/citizenship debate at EU level to focus on employment-related matters (and hence to ignore wider quality of life issues and matters of domestic social policy), this does not, of itself, explain the focus on motherhood and the failure to address the labour market implications of other forms of caring relationship. It may, however, reflect a 'pragmatic' assumption that such women are generally older and less inclined to be active in the labour market. The inadequacy of this assumption may similarly reflect the composition of the women's lobby at EU level and the domination of younger, middle-class 'femocrats' in the decision-making structures whose presumptions about gender inequality and the lived experiences of women are based, not on sound research, but on their own experiences. To that extent it could be argued, as Ruth Fincher[15] suggests, in relation to Australian social policy, that those women who have managed to enter the corridors of power represent a relatively narrow cross-section of women who share similar interests and characteristics, one of which is their life-course position (and a preoccupation with juggling children and career).

In a similar vein, Rosser locates the neglect of feminist life-course studies in the composition of feminist scholars who have not only been predominantly white, middle-class and Western, but also relatively uniform in age (20-45 years). Rosser suggests that it is only as such women have

---

[14] Pratt, G. and Hanson, S. (1993) 'Women and work across the life-course: moving beyond essentialism', in Katz and Monk (1993, p 28) supra, note 3.
[15] Fincher (1993, p 249), supra note 12.

begun to age that we have seen any serious attention paid to issues facing older women[16].

The focus of interest, within the EU women's lobby, has thus led to a preoccupation of feminist concern with the development and evaluation of Community sex equality law[17] to the neglect of other areas of evolving Community influence in which, arguably, a wider range of women's interests over the life-course are more effectively represented. As such, the opportunity to exploit a narrow, but symbolic, window of opportunity, albeit deriving from a very restrictive economic principle (the 'facilitating mobility' test), has, to some extent, been overlooked.

The evolution of a more holistic approach to family policy – and to individuals as economic actors with social needs – under the free movement of persons provisions was documented in some detail in Chapter Four. We saw here how a more explicit acknowledgement of caring responsibilities and familial ties has developed, blurring the boundaries between social and economic policy and the parameters of legal competency. In practice, these 'family' rights amount to an extension of the personal scope of the provisions to include family members in the ascending and descending line of the worker (and *his* spouse) and the extension of the material benefits, under the social advantages formulae to these persons (representing a move in the direction of a 'social dimension' to European citizenship).

The rational for this incursion into domestic social policy lies in the presumption that a failure to extend such rights would amount to a fundamental barrier to labour mobility and the successful completion of the internal market (reflecting various presumptions about households and migration decision-making processes). Little attempt has, however, been made to evaluate either the presumption itself or the impact of these interventions in family policy on the citizenship experience of EU migrants and the extent to which formal legal rights translate into citizenship experience.

---

[16] Rosser, S.V. (1991) 'Eco-feminism: lessons for feminism from ecology', *Women's Studies International Forum*, vol 14, no 3, pp 143-51, cited in Monk, J. and Katz, C. (1993) 'Where in the world are women?', in Katz and Monk (1993, pp 1-26), supra, note 3.

[17] Ackers, H.L. (1994) 'Women, citizenship and European Community law: the gender implications of the free movement provisions', *Journal of Social Welfare and Family Law*, vol 18, no 4, pp 391-407.

Migration and caring: the importance of space

The discussion above has emphasised the importance of taking a more holistic view of caring and citizenship through a life-course perspective. The literature referred to does not, however, generally refer to the spatial implications of this perspective. Save from an increased awareness of the effect of intra-regional migrations on the supply of informal networks, at the local level, to support community care, relatively little attention has been paid to the geography of dependency and its implications for women. Indeed, to the extent that cultural factors have been taken into account at all in the community care literature, it has generally been to critique racial and cultural stereotyping (and the notion that the Asian families have, by virtue of their culture, greater access to unpaid caring resources via the extended family).

The spatial manifestation of this spread of caring resources and obligations over the life-course is, however, of prime importance to the lives of many women who have undergone migrations at either intra-regional, international or intra-Community level, as the geography of dependency creates its own dynamic of choice and constraint. In some cases it may permit women to 'opt out' of caring, while in others it may seriously constrain and circumscribe their autonomy, putting pressure on both financial resources and personal relationships. In other cases it may result in further migrations. In their conclusions to a collection of essays on the geographies of women over the life-course, Katz and Monk note the importance of 'place' to an understanding of women's lives:

> A peculiarity of the juxtaposition of two life-course characteristics in the industrialised West – the postponement of child-bearing and wide-spread increases in life expectancy, along with the stubborn relegation of caring work to women – often results in women in their middle years juggling not only paid work and child-rearing, but also the care of their older family members. The dispersal of families across cities, regions and even nations make these intersections even more difficult to negotiate. These extensive webs of care which absorb women's time, as well as emotional and physical energy are made simpler or more difficult to deal with depending upon their particular spatial form.[18]

---

[18] Katz and Monk (1993, p 275), supra, note 3.

This tendency to distinguish between two temporally delimited periods of caring – and to locate them in conceptually distinct analyses of citizenship (as 'citizen carer' and 'citizen mother') – is evidently problematic for the majority of women. The experiences of migrant women, while empirically distinct in some important respects, also serve to emphasise fundamental flaws in the existing debate and public policy affecting all women. This chapter examines the adequacy of this debate (and public policy) in the context of the lived experiences of migrant women. It considers the family structure of migrant women, the geographical and temporal spread of caring relationships and dependencies and women's interpretations of, and responses to, these. Case studies presented in these sections emphasise the importance of seeing these aspects of women's lives as components of a complex web of caring resources and obligations, forming a framework of opportunity and constraint which shape women's freedom of choice over time and space.

Chapter Five emphasised the dominance of the 'male breadwinning' model within traditional analyses of migration behaviour and contrasted this with evidence indicating that the majority of migrant women were, in fact, single at the point of migration. The male breadwinning model of migration behaviour not only simplifies and distorts our understanding of migration processes, but also encourages various assumptions about the temporal nature of the migration (hence the frequent reference to 'mobility' in EC literature) and the geography of dependency. The image is of a young, economically-active male, migrating for work purposes and bringing with him a female partner who either fulfils a secondary labour market role, or works full-time in an unpaid capacity in the home. In the latter case she may have child dependants in the household[19]. All other family members, in this simplistic model, are resident in the country of emigration and the onset of dependency is responded to by either return migration or, in relatively less common cases, by the migration of those persons to reside with the migrant family (exercising their rights under Community law).

The evidence presented in Chapter Five suggests a migration dominated by single women who then create a second home or family, typically on a permanent basis, in the 'host' State. As a consequence of this, the extended

---

[19] Indeed, the priority attached to the development of rights safeguarding the children of migrant workers, particularly in relation to language support in schools and cultural integration programmes, reflects the preoccupation with the idea of a migration dominated by same-nationality couples.

family structure of these households is distorted, resulting in a complex spatial distribution of informal support networks and dependencies with many migrant women having 'family' resources and obligations spread across at least two Member States. 'Same-nationality' couples may lack any informal support in the country of residence (to help with childcare etc) while retaining caring obligations in their country of emigration. For couples of mixed nationality, particularly where the woman's partner is a national of the host State, there may be more support in the immediate locality (although in-law relationships were often themselves problematic), but the geographical spread of potential dependencies may cause tremendous tensions and pressures for the women concerned. This situation is further exacerbated by the significant incidence of multiple migrations – of both the woman herself and also of her siblings and, on occasions parents – and by the breakdown and reconstitution of families[20].

The following section considers some of the evidence collected in the interviews on the structure and geography of migrant women's families. It then goes on to examine the implications of this for informal care-giving and receiving, and the consequences in terms of women's autonomy.

Family structure: the extended family over space

Caring and dependency in the country of residence

The first part of the following section considers the family structures of migrant women in their country of residence. For the majority, this includes caring for their 'biological' children. For that group of women with partners who are nationals of the host State, this may also include in-laws and the extended family on the male partner's side. In a number of cases, migrant women also had obligations towards step-children from their partner's previous relationships. Furthermore, a number of migrant women had members of their own extended family who had migrated, usually some time after their initial migration, to join them in the host State, mainly to be cared for by their daughters. The next section thus considers, firstly, the impact of having children on migrant women, the overwhelming majority of whom have no family (or sources of informal support) of their own nearby. The focus here is thus on women as mothers of young

---

[20] Many women came from families in which there was a tradition of migration. As a consequence, their siblings – and parents, in some cases – had also migrated either to the same location or to other more disparate locations.

children and as potential recipients of informal support themselves. The discussion then goes on to consider the wider caring obligations these migrant women have in the country of residence towards persons other than their own children.

The second section shifts the focus to assess the extended family situation in the country of emigration and their responses to potential or existing caring obligations. Rather than focusing on these two different locations as geographically and temporally delimited, a series of case studies are introduced to illustrate the complex web of tensions and pressures that shape the lives of many of the interviewees.

The demographic structure of the female EU migrant population

Figures from the European Labour Force Survey (ELFS) show a concentration of EU migrant women in the 25-49 age group with a lower representation of elderly and young persons, compared to nationals. The majority are at the stage of their lives associated with child bearing and rearing (see Table 8.1). However, some countries, notably the UK, have a significantly 'older' migrant population (reflecting to some extent the long history of Irish migration).

Table 8.1: Demographic structure of the EU migrant population, by broad nationality and gender

Age (years)	Male national	Male EU migrant	Female national	Female EU migrant
0-14	19%	13%	17%	13%
15-24	14%	14%	14%	15%
25-49	36%	45%	34%	**44%**
50-64	18%	20%	18%	18%
65+	12%	9%	18%	10%

Source: 1992 Labour Force Survey, Eurostat (1994)

The age structure of the interview sample showed a greater concentration of younger women than one would expect from the ELFS data. To some extent, this reflected the sampling policy which sought to include only women of working age (see Table 8.2).

Table 8.2: The age structure of the interview sample

Age (years)	% of sample
16-24	3
25-39	55
40-54	34
55-64	6
65+	2

Source: Survey of Migrant Women (1995)

As could be expected (and illustrated in Figure 8.1), younger women aged 20-24 are less likely to have children present in the household. The peak years of parental responsibility are those of 30-39 during which time over 80% of both national and EU migrant women have children present in their household. The sample interviewed included higher than expected proportions of childless women and women with two or three children (see Table 8.3).

Figure 8.1: The presence of children in migrant women's households, by age group

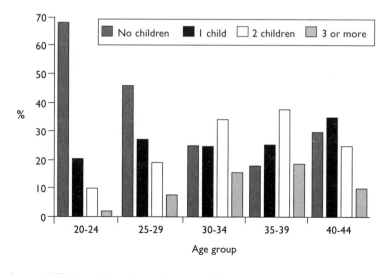

Source: 1992 Labour Force Survey, Eurostat (1994)

Table 8.3: Female fertility of the interview sample

Number of children	% of sample
No children	39
I child	21
2 or 3 children	37
More than 3 children	3

Source: Survey of Migrant Women (1995)

Some 61% of the women interviewed were mothers. Many of them talked, during the course of the interview, about their experience of motherhood in the period following migration, referring frequently to the lack of emotional and practical help. Dislocated from kinship ties in their country of origin, they lacked the kind of support that many national women rely on in order to be able to manage the relationship between paid and unpaid work and to sustain healthy relationships with their partners. A recent survey in the UK found that grandparents constituted an important source of childcare in Britain, with 23% of pre-school children cared for regularly by their grandparents when their mothers were absent (a greater proportion than those cared for by fathers). A similar proportion of school-age children are looked after by grandparents outside school hours[21]. This situation has also been held to be the case in Mediterranean countries, characterised by Langan and Ostner as 'mother–daughter' economies or 'welfare societies'[22].

The lack of family support in helping to bring up children was referred to by many of the women, particularly those coming from Southern European countries where the expectation of family care was more prevalent. One woman described her experience of motherhood as a migrant woman as follows:

"You have no family if you are a foreigner and that is one of the difficulties. I felt that if I had stayed in Spain I would have

[21] Meltzer, H. (1994) *Day care services for children*, London: OPCS. See also, Melhuish, E.C. and Moss, P. (1991) *Day care for young children: International perspectives*, London: Routledge.

[22] Langan and Ostner (1991), supra, note 2. This material is discussed in more detail in Chapter One. For a general discussion of family policy in Europe see also, Hantrais, L. and Letablier, M.T. (1996) *Families and family policies in Europe*, London: Longman; Cochrane, A. and Clarke, J. (eds) (1993) *Comparing welfare states*, London: Sage.

lots more help from my mother and family."[23]

Another woman simply echoed the feelings of the majority of women when she said that she missed having, "a grandmother ... somebody who'll take care of them"[24].

One might reasonably assume that those women who have family resources in the host State (by virtue of their partners) were less isolated and received more practical help. The interviews suggested, however, that this was rarely the case; relationships with in-laws were often complex, frequently disappointing to the migrant women and, on occasion, contributed to their sense of isolation. The following case evidences the problems experienced by many migrant women who, although married to nationals, nevertheless lacked informal support from their husband's family and suffered, as a result, from high levels of isolation and loneliness. It also brings out the importance of economic resources as a dimension of social support.

> One woman came to the UK from Luxembourg initially to work as an au pair. She returned after a year when her work permit expired and came back to join her English boyfriend after the UK joined the EC. They then married and had two children: "I didn't have any relatives here except my in-laws and that was not an easy relationship. So that was difficult, I found that very difficult, very lonely, very lonely, terribly lonely. And of course I didn't have much money to telephone anybody so yes that was hard. I think if I'd had more money I would have gone back [to her parents] more often – I don't know. But it would have been nice to have mother to baby-sit you see and have somebody. You couldn't do anything because we never had a baby-sitter. We didn't have money to pay". This marriage subsequently ended in divorce and she is now cohabiting with another Englishman. During the time of her divorce, this woman's parents also died within a very short space of each other: "It was all quite traumatic that year and I didn't know what to do. I was thinking shall I go back to Luxembourg, shall I stay here, but of course my daughters

---

[23] Interviewee D008 (UK).
[24] Interviewee D502 (Ireland).

> **were then eight and 10 and they were English and I didn't think it would be fair on them to take them back."**[25]

Many women with pre-school children achieved a level of informal support by regularly returning home for extended visits to their own mothers, sisters and friends. This was clearly less common among those who had limited access to funds or had partners who were unwilling to 'release' funds for that purpose. It also became less of an option even for women who could afford it, however, once children reached school age and developed a much stronger sense of identification with the host State (particularly when they lacked the linguistic skills to communicate with their family abroad). The heavy responsibility faced by many migrant women is also clear from the case above, divorced at a time when her children were still quite young, and with her own parents sick and dying in Luxembourg, she was effectively caring on her own and experiencing a high level of guilt and stress at being unable to care for her parents.

In some cases, women had received help from their 'natural' families (mainly their mothers) with child rearing. This may involve the child returning to stay with family in the country of emigration. In one case, a young French woman, separated from her daughter's natural father sent her daughter home to France for two months during a period of full-time study in the UK. While acknowledging the importance of this help to her, the woman commented, "when I went back [to collect her] she wasn't my daughter anymore and they wanted to keep her"[26]. More commonly the woman's parents, or just her mother, visited for short periods following the birth of a child. The following two case studies give some idea of more complex arrangements some women had made in order to facilitate their migration and manage their dual roles as mother and paid worker. They also illustrate the impact of migration on the 'geography' of dependency:

> **Julia came to Sweden in 1978, aged 16, in what was more or less an arranged marriage to a Greek friend of her family, resident in Sweden. The husband already had relatives in Sweden (his mother's brothers and cousins). Following the marriage she worked in a factory until her children were born and then gave up work for a while to care for them. They then sent the**

---

[25] Interviewee D087 (UK).

[26] Interviewee D009 (UK).

---

children back to start school in Greece where they were cared for by her sister and she returned to work full-time. The husband's mother subsequently came to live near them in Sweden. Julia's own parents live in Greece and are looked after by her brother who lives with them. Julia commented at this point: "I often feel that it is a burden to me not to be close to my parents – being able to take care and help them out. It is difficult to be in another country when your parents are getting older. I speak with my mother frequently on the phone...." [Husband]: "And she often phones to the children when they are in school in Greece ... almost every other day she phones!" Julia said that she found it hard not to be with her children (now aged 15, 14 and 12) but she works overtime for 10 months of the year so she can afford to go to Greece every autumn for two months and the children visit in the summer.[27]

In this complex case the woman and her husband had effectively 'exported' some of their caring obligations (towards their children) and 'imported' others (towards her husband's mother).

The family, in another case, had made a series of migrations (which was, in fact, quite common) resulting in a dislocation of family structures, further complicated by marital breakdown and employment conditions, which prevented the family actually living together for many years (and the prospect of bringing a child over).

Anna married her Portuguese husband at the age of 14 and they migrated together to Venezuela where she had her son. They then returned to Portugal. Her mother then migrated to London and was subsequently joined by Anna's husband. Some time later Anna moved to London, leaving her son in Portugal with her aunt. She was, however, unable to live with her husband or mother as they all had live-in jobs [domestic work]. Some four years later she decided to go and fetch her son, "... and then one day I decided to bring my son from Portugal. I went straight to my aunt's to see him and he just stood there staring

---

[27] Interviewee D240 (Sweden). Interviewer comments on this interview suggest that the (unplanned) presence of the respondent's husband during the interview, and his insistence on answering on behalf of his wife, may well have resulted in a more guarded response to this situation on the woman's part.

at me and then he said 'mummy'. Poor thing! From that day
I will never leave a child of mine behind. I will take them
everywhere with me." All four of her brothers now live in
London, one with her mother and her sisters remain in Portugal.
Anna's parents are divorced and her father lives in Newcastle.
She goes home every summer so that her aunts can help to
look after her son.[28]

The woman in the following interview has experienced multiple and
substantial caring relationships since her migration. Much of the interview
was taken up in discussing the impact of these on her working life. Caring
for her own children, with little parental support and with evidently little
help from her husband who worked long hours himself, she then assumed
the role of step-mother with an additional responsibility for five children.
Because of complications connected to her and her partner's marital and
financial status (in Ireland), the interviewee also had to contribute financially
to the maintenance of her five step-children; she had to both 'care for' and
'care about' the se children. Together, she felt that the pressures of caring
contributed to her own ill-health and evolving dependency. The
geographical separation from her parents has meant that she can neither
effectively support them nor them her, resulting in tremendous emotional
pressure and guilt.

Helen met and married her Irish partner in England and
subsequently moved to Ireland with him. Her partner had five
children by a previous marriage and they had two children
themselves. Helen has had considerable problems stemming
from her partner's previous marriage and divorce (in England),
affecting her own marital status (in Ireland) and the legitimacy
of her children. In practice, this meant that for a long period
she was looking after her own children during the week, as
well as working full-time and had her five step-children at the
weekends: "I was surrogate mother to five kids, not quite an
Order, but Court instructions". She now suffers from multiple
sclerosis and is on long-term disability benefit. As a result she
is no longer able to make regular visits to see her very elderly
parents in England (as she used to) and they are no longer fit
enough to visit her: "I am not able to go so easily now as I find

---

[28] Interviewee D056 (UK).

travelling on my own on the ferry, for instance, very difficult. My parents don't live in a town close to an airport so therefore it is a lot of travelling to get to see them. Equally, a lot of travelling for them to come here. I worry about what will happen as they get older still. My sister doesn't live near to them so there is nobody there. They don't have any family nearby, it worries me and also it worries me they don't tell me when things happen. My mother was in hospital and it was very serious, she didn't tell me until afterwards not to worry me. She could have died."[29]

While the problems of sole caring and lack of family support affect all women, the experience is particularly marked for single mothers and for those women caring for children with disabilities. The tensions that this creates are evidenced in the following interview with a mother of two disabled children, one of whom had quite a severe disability. As a consequence of this, she received even less help from her own mother (who felt unable to cope in a foreign country with disabled grandchildren), was less well integrated in the local community and less able to support her parents.

Marie migrated initially for her own career, subsequently married an English man and then made a number of intra-regional moves for his career: "Being foreign you don't have any family around. I think when I compare myself to other people – a sister in the village, a mother [nearby] .... The friends I have are usually in the same situation as me. We find it very difficult with the two children. In fact last September we paid [a childminder] to have both children for 24 hours. We stayed in the house – we went to that extreme – we just wanted 24 hours. I've got some in-laws but they've never done anything – now they're getting old but they haven't always been old. My husband is a bit furious because his mother had a lot of help off her own mother so she should have reciprocated but she

---

[29] Interviewee D555 (Ireland). The concealment of family illness was a common concern for many women who felt that they lacked full knowledge of the situation 'back home': "At the time I didn't know how serious it was, but my mother couldn't do anything so my sister and my father took care of her without letting me know how serious things were ... I don't know what I would have done if they would have told me. It is very hard to say", Interviewee D232 (Sweden).

never did. Fair enough, I'm not her daughter but she has no daughter only two boys. Oh, she'll help in a crisis – like when I was in hospital. I'd love to be able to go away for a weekend without the children but this is something I cannot really do with my parents when they are here – much as I would love to do it – given the type of children we have. My mother would like to offer that but she would not like being responsible in a foreign country where she doesn't know the language and I understood. She said if anything happened ... but when we went to France we could do it a little bit – not any more because they're too old. Even when we moved [house] they are there all the time, there is nothing you can do about it. With my husband we really suffer from that and in France it's a bit different – the family bond is a bit stronger – I think that's a big thing in the Latin countries."[30]

This woman subsequently suffered severe problems of depression resulting in her hospitalisation for a period of several months. In another case the woman cared for a disabled child on her own, as a single parent, with little support from either family.

Claudia met her English partner while he was based in Germany in the army. They moved to England, had a child and separated only five months later. They never married. At this point the woman moved to another part of the UK to be close to her sister (who later returned to Germany). The child is now six and suffers from a mental illness (autism); he has severe communication problems and attends a special school for disabled children. As a consequence, she is unable to work full-time. Part-time work also proved not to be an option as it meant that she lost all her benefits (including the child's disability allowances). She is now unemployed and her life revolves around her son who consumes all her attention: "My son is all there is for me ... as soon as he gets home from school, my life stops and it's just him". The child's father and English grandparents have kept in contact with the child but otherwise she receives no family support.[31]

---

[30] Interviewee D001 (UK).
[31] Interviewee D017 (UK).

Many of the women interviewed had experienced caring for children as a single parent at some point since their migration, even if they had a partner at the time of interview. In some cases, migration was itself triggered by a relationship breakdown and, in others, precipitated such a breakdown. Where children are involved, family breakdown typically results in high levels of sole caring.

The discussion above has focused on the informal support structures experienced by migrant women caring for their own children. Although childcare was the most common source of caring responsibility in the country of residence, other women referred to obligations towards other members of their and their partner's families, including step-children and siblings. In one case, an Italian woman who came to England after the war to be with her recently widowed sister is now caring for her following a deterioration in her health in a relationship characterised by a very high level of interdependency.

A significant proportion of women not only cared for their own children but also for the children of their partners and, in some cases, ex-partners (as in the case of Helen [D555], above) – one of the most common forms of caring obligations outside motherhood. This often takes the form of intermittent care, with children perhaps visiting for summer vacations but, in some cases, involves an ongoing parental relationship. Some examples are given below.

Caring for step-children

Maria moved to Sweden from Portugal with her Swedish husband where they had three children together before the relationship broke down. She subsequently met and married another Swedish man who had two children from a previous marriage. Maria is currently on maternity leave following the birth of another child and is now responsible for looking after six children between the ages of one and 18 years (including three 12-year-olds!).[32]

Isabel lives in England with her husband and their new baby. She would like to return to Spain with her family but is unable to do so until her husband's three children from a previous relationship, who live nearby, have left school.[33]

---

[32] Interviewee D247 (Sweden).
[33] Interviewee D014 (UK).

"My family is sort of mixed up. I was married for many years to the father of my two boys and the boys are 24 and 20 and I divorced him some years ago. Then I remarried and together we have five children from 16 to 24. And last year we had two of them, my son who is 20 but he is back in Gothenberg now for his studies and we have still my husband's youngest son and he is in the Swedish school. So I have my two boys, my new husband and my step-children and his parents too. They're very old."[34]

In such cases involving 're-constituted' families, the period of caring is typically extended and the age span of children quite broad, thus distorting simple models of mothering. The importance of seeing caring as a life-course phenomenon is also emphasised in a couple of interviews in which women had resumed caring for children in their adulthood. In one example, a woman is now caring for her 45-year-old son. The whole of this woman's life, and her migration history, has been shaped by caring relationships of one form or another.

Helen came to England after the war to stay with a friend and look after her child while she went out to work. She then returned to France to care for her own mother who had become ill. While in England she had met a young man who subsequently asked her to marry him: "Obviously I refused, I didn't want to leave my country. My mother was already a widow and she had only me to rely on". Eventually the man moved to France to marry her, where they lived for 18 years with their son and her mother. When their son reached the age of 18 (and the mother died), the son decided he wanted to be English, so they moved to England. Her husband died five years ago and the son, now aged 45 and unable to work because of illness, has returned to live with his mother.[35]

Another important source of caring obligations in the host State derived from their relationships with nationals of the host State and the extended family thereof. The existence of dependencies on the male partner's side of the family had an important influence on the migration and location

---

[34] Interviewee D093 (UK).
[35] Interviewee D033 (UK).

decisions of many migrant households. While such decisions (to locate near dependants) clearly affected the personal autonomy of the women concerned and their ability to work and care for their own children, for example, given the gendered nature of even in-law caring relationships, they also restrict the woman's ability to expend her caring resources within her family back home. The following examples give some typical scenarios in which women had taken on caring for members of her partner's family.

Caring for parents-in-law

When Louisa's mother-in-law died she refused to allow her father-in-law to move into residential care – a preference for family care which she attributes to her cultural background: "Nothing compares to living in one's own family and growing old with them ... because in Spain family bonds are the strongest. The family is so important for us. You see, my husband is an only child and when his mother died five years ago his father tried and lived for a while by himself in their flat in London, but then became incapable of looking after himself and was ready to enter a nursing home. But I didn't want him to, I mean nursing homes in ... are supposed to be very nice but I just couldn't get rid of him, sending him to one of them. We are his family, we have to keep him with us, he's happy, my children are happy – they adore him, and I'm happy as well, even though it is not always easy to put up with elderly people, but I think I did the right thing."

It is interesting to note that later in the interview, talking about her own daughter, however, she said that she expected her to 'return' to live in Spain, thus reducing the possibility of family care for herself in her old age.[36]

Helga moved to Greece, married a Greek man and has two children at home (aged 14 and 19). She also looks after her husband's father and brother who live next door. Until recently she made regular visits to Germany to look after her sick mother, until her mother died.[37]

---

[36] Interviewee D035 (UK).
[37] Interviewee D407 (Greece).

> Jane migrated to Greece as a single person, subsequently married and has two young children (aged two and five). Her parents and brother later moved to join her but are not presently in need of any care. Her husband's mother, however, lives in a separate apartment very close to theirs: "We help her because she is old, she has kidney illness and she needs our help very much".[38]

While the overall impression was one of loneliness, isolation and sole caring, a small number of women had received informal support from other women in the community – from neighbours and friends. In one example, the neighbour of a single mother, who worked shifts, had provided considerable support, taking and collecting her child from school every day[39]. Another woman referred to the local mother and toddlers group as a 'lifeline'[40]. In an unusual case, several of the English women interviewed in Sweden had got together and effectively 'pooled' resources:

> "We were three families with English-speaking parents, who had children of the same age and we were all working part-time. So all the children went to one house one day, then they went to another house one day and so on ... we shared the five children between us. It was very good actually because they all spoke English all the time, even in the day care. It was mostly the women who took care of the children, obviously. Sometimes the men helped out, because we all had fairly flexible jobs. But the main responsibility was the women's, since the men were working full-time."[41]

Caring responsibilities in the country of origin

In addition to the caring responsibilities women had in the country of residence, virtually all the women interviewed had family in the country of emigration. In some cases, their own families had dispersed as a consequence of migration, to other countries. Indeed, it was quite common

---

[38] Interviewee D437 (Greece).
[39] Interviewee D009 (UK).
[40] Interviewee D554 (Ireland).
[41] Interviewee D208 (Sweden).

---

for siblings to have also migrated, either to the same location as the women interviewed or to other countries. This spread of constantly evolving family resources and dependencies presented the migrant women with complex dilemmas. A few general points can be made about the interviews. Firstly, where there are a number of siblings remaining in the country of origin, the problem is less acute. In families with a large number of children, the women generally experienced less pressure both at an emotional level and, in practice, to take on caring responsibilities. In many cases, even where siblings existed, however, they also lived long distances from their parents. The gender of proximate siblings was also a factor for although it was quite common for the women's brothers to have taken on a caring role, this was more usually in cases where they were the sole remaining sibling (in other words, no sisters were present). It was generally more common, and expected, for daughters to take on caring roles *even when they lived in another country*. In some cases, this derived from women's own sense of obligation. As one woman put it, "It's always the girls who feel most responsible when it comes to taking care of parents"[42]. A French woman, living in Portugal, said that she felt more responsibility than her brothers in France because she was the only girl and, "... as a daughter I feel I should be the one to look after them"[43]. In other cases, the women's response appeared to reflect a sense that their parents had gendered expectations. One woman felt that she may have to return to Greece to care for her father, despite the fact that she had brothers close by because, as she puts it, "It is the daughter who would give the glass of water rather then the son, so he [her father] would expect me to do it"[44].

The gendered nature of caring obligations was sometimes reinforced on a more pragmatic level by the lack of support provided or anticipated by male siblings: "they [her brothers] do not at all take care of [my mother] or feel that they have any caring responsibilities towards her. But anyway, my family is very traditional when it comes to who did what and what you were supposed to do if you were a boy or girl"[45].

This inability to rely on support from male siblings was also emphasised in the case of an Italian woman resident in Sweden. Having recently returned to Italy for a month to look after her father and support her

---

[42] Interviewee D209 (Sweden).
[43] Interviewee D322 (Portugal).
[44] Interviewee D060 (UK).
[45] Interviewee D213 (Sweden).

mother in the period leading up to his death, she reflects on the prospects of her mother's need for care in the future:

> **"Even though my brothers are living in the same house as my mother now, I don't think that they will take the caring responsibility for our mother if she would become ill. I think that if that happens – God forbid – my sister or I will probably go back to be close to her."**[46]

Respondents' perceptions of their caring responsibilities were particularly acute when they were the sole child or sole female sibling. Family responsibilities in the country of origin extended not only to parents (and in-laws), although this was most common, but also to grandparents, siblings and other relatives. One woman expressed a strong sense of responsibility towards her mother-in-law from a previous marriage:

> **"I have another mother-in-law who's my first husband's mother and she lives on her own now and it's difficult to look after her; she won't come over here. I was widowed when I was 30. My husband who died was an only child and his father died as well and I feel sort of responsible for her. And it's very difficult to help her, I can't really do much 'cause she's depressed but if I lived in England I would visit her more often than I can now."**[47]

The nature of caring responsibilities ranged from ongoing intensive 'hands-on' personal care to prolonged vacations to care or relieve other sibling carers or to undertake other forms of caring, such as sending money, making arrangements for residential care, offering advice and emotional support (often by telephone although there were a number of women in Sweden who communicated by e-mail). Some women were in telephone contact on a daily basis with parents in their country of origin, fulfilling an important role in supporting family 'back home'.

Faced with the reality or prospect of caring obligations in their country of origin, women responded in a variety of ways. Some brought family over to join them in the host State; others returned either for regular short visits to care or to support sibling carers or by spending extended periods back home (particularly in cases of serious illness). In other cases,

---

[46] Interviewee D249 (Sweden).
[47] Interviewee D533 (Ireland).

women, perhaps unable to give personal care, provided support through financial contributions, by liaising with welfare organisations (making arrangements for residential or domiciliary care) or by 'organising' informal networks of support.

It was quite common for migrant women to be joined by family members, particularly when care was needed or anticipated. The right to free movement and residence in Community law extends to family members in the ascending line of both migrant workers and their spouses and provides for full access to the social advantages of the host Member State. It is clear from the interviews that this right was being exercised without too much difficulty. The following cases are typical.

Bringing dependants over to care

After the death of her father, Tania's mother, who suffered from Alzheimer's Disease, moved to Portugal to be cared for by her daughter.[48]

Tracey moved to Italy and married an Italian man. They now have two children aged 13 and 16. Her mother (who was originally from Italy but had moved to England as a young woman) then moved to Trieste: "She wanted to come back and we thought it would be the best thing to do also in order to be able to look after and support her".[49]

Mary, her husband, their children and her mother are living in Sweden. Her mother came over shortly after the initial migration, when she was 80 years old and is now 93:

"My mother has been in need of extra care for a long time now, and her migration to Sweden was a result of this. I wanted to be closer to her. A year before she came, my mother was very depressed and socially isolated and we felt that the only thing that we could do was to look into what the possibilities were for her to come to Sweden. We suggested it and she accepted. She didn't have anything to lose, all her friends were dead, she was retired and I was her only child. So the first four

---

[48] Interviewee D363 (Portugal).
[49] Interviewee D602 (Italy).

years she stayed with us, then she moved to her own apartment where she got extra help whenever she needed it. Today she is in an alms house and thinks that she couldn't be better off... We are also starting to prepare ourselves for getting old, and none of us believe that we would like to stay here when we are retired, since our jobs mean everything to us while we are here. So we are planning to live in England for six months a year and in Sweden for the rest of the year for some years and try to figure out how Swedish we really are. I don't care much for the way elderly people are being treated in Sweden, so I think we will be better off in Britain. Also we do not want to stay here just to be close to our children, even though we were overwhelmed when our youngest son addressed the issue and, very concerned, asked 'But who will take care of you if you go back?'. But I never want to become a burden to my children.'[50]

The last case here illustrates very well the geography of dependency over the life-course as the woman reflects upon her own old age, the onset of dependency and the implications for her children, now fully integrated into Swedish life.

Many women were faced with the dilemma of whether to bring their parents over to stay with them in the host country or whether to return, themselves, to care. While these women may have the legal right to bring their parents over to live near to them, this was not always practicable or desirable from either the woman's point of view or that of the dependant. 'Moving to join' daughters was often considered to place family relationships at risk and also to be a poor solution for the parents themselves, mainly due to language problems and concerns about their ability to integrate and the implications in terms of welfare entitlement. The 'option' of moving dependants to be closer to their daughters was less likely to be exercised in cases of sudden unanticipated or acute illness and more common in cases where relatives anticipated the onset of dependency well in advance, or where they were suffering from long-term chronic and degenerative diseases, such as dementia. The following cases give some example of the problems women experienced or anticipated in bringing their parents over and the impact of migration on family structure.

---

[50] Interviewee D219 (Sweden).

Cases where women had experienced difficulties in bringing their parents over to join them

"They are quite old – my father is 75 and mother 81. They are OK at the moment. My brother pops in and sorts them out; it's difficult for me – it's too far but there is no way they could come and live in England. They don't speak English for a start and they wouldn't want to. If one of them did become ill, we have talked about it ... they have made arrangements; my father had a brother in a neighbouring village and there is a sort of home there and they would go into that set up ... I don't like it – I don't have a choice – purely because we are too far and also I couldn't possibly take them in to live with me – purely because I am in England – and an 85-year-old can't just come and live in another country. I couldn't uproot my family and go over there because my children are English children with an English education and you can't just ... as I say, I don't like it, I would have considered it, not my duty in the sense of it being a chain around my neck, but to look after my parents, but that's not going to be possible."[51]

Jade lives in England with her English husband and two young children. Her father died in Germany two years ago aged 80:

"He just got senile and very slow. They tried to adjust his medicines and then within a week he just died. My mum rang on the Saturday so I took a flight on the Monday but by the time I arrived he had already died. I was really sad because I would liked to have seen him. On the other hand I'm glad he died so quickly. The only hitch was getting the children together and getting out there. [Mary] wasn't on my passport so we had to dash to the embassy – it was a bit traumatic. I worry about my mum now, she's 75 and my sister has three children of her own and health problems of her own so I don't think she would be able to look after her. If she became dependent I couldn't bring her over here because she doesn't speak English. I don't really know what would happen. I just really hope that she will just die in her sleep one day while she is still ... I hope

---

[51] Interviewee D020 (UK).

that for us, because it would be really difficult – I wouldn't know what to do with the children. I would have no problems going back for a couple of months and looking after her but I couldn't do that forever. Also they are starting school now and also I wouldn't want to take children to look after. I don't mind them seeing someone dying but it wouldn't be comfortable for my mum to have three screaming brats around! It does worry me. My husband's parents are old too but he has three sisters so it's less of a problem but I have said to him that I would have them here. It's more difficult for my mum because she doesn't speak English. If she had Alzheimer's I might bring her over – then again I'm not sure about her healthcare. She has good insurance in Germany. I don't know how she would be looked after here – she doesn't have a GP. She has good health insurance in Germany."[52]

The point this woman raises about health insurance and the comparability of social arrangements between the Member States concerned was frequently raised. Most commonly, this concern reflected a lack of awareness of domestic provision and entitlement, both in the country of emigration (which many had left some years before) and in the host State. This lack of knowledge makes it very difficult, in practice, for women to exercise citizenship and make informed decisions. Not only does this apply to women at the point of making the migration decision (when issues about career or relationships may take precedence), but also subsequently as circumstances change, in re-negotiating their position, in response to evolving family obligations. In some cases, women were making informed 'choices' based upon their understanding of the different welfare systems, "For me it will be complicated to make her come mainly because the structures existing in Portugal have nothing to do with those in France, in terms of health for instance"[53].

Clarissa, now living in England, was fairly confident that her parents would be well cared for by the state in Sweden: "You go from one care-taking into another one so I think I feel very secure in Sweden about that. I'm not so sure that I would feel safe here. But, well I have friends, female friends in Italy and

---

[52] Interviewee D013 (UK).

[53] Interviewee D346 (Portugal).

they have been living there for 20 and 30 years. And they always said, 'Oh! you must be happy that you have your old parents in Sweden – you can't understand how it is in Italy!'. They take care of old people in Sweden."[54]

It is important to note that many women reported satisfaction with residential care facilities in their 'home' country. To some extent this may reflect the fact that such provision is more widely available and of higher quality, but also, and partly as a consequence of that, there was less cultural pressure for women to perform informal care tasks as a matter of duty. Where this was the case there was clearly less pressure on the women concerned to restructure their lives in order to be able to provide informal care. This was particularly evident in cases involving Swedish and German women who were, in general, more prepared to accept residential care as a solution to dependency in old age. Italian and Spanish women, on the other hand, were less inclined to see this as a solution reflecting, to some extent, the under-development of statutory welfare provision for elderly people, the expense of private care and the stigma attached to using 'formal' services. It is interesting to note that migrant women in Sweden also appeared more ready to accept the idea of residential care for their parents, irrespective of their country of origin, suggesting that the 'culture of care' in Sweden had affected their own judgements.

Recognition of the implications of welfare retrenchment, even in Scandinavian systems, was evident, however, and raised, for some women, the prospect of a future of uncertainty. The following quote from a Danish woman living in Sweden evidences this problem of planning for old age in a period of welfare restructuring:

"If my mother would need help ... she would probably go into a nursing home. I hope so, at least. But you never know. The social welfare system in Denmark is degenerating and people have to start saving and investing their money in all sorts of insurances to be used when they get older."[55]

Returning to care

'Returning to care' often involved women giving up careers (even when

---

[54] Interviewee D093 (UK).
[55] Interviewee D218 (Sweden).

the visits were relatively short) and caused considerable stress within families. For women with young children in the host State this dilemma was most poignant and painful:

> **"I don't think it would be possible for me to move to Germany in order to help my father at this time because my children would have a hard time getting adjusted to another migration and another culture once again. My father wouldn't like to come to live in Sweden. He needs his own social network and his own doctors."**[56]

Indeed, the majority of women who said that they either had or were prepared to return to care did not have children to care for. The age of the children was also an important factor here; women with pre-school children were, in some respects, more 'footloose', while women with children at primary and secondary school were particularly tied to the host State. Walker has used the concept of a 'new generational contract' to describe the impact of welfare restructuring, characterised by service withdrawal and reductions in social expenditure, on caring obligations creating profound and complex tensions within families which, he suggests, "has all the pent-up potential of a pressure cooker to create new conflicts both between carers and older relatives and within carer's own nuclear family"[57]. The interviews illustrate the specific manifestation of this dynamic over time and space. In other cases, women were torn between their responsibilities towards their partner's parents and their wish to be with their own parents:

> **"The problem is I should like to go to Italy, not every Christmas, but once. But now we can't because of his parents. He told me last year if you want to go, you can go, but I can't. They are like parents to me so I can't leave them. They're so old – 86."**[58]

As is often the case in relation to caring, partly because state services increasingly take the form of crisis management rather than intervention

---

[56] Interviewee D209 (Sweden).

[57] Walker, A. (1996) 'Intergenerational relations and the provision of welfare', in A. Walker (ed) *The new generational contract: Intergenerational relations, old age and welfare*, London: UCL Press, p 35.

[58] Interviewee D563 (Ireland).

to prevent situations deteriorating into crises and partly because of the difficulty of moving persons who become sick, women were often presented with a situation which required them to return or stay 'home'. For some women caring obligations deferred their initial migration.

Delaying moving to care

"My mother died in 1985 and it was foremost my family who helped my father and stayed with him every weekend. And it was my children actually who helped him through the crisis. I was hesitant for a long time to go to Sweden. I thought that no, I can't move. I feel that I have a responsibility for my father's well-being even though I have two brothers and one sister still living in Germany."[59]

"At the time of the migration my father was pretty ill. At one point we thought he might die. Then it felt terrible having to move so far away. So I decided that I'd only go if his condition was improved and it was. But for a long time after the migration I felt very guilty for moving away from my father especially ... When he was sick it was mostly my mother and I who took care of him, you see, and I didn't want to leave my mother alone with the responsibility. I do have a brother but he doesn't feel that he has any obligations towards our parents, but I feel that I really want to help them out, especially if they are ill."[60]

In other cases, women had returned home after the initial migration because of caring obligations. The following cases illustrate the type of migrations women are involved in, as carers, in managing a complex web of dependency.

Orla moved to London, with her cousin, in search of work in 1959 where she met her Irish partner. Following the death of her mother, she gave up her job and returned home to care for her sick father for a period of over two years during which time her brother also died. She then married her partner and returned to London where they had three children.[61]

---

[59] Interviewee D209 (Sweden).
[60] Interviewee D229 (Sweden).
[61] Interviewee D058 (UK).

> Karen had to leave her job in England and her two sons (then aged about 18 and 20) for a period of just over two years when her widowed mother in Denmark became ill herself (and eventually died). During this period she describes herself as, "constantly moving backwards and forwards".[62]

> Liz moved from Italy to England to work and then married her English partner. She is an only [adopted] child and sees the care of her mother as her responsibility: "My husband knows quite well that if anything happens to them, I will be going back there for as long as it takes – it's the way I was brought up. It's always been like that so I automatically grew up knowing that I would have to look after my parents". Although her mother is not currently in need of care herself – she cares on a full-time basis for her own mother. Liz currently returns home on a regular basis for several weeks at a time to give her mother a break from caring for her 96-year-old grandmother.[63]

Issues of spatial proximity mediated the effects of migration in some cases. This was particularly evident in the case of migrations between Finland and Sweden and Ireland and the UK, where intra-Community migration posed broadly similar problems to intra-regional migrations. In such cases, migrant women's location decisions (in the host State) were often influenced by the need to remain as close as possible to their parents. This phenomenon was also identified in some of the other interviews, however, where access to specific rail or air links and location in a particular region, in practice, meant that the women effectively remained the closest carer. This was evident in some of the interviews held in Plymouth, for example, where access to France and Spain was quite good. For those women interviewed who worked in areas connected with tourism, which was quite common, this also often afforded them special travel concessions enabling them to make regular visits home. In one case, a French woman's decision about her prospective career was guided by issues of proximity. Although she has a sister in France, the fact that her sister is married, and the interviewee single, places greater pressure on her to be available to help should the need arise. In practice, because of her location and access

---

[62] Interviewee D072 (UK).
[63] Interviewee D002 (UK).

---

to travel (as a language teacher) she says that she now sees her parents more often than she did before she migrated:

> "That's why in a way when I was looking for a job I always look for somewhere where I can go fast – I can be home today. I have always considered it. It depends how bad they were, perhaps I would consider giving up my job for some time but I would probably come back – I don't know. My sister's married and works full-time – she's more busy than I am. If I was needed probably I would have to go. They live one hour's drive from Roscoff so I go back every six weeks – it's OK – expensive but...."[64]

This interview illustrates some of the economic costs of caring for, and maintaining contact with, family abroad. The financial implications of migration, in terms of long-term caring obligations, were referred to by many women in the interviews. In some cases, this involved sending remittances home to pay for care (nursing, home helps etc) or as a form of income support, while in others, women referred to the prohibitive cost of returning to care and the measures they had taken to ensure that they could, if necessary, return to care for family in their home State. Many women expressed considerable guilt at their inability to provide support both to the dependent parent and also to their siblings left with sole care:

> "Well my parents are really old now and it is my sister who has been taking care of them ever since they started to need extra care. She lives very close so she takes care of them because they don't want to have some stranger coming home to them taking care of them. But I sometime wish that I could be closer to help my parents but especially I feel that I should help my sister. It is really hard on her and it is not really fair that she has to take care of them all alone just because I live so far away. My father is 87 years old and he is very ill. I feel a bit guilty since my sister is pretty ill herself and in no condition to take care of anyone else but herself ... But I can't say that I've ever considered moving back just to be able to help my parents and they would never like to come here."[65]

---

[64] Interviewee D021 (UK).

[65] Interviewee D238 (Sweden).

Martha lives in England with her husband and two grown-up sons. Her mother, in Sweden, is a widow in need of constant care. Her sister who has three children to care for, has taken on the role of prime carer for the elderly mother. At the time of the interview, it became apparent that this 'arrangement' was beginning to show signs of strain. Talking about care for her mother, the woman replied:

> "That is a very, very pertinent question because I've just been told by my sister who, as I've told you, is a teacher, she's got eight weeks holiday and she told me she is not going to look after mother for eight weeks but wants my help. And I said to her that I'm happy to help but that I have not got eight weeks holiday. Yes, if my sister seriously asked me to come and help her look after mother I would certainly consider it very, very seriously...."[66]

The stress in this case clearly arises from the need to support her sister as sole carer in a relationship of increasing dependency. The respondent's words suggest a defensive reaction to a situation which presents real dilemmas for her as a woman with a good full-time career, a husband and two grown-up children in Sweden. While she has been unable, to date, to provide much practical help, the interviewee later said that she telephoned her mother every day.

For other women, the guilt of being unable to care in the past, because of distance, children or career, particularly when the dependent person subsequently died, is carried by them for years ahead:

> "My mother turned ill about 10 years ago and died in 1989. At that time I had just had my third child and didn't have the possibility to go to her to visit as often as I should. Ever since she died I've felt somewhat guilty for not having been there more often. I should have been there. A long time after her death these kind of thoughts have appeared and I still feel bad about this."[67]

Many women who had not yet needed to care for their parents, nevertheless experienced constant anxiety over the prospect and its impact on their lives, torn between family commitments in their country of residence,

---

[66] Interviewee D069 (UK).
[67] Interviewee D239 (Sweden).

career and a sense of obligation towards their families back home. Indeed, this was the single most difficult issue facing the interviewees. In all, 94 women expressed real concern at the prospect of having to care for someone back home in the future.

Conclusion

This chapter began by referring to the tendency, in academic research and within EU policy agenda, to treat 'mothering' and 'caring' as distinct activities and, furthermore, to locate them in distinctive philosophical debates. This apparent polarisation of the citizenship debate between motherhood and paid work on the one hand, and carers and services on the other, has failed to capture the complexity of caring relationships over time and space. By focusing interest on two, apparently distinct, periods, there is a tendency to view caring as simple, practically unrelated, phases in most women's lives. In practice, this is evidently not the case. The findings of the interviews suggest a far more complex reality characterised by periods of tension and reciprocity throughout the life-course. To the extent that such 'phases' were ever significantly distinct, they increasingly eclipse one another in modern Western societies. The impact of demographic change, delayed marriage and family formation, declining fertility, the extension of the concept of youth and parental responsibility, increasing levels of separation and divorce coupled with re-marriage, set in the context of widespread welfare retrenchment and the privatisation of social responsibility, all lead to a reality in which reference to a simple, biologically-determined chronology becomes increasingly meaningless. In practice, a complex interplay of dependencies, interdependencies or reciprocities and new forms of exploitation coexist. It is only by disentangling these and evaluating their impact on different groups of women that we can begin to understand women's experiences as citizens.

This multitude of tensions and opportunities have an important, typically overlooked, spatial dimension which is present for all women, but is particularly dramatic in the case of international migrants juggling not only sheer distance but also different jurisdictions. The development of social rights under the free movement provisions begins to create a framework of entitlement at EU level with the barebones of a 'family policy' enshrined in legal provisions. The effectiveness and impact of that policy, even when judged against its own narrowly economic objectives, is likely to be limited. Implicit in the provisions is the assumption that European citizens are aware of their rights and are thus able to make informed decisions. The right to non-discrimination implies that potential migrants will not be deterred from migrating on the grounds that they will have unrestricted access to social advantages in the host State. Of course what matters to migrants is not the non-discrimination principle as such, but their material entitlement. In order to be able to behave as active citizens, migrants require full information on their rights – and knowledge of the practical implications of their migration – prior to their decision. Simply providing the theoretical entitlement to bring dependants over to join the migrant worker is not adequate. The implications of caring obligations for migrant women vary considerably, depending on the nature of provision in their country of emigration and the host State. Many women had little knowledge of what their social entitlement (as mothers and carers) was in either State and were thus unable to fully assess the implications of different options. This problem is further complicated by the fact that forms of social support which have most immediate benefit to women (childcare services and community care) are typically discretionary and generally provided by the local state[68]. The result is considerable 'unevenness' in entitlement over space at national level. The persistence of territorial injustices in social resources is further exacerbated by the fact that even these arrangements are highly fluid and subject to sudden reduction and withdrawal. While some women had an awareness of what existed 'back home' when they left, very few had an impression of what their parents could rely on today – or next year. The ability of women to access relevant information on welfare rights in the host Member State is also likely to be restricted by their migrant status[69].

---

[68] For evidence of territorial injustice in community care provision within Member States see, for example, Ackers, H.L. and Abbott, P. (1996) *Social policy for nurses and the caring professions*, Buckingham: Open University Press, pp 143-64; Johnson, N. (1990) 'Problems for the mixed economy of welfare', in A. Ware and R.E. Goodin (1990) *Needs and welfare*, London: Sage, pp 145-65; Glendinning and McLaughlin (1993), supra, note 5; Fincher (1993), supra, note 12; Giarchi, G.G. (1996) *Caring for older Europeans*, London: Arena Publishing/Gower; Melhuish and Moss (1991), supra, note 21.

[69] I am not aware of any research specifically addressing European migrants. Existing research, however, suggests that characteristics such as social class, culture and ethnicity are important determinants of access to information (Tester [1996], supra, note 4; Twigg and Atkin [1994], supra note 10). Certainly some of the interviews suggested not only a lack of awareness of sources of information but also some cases in which benefits officers were either confused or discriminatory in their approach to migrant women.

Enabling women to make informed decisions on matters as important as whether (or where) to migrate or whether to bring a dependent relative over (or to return to care), demands far more than a formal entitlement to residence and non-discrimination. At the very least, it requires the EU to take a much more active role in the collection and dissemination of information as the basis of active citizenship enabling women to consider fully the material implications of any particular decision.

At a more fundamental level, however, any attempts by the EU to safeguard women's interests and protect the rights of migrant families are entirely undermined by wider global economic and political trends (and their specific European manifestation in the lead up to monetary union). Taken together, these trends point to important pressures towards policy convergence in the form of residualisation, deregulation and retrenchment in domestic social policy. The extension of formal legal rights in the context of present macroeconomic policies, aimed at sweeping away the very infrastructure of European welfare states, suggests little genuine commitment to family policy. Any further reduction in social redistribution on needs-based criterion (to children or elderly and disabled dependants) signifying a return to 'individual responsibility', will have serious implications for migrant women as sole carers in the host Member States and as the daughters and sisters of dependants in the country of emigration.

Furthermore, recognition of the effect of this web of caring obligations, over the life-course and over space, on migrant women's abilities to maintain active labour market roles indicates the potential impact of an approach to citizenship which ties social entitlement so closely to employment status.

NINE

Conclusion

Introduction

This book, and the research project on which it is based, has tried to achieve a number of goals. At one level it has focused on a particular aspect of Community law – the right to freedom of movement for Community nationals within the European Union (EU) – and sought to evaluate that right and the associated entitlements. Focusing first on the material basis of these rights, Chapter Four demonstrated the important substantive basis of entitlement and the very real material benefits at stake. The purpose of this discussion was to emphasise a key contention underpinning the research, that the concept of 'citizenship of the Union' is not simply one of rhetorical or symbolic significance, but carries tangible and meaningful social benefit. In that sense, I have argued that it is indeed legitimate to use the language of citizenship as the basis for evaluating this area of Community law.

An examination of citizenship requires not only a description of the range of benefits on offer, however, but also detailed consideration of systems of entitlement and conditions of access. Despite the inference of a broad universality of status in the wording of Article 8, deriving from Community nationality, very rarely can claims to benefits or rights be made on the basis of citizenship as such. In practice, access to the panoply of material benefits described, hinges on more complex notions of social contribution – and the primacy attached to certain forms. Furthermore, any understanding of the effect of formal policy on people's lives demands analysis, not only of a quantitative nature, but also of the quality of that relationship and its impact on wider social relations. In particular, I have emphasised the important distinction between independent and derived entitlement. The discussion of the personal scope of the provisions thus shifts to consider what I have described as the 'tiering' or hierarchy of entitlement. In particular, given the focus of this project, Chapter Four assesses the gender implications of the rules governing access. In some respects the gendered nature of Community law in this area is quite evident, as in the interpretation of the concept of spouse. In others, the discriminatory consequence is less explicit and derives from the failure to recognise the 'economic' contribution of unpaid work and the specific barriers faced by women in gaining access to and maintaining continuous employment histories.

The very notion of policy evaluation almost suggests that policy-making processes themselves are neutral and objective and that, as such, the gendered impact lies at the implementation stage and falls into the category of 'unintended consequence' or covert discrimination. The evaluation of the legal framework governing the free movement of persons has endeavoured to move beyond a simple description – or statement of the legal position – to consider the rationale behind the inclusion of provisions and their specific extension through secondary legislation and ultimate interpretation by the European Court of Justice (ECJ). An understanding of this first 'phase' of the policy implementation process is necessary in order to appreciate the dialectical relationship between society, social relations and policy making. The introduction of measures, such as the extension of personal entitlement to families, reflects a specific interpretation of the 'problem' (barriers to mobility) and that interpretation will shape the response. It is unsurprising that the prevalence of 'common-sense' ideas about international migration (and relationships within migrant families), reinforced by the work of academic theorists, has influenced the definition of the 'phenomena' (or objective) and become manifest in the policy response.

Particular views about labour mobility, families and social relations in general, herald a specific response which, in the process, reflects and reproduces those relations, or at least the framework of opportunities and constraints that we call citizenship. Understanding the gendered nature of laws or policies demands that our evaluation extends beyond a consideration with the policy implementation process, however, and the identification of discriminatory potentials to consider the effect of policies on people's lives. This not only includes consideration of policy interaction (with the welfare systems of host Member States, for example) and the translation of EU policy into tangible material benefits (such as levels of maternity leave, unemployment benefit or the availability of childcare), but also the subjective response of the beneficiaries. Women are not passive recipients or victims of policy; in some cases they are completely unaware of their legal rights (and in that sense may be denied both entitlement and the concomitant pressures to structure their lives in accordance with those policies). In other cases, women may be fully aware of opportunities or constraints and may skilfully negotiate around those, sometimes 'choosing' not to take up certain benefits (such as nursery care) and, in other circumstances, making decisions which delimit the effect of constraints (such as returning 'home' to marry). In trying to understand citizenship we cannot, therefore, simply infer a relationship between policy and outcome. The project thus moves from an understanding of the legal framework to detailed empirical work with 'policy recipients' in an attempt to understand the material impact of the law.

The specific reference to the concept of citizenship in the Treaty on European Union itself, in the context of evaluation research, immediately suggests a reference point. Notwithstanding the problems inherent in this concept, well rehearsed in the academic literature, and discussed in some detail in Chapter Two, particularly as a benchmark for the evaluation of the quality of life of women, this project has 'stuck with it' and attempted to define the concept, as a measure of autonomy, and operationalise it using the method of life-history interviews. This approach has allowed migrant women to define, themselves, the impact of moving on their autonomy in a fairly holistic sense. As such, they have provided us with a richer understanding of the complex intermeshing of the public worlds of work and welfare with private ambitions and relationships, not at any one point in time, but over their life-course. The notion of life-course did not explicitly inform the original design of the research; at that point I had intended to compare pre- and post-migration experience. In practice, life is not like that and such a comparison would have yielded a very misleading impression; in many cases it was not so much the shift in geographical spaces that transformed a woman's autonomy but the relationship between that transition and a whole variety of other factors.

Other 'transitions', such as shifts in legal status on marriage or divorce, or the evolution of a complex web of caring needs and obligations, over time and space, shaped their interpretations of migration. The limitations of assuming a simplistic 'before and after' effect is also evidenced by the stories women told us about their moves; in most cases, women did not make one single, unilateral, migration but shifted to and fro in response to their circumstances, negotiating their lives over a number of geographical and legal spaces.

The remainder of this final chapter identifies some of the issues raised in a piece of research that has developed in a number of different directions, drawing on work across several disciplines, and attempts to synthesise some of the key themes.

The legal framework

To the extent that the evolution of citizenship rights under the free movement of persons provisions form, the basis of an incipient European citizenship, the evidence presented in Chapter Four suggests a hierarchy of entitlement based on gendered assumptions about the labour market, the family and migration behaviour. At the top of the hierarchy, those Community nationals in paid employment have full independent entitlement to equal treatment in the social advantages of the host Member State. A second tier provides derived entitlement for the legally married spouses and children of EU migrant workers for as long as their marriage and their spouse's status as a 'worker' subsists (that is, the 'worker' is not voluntarily unemployed or deported for any reason). Finally, a third category of citizenship exists which gives rise to very minimal social entitlement, requiring those who claim a right to free movement to demonstrate financial autonomy. This group includes all non-working, non-married partners of migrant workers, jobseekers, pensioners, students etc. For this group, the right to free movement itself is circumscribed by the requirement that they, "avoid becoming a burden on the social security system of the host Member State"[1]. In other words, they have no effective right to welfare.

Analysis of the provisions and their interpretation by the ECJ suggests that the development of law in this area has been influenced by presumptions based on 'traditional', ideologically-loaded and outmoded models of family relations and migration behaviour. Guided by the 'facilitating mobility' test, the Court has generally expanded its competency, extending important social rights to economically inactive members of worker's families. The rationale for the extension of these rights, however, rests on the notion that they directly or indirectly benefit the Community worker and promote his [sic] mobility. Evaluation of the case law suggested three broad areas of concern[2]:

- access to privileged status of 'Community worker' as the source of independent entitlement;
- the limitations of derived entitlement for spouses and worker's families;
- specific problems concerning the concept of 'spouse' restricting access even to derived rights.

---

[1] Council Directive 90/365.
[2] Points adapted from the Report of the High Level Panel on the free movement of persons, EC 1997.

The first area concerns the status attached to specific forms of social contribution as the fundamental determinant of citizenship status – and the primacy attached to paid work. It is not simply the fact of an 'economic nexus' as Steiner[3] suggests, but the narrow definition of this that is at issue and the exclusion of forms of work that have important economic implications (such as caring and unpaid family work, for example) but which do not fall within the definition of 'employment'. It is employment status then, as a distinct form of social contribution, that triggers the most highly privileged form of social status. The concept of worker has been interpreted generously by the ECJ to include part-time work and levels of remuneration below state subsistence levels resulting in resort to state means-tested benefits. While such interpretations are generally beneficial to women, some outstanding issues require consideration. The interpretation of the concept of 'purely marginal activities' (following *Levin and Raulin*[4]) raises some questions about the status of persons in short-term, part-time and 'on-call' forms of work.

Women involved in unremunerated caring work in the home are excluded from Community protection (unless they derive entitlement via breadwinning husbands[5]). Such activity not only fails to qualify as a recognised form of social contribution but also restricts women's abilities to undertake paid work outside the home, and qualify in their own right as workers. This problem will increase with welfare retrenchment across European societies and increased reliance on 'family care'.

Just as unpaid caring work fails to meet the requirement for remuneration (despite its economic contribution), caring obligations frequently interrupt women's abilities to undertake paid work. Women who stop 'working' in order to look after children or other relatives may lose their status as workers (and independent entitlement) if their unemployment is interpreted as 'voluntary' by the competent employment office. Regulations relating to the payment of Jobseeker's Allowance to mothers in the UK and Ireland (and the interpretation of the 'availability for work' test), at least, suggest cause for concern. The Court's refusal to take into account a person's pre-migration employment history further limits the access of many women to independent entitlement.

Furthermore, the requirement of some form of remuneration excludes from full Community protection all those women engaged in unpaid

---

[3] Steiner, J. (1996) *Textbook on EC law*, London: Blackstone Press, p 261.

[4] Supra, Chapter Four, notes 81 and 85 respectively.

[5] This, of course, places single mothers in a particularly vulnerable position.

family work, in family businesses. Although not a factor affecting many of the women included in our sample, it is important to remember that about 25% of female workers in Southern European countries undertake this type of work[6].

'Economically-inactive' partners and the families of migrant workers do not, therefore, currently derive independent entitlement under the provisions; their rights are coterminous with those of the worker and depend on the continuation of his status as worker and the subsistence of marriage or relationships of dependency (in the case of children). This creates the conditions for very high levels of personal dependency on working spouses.

Citizenship is not solely concerned with matters of material status, but also with the conditions of access to benefits and the impact of certain forms of entitlement on a person's autonomy; the fact that many married migrant women have good access to social advantages in the host State does not therefore compensate for the high levels of dependency of women whose relationships break down or who simply wish to preserve their autonomy, as individuals in their own right.

The final area of concern is with the limited definition of spouse restricting entitlement to derived benefits. We saw how the concept of spouse in Community law is not broad enough to include cohabitants, same-sex marriages, or divorced partners. Unless these persons are undertaking paid work, they are denied entitlement under the social advantages formulae. While Community nationals may retain a basic right of residence (provided they make no claims on the host social security system), partners of third country nationality, who are not legally married, may be denied residency. I have already referred, in the introduction, to the relationship between law-making and wider social relations; the effect of this narrow interpretation of the concept of spouse may be either to pressurise women into marriage (in order to preserve their legal status) or, for those who do not wish to, or cannot (perhaps because they are in same-sex partnerships or, as in Ireland, because they or their prospective partners were divorced), seriously reduce the claims they can make on the basis of citizenship. We saw in Chapter Seven how some women had gone to great lengths to negotiate this problem.

In order to understand the reasons for these loopholes and the unacceptability, for example, of Ms Reed's contention that, in order for the law to keep pace with contemporary society it ought to recognise

---

[6] European Labour Force Survey (1996).

cohabitation rights, we need to remember that the fundamental concern was not to develop a coherent approach to family policy, in a migration context. The policy objective was not to secure a comprehensive citizenship status for the partners and children of migrant workers, but rather to promote the mobility of workers themselves. Any family rights exist in order to advance that objective. As such, family policy has developed in an uneven and, to some extent, incoherent fashion, responding to changing perceptions about migration behaviour (and the identification of 'new' barriers to mobility) rather than seeking to adapt to changing patterns of family life. Family rights have thus evolved 'through the back door' through the Court's interpretation of the 'facilitating mobility' test. The Court has made no attempt to disguise this fact. Even in extending entitlement to Ms Reed on the grounds that cohabitation was recognised in The Netherlands, the Court made it very clear that this was not for her benefit, as a citizen, but for his benefit as a worker, "to assist his integration in the host state and thus contribute to the achievement of freedom of movement for workers"[7].

This summary of some of the key issues arising from an evaluation of the legal provisions indicates the influence of the male breadwinning model of migration behaviour on the evolution of the law. The second 'phase' of the research undertook to 'test' this model against the empirical reality of intra-Community migration using available secondary data on migration flows and the in-depth interviews with migrant women.

The material presented in Chapter Five demonstrates how, contrary to popular belief and academic literature, women make up around half of all Community migrants and, in many cases, dominate European migration flows. The numbers of women moving to live in another Member State outnumbers that of men in nearly every country. Of particular interest here is the destination of many migrant women. Women dominate both out-migration from countries typically regarded as 'woman-friendly' with more progressive family policies (such as Denmark, for example) and migration into the most woman-hostile countries (such as Greece). The data does not support the theory that female migration is characterised by subsequent family reunion; the length of residence of male and female migrants being broadly coterminous. The evidence on marital status, furthermore, suggests that the majority of migrant women were not

---

[7] *Netherlands State v Reed*, Case 59/85 [1986] ECR 1283.

married when they first moved[8]. While aggregate data suggests a figure of around 54% were married at the time of survey, our own research, which looked at changes in marital status before and after migration, found that only 27% of women were married when they moved (and of these, not all moved with their partners). Indeed, some 65% migrated as single women, corroborating the findings of Pauline Jackson's study of Irish emigration which found that, in the 1961-71 period, 87% of Irish women emigrants were unmarried and a further 8% were widows, "Thus a full 95% of women emigrants left Ireland without male protection"[9].

The figures on marital status at the point of interview (post-migration) paint a different picture. At this time, some 60% of women were married, 8% were either divorced or separated (a figure somewhat higher than indicated in Eurostat data, perhaps because it fails to enumerate cases of separation) and a further 11% were living in cohabiting relationships. In many cases, these women had met partners in the host State (predominantly host nationals). In addition to these ball-park figures, the interviews have demonstrated the fluidity of relationships, with many women shifting from one status to another and back again over the life-course, in response to changing circumstances.

These findings, together with the data on employment, draw attention to the fact that many migrant women, at least for periods of time, fall outside the categories of citizenship which attract optimum social protection. Moreover, this transformation in the post-migration marital status of women typically reflects a period of family formation in which almost 70% of EU migrant women with young children 'withdraw' from the labour market[10]. It is at this point that the 'rational household strategy' of male economic maximisation becomes a determining factor, shaping

---

[8] The predominance of single women in our sample of migrant women may support Linda Hantrais' suggestion (detailed in Chapter Seven) that a lack of attention to family policy – and evidence of divergence in provision – may constitute a barrier to migration for married women with families. As we did not interview women who decided not to migrate, we cannot specifically corroborate this view. What we did find, however, was that having established families in the host State, many women were reluctant to return home or migrate elsewhere, largely because of concerns about their children's integration and the comparability of education systems.

[9] Jackson, P. (1987) 'Migrant women: the Republic of Ireland', Commission of Europe, DGV/139/89, p 5.

[10] European Labour Force Survey, 1996.

women's autonomy. While the male breadwinning model proved to be a poor predictor of migration behaviour, its significance in understanding the post-migration experience of migrant women (and their relationships with partners and the welfare state) becomes painfully apparent.

Women's relationships with the labour market are highly complex and reflect a whole range of factors and attitudes; one of the most important messages coming from this research has been the need to avoid simplistic, deterministic, responses to 'social facts'. Evidently, labour market withdrawal may reflect a clear and conscious choice on the part of some women and the material discussed in Chapter Seven highlights the problems of aligning labour market participation too closely with indicators of autonomy. Nevertheless, the results of the interviews (reported in Chapters Seven and Eight) suggest that migrant women have limited access to family support with childcare at a time when family care (and care provided by grandparents) is increasingly common[11]. Migrant women lack access to the infrastructure of interdependencies and reciprocities (within the bonds of kinship and community) which provide the foundation of many women's lives, often concealed from academic research, but so important to their ability to exercise autonomy. This lack of informal support lays bare the relationship between public and private patriarchy. Migrant women in Sweden, while evidently aware of the lack of informal support, were cushioned from private dependency by public policy measures which enabled them to reconcile more effectively their caring and employment roles. Elsewhere, the situation was more stark and women had little choice but to give up employment to 'care'.

In addition to the lack of support in the bringing up of their children (and in some cases their husband's children), migrant women do not 'escape' the pressure to provide care and support for elderly and disabled members of their own, and their husband's families. Chapter Eight has discussed, in some detail, the persistence of caring obligations over space and the impact of these on migrant women's abilities to manage their roles as mothers and workers in the host State. In many cases, women have to return 'home' to care or bring their dependant relatives over to live with them. While the opportunity for ascendant relatives to join their families in the host State constitutes an important and exercised Community right, the research has shown how, in many cases, this form of 'family policy' fails to provide a solution to the evolving caring problems faced by many families. Not surprisingly, it is particularly inadequate in cases of family crisis, when

---

[11] Meltzer, H. (1994) *Day care services for children*, London: OPCS.

a relative is faced with an emergency. In the majority of non-emergency cases, however, it is also inappropriate, given the problems of integrating elderly or disabled people, often with limited language skills, into a new culture and policy context. Faced with this situation, what many women really require is a greater degree of harmonisation, coordination and generally improved provision of domiciliary services. This may not only prevent the need for another migration (of the elderly person or carer), but also relieve the amount of emotional stress placed upon women who cannot support sibling carers in the host State. The problems of divergence in policy frameworks, ever shifting goal-posts and poor communication and liaison often make care planning a difficult and distressing business for the migrant daughter.

Chapter Five referred to Bonney and Love's work on inter-regional mobility (within the UK) and its impact on the autonomy of migrant wives which concludes:

> **... unfortunately, the dilemma facing many women is that sex inequality in the home and workplace serves to attenuate the link between geographic and social mobility, which in turn perpetuates existing sex inequalities.**[12]

If these conclusions hold for inter-regional migration, then married women moving between Member States are likely to be particularly disadvantaged as systems of social entitlement at EU level are so tightly linked to employment status and marriage and informal support networks fractured by the migration process.

On a more 'positive' note, Bonney and Love speculate that the impact of inter-regional migration on women may be tempered by the fact that many wives will have played a 'secondary labour market role' prior to migration and, in any case, some occupations (such as teaching) "positively facilitate discontinuous careers". In a European context, however, this argument does not hold as these careers, particularly teaching, may prove especially difficult for migrant women to enter, as the interviews in Ireland demonstrated. Indeed the ECJ has held that the requirement of specific linguistic competencies may not contravene the non-discrimination principle. Wider concerns over the recognition of teaching qualifications were evident in many of the interviews, preventing women from resuming

---

[12] Bonney, N. and Love, J. (1991) 'Gender and migration: geographical mobility and the wife's sacrifice', *The Sociological Review*, vol 39, no 2, pp 335-48.

teaching careers in the country of immigration and also, in some cases where the woman has trained in the host country, from returning to their home state.

While marriage may constitute a constraint on the autonomy of many migrant women, the effect of divorce, in a migration context, is of even greater concern. Lichter's study of the socioeconomic returns to migration among married women concluded that:

> ... **whilst most married women do not receive positive returns to migration ... migration-induced dependency may have serious adverse effects on the socio-economic well-being of women should they become separated or divorced.**

The effect of divorce, on a non-working spouse, may, for example, be to extinguish her derived entitlement as she loses the status of the spouse of a Community worker. In cases where the male partner returns home or makes another international move, the migrant mother may also experience great difficulty in claiming maintenance for her children[13].

Any understanding of the citizenship experience of women in Europe requires an analysis of the impact of a complex web of inter-related dependencies. Women under different social systems effectively 'spread' their dependency between male partners, the welfare state, female members of the wider family and the labour market (depending on the welfare system and cultural and economic climate). For migrant women, the 'choices' are particularly stark when reliance on informal support by other women (particularly mothers and sisters) is reduced through the dislocation of extended family networks. The achievement of financial independence (and independent social entitlement) is also threatened by the fragility of migrant women's relationship with the labour market, particularly during child-rearing years. Discontinuous employment and higher levels of short part-time work, coupled with problems of unemployment, seriously undermine the value of occupational-based benefits, shifting dependency very much into the private sphere and onto male partners (where they exist). While the migration of single women signifies high levels of personal autonomy, subsequent changes in marital status and associated male-

---

[13] This is an issue we are currently taking up on a new project directed by the author on children and migration. It also forms the focus of a paper by Kirsten Grotheer entitled, 'Cross-border maintenance claims of children' in V. Gessner (ed) *Cross border legal interactions*, Aldershot: Dartmouth (forthcoming).

---

orchestrated inter-regional migrations, coupled with the arrival of children, throws many of them into high levels of dependency.

What becomes clear from the above is that both Community law and migration theory are out of step with the contemporary reality of internal migration. Models of migration based upon male breadwinner, utility-maximising, behaviour render migrant women invisible. Even those studies which attempt to examine the 'problematic connection' between individual action and the household, subsume women within the broader family failing to see them as individual actors in their own right. Thus, Lichter concludes,

> ... **migration would appear to be rational from the standpoint of the family as a whole ... [furthermore] ... many married women may willingly sacrifice their careers provided that migration improves the economic well-being of the family.**[14]

The decision of a household to migrate may appear to be 'rational' in any narrow cost-benefit analysis of aggregate family income, but at the cost of increased levels of dependency and loss of personal autonomy for female partners. Findings from the interviews suggest that, ironically, the superior language skills of the female partner (in mixed marriages) appear to underline the justification of the male breadwinning strategy. In other words, it makes rational sense to locate in the country of his nationality, as his lack of linguistic competency would adversely affect his career in another Member State. This appears to hold even in cases where women's career prospects prior to migration were objectively better than those of their partners.

We have talked, at various points in the book, about the concept of welfare tourism and the notion that the relative merits of different social systems may influence the decision to migrate or, at least, the location decision. At each point, we have presented evidence to suggest that this phenomenon is more a myth than a reality, with many women moving to areas generally considered to be 'hostile' to women. The very notion of welfare tourism, however, raises two problems. Firstly, that women can effectively weigh up the pros and cons of each anticipated move in an informed cost-benefit analysis and, secondly, that it is possible to rank domestic welfare systems along some linear continuum of gender-friendliness (on the basis that women have universal needs and goals).

---

[14] Lichter, D. (1983) 'Socio-economic returns to migration among married women', *Social Forces*, vol 62, pp 487-503.

The evidence presented in this research suggests the need to re-examine not only explanations of migration behaviour, to the extent that women do not appear to be moving in the direction predicted by economically-weighted models, but also academic preoccupation with the social status/labour market participation axis as the central determinant of citizenship[15].

The presumption of informed decision making on which the concept of welfare tourism is based requires that women are fully conversant with both their Community entitlement and the relative merits of domestic social systems. In practice, most women had quite limited awareness of their Community rights and the host social security and welfare systems (in a general sense)[16]. That this was the case does not infer a lack of intellect on their part, but rather the reality that most people only know what they are entitled to when they make a claim, or when a need arises. A woman might seek information about her unemployment benefit if she is moving in search of work but, in general, people do not research all eventualities. For one thing, they may not predict any changes in marital status or the arrival of children. Many women did not even plan to remain let alone start a family in the host State! Furthermore, in the discussions about caring obligations in the future, many women expressed concerns about the shifting basis of social entitlement (due to welfare retrenchment); as such, they could not view with any degree of certainty what their relative status might be in a few years time. Neither was it simple (or in many cases comfortable) to attempt to predict the evolution of one's own situation over the life-course (and the possibility of having a severely disabled child, for example or a dementing mother). I am not suggesting here that women respond passively, or irrationally, to different environments, nor indeed that they bury their heads in the sand but that, in practice, the level of awareness of social policy provision at national and regional level is very limited – much more so when we expect people to compare objectively across borders; that policies are constantly in flux and that life circumstances are constantly evolving (often in an unplanned fashion).

Women often referred, during the interviews, to the disjunction between formal policies and popular attitudes, resulting in the lack of take up of provisions. A very interesting example of this situation can be seen in two

---

[15] A point which applies equally to non-migrant women.

[16] This is an area in which the European Commission could do more to publicise and inform people about their rights – a concern raised by the High Level Working Party on the Free Movement of Workers and reflected in its 'Citizen First' campaigns.

of the interviews with French women in the UK. Here the women compare not simply their formal status under the two systems, but demonstrate a subtle awareness of the articulation of marital or family status with citizenship. Their views about which system best promoted their interests depended very much on their specific circumstances and the value they attribute to different dimensions of autonomy:

"I think as a single or individual, a woman is better off in France with education, childcare ... but, as a married woman, you are better off in England. As a married woman in France – I have no experience of a [French] husband but from the husbands I see in my family or friends – they seem to treat their wives in a way that is not to my liking. They certainly want dinner on the table and, 'I'll go shooting and hunting and you will look after the children'. Maybe I see it from an outsider's point of view but I wouldn't want that sort of thing – chaps would all get together and go to the cafe, shooting, rugby and the wife will go with the kids to his mother's or her mother's and get parked there for the day. Whereas in England, I haven't been parked off...."

"As a married woman I think I am better off in England but if I was divorced or single I think I'd be better off in France because there is far more support ... I am saying this because recently we did have a near divorce and because I was going to be isolated. But with the childcare ... because my husband does his share it is working out reasonable but if I didn't have a husband, which I wouldn't have if I divorced, it was going to work out horrendous. I then questioned the fact of coming to work altogether because why should I come to work just to pay childcare – you're better off on benefit looking after your own children. I then made enquiries about going to France and school was until half past five for a start and I certainly considered it, although in my position it was going to be difficult because I was going to uproot three English-speaking children to a foreign speaking country. I think if I was to be divorced with three children I would rather be in France."[17]

---

[17] Interviewee D020 (UK).

> "It's very different. English men are less macho – the way you
> can talk to a man – in France it's always a sexual thing. I don't
> see that in this country but money-wise and jobs, well ... most
> of the women I've met in England have crap jobs, crap education
> and had their kids so young, it's amazing – teenagers with
> pushchairs, my God...! In terms of male attitudes its better
> but everyday life for a woman is hard in England – if you don't
> work in France you can still put your child in a nursery and
> have time for yourself. You get a lot of help from the French
> government – and we have a minimum salary – you haven't.
> In England you can go to work just to pay the nursery school
> – that's crazy – that's nuts – I'm very happy here but life is
> easier in France."[18]

These two examples illustrate what women have identified as the
disjunction between family policy in France, at the public level, and gender
relations in the private sphere and perhaps reflect the fact that gender
equality was not the engine of French family policy, but rather procreation[19].

To the extent that women could evaluate and compare different systems
(and thus the impact of moving on their status), it was rarely a case of
ranking national systems; it was apparent from the interviews that
citizenship is not simply commensurate with measures of formal status or
material entitlement. The findings discussed in Chapter Seven highlighted
the problems of assuming universal objectives and identifying material
solutions. In order to understand citizenship, as it is experienced by women,
we need to consider systems of entitlement, in their social context, to
understand the motivations and ideological objectives underlying them
and their articulation with popular culture and the attitudes of men and
women, which together mould environments of opportunity and
constraint, shaping women's freedom to exercise choices at any point in
time. A focus on indicators of formal equality not only fails to take account
of culture (both in the host State and from the woman's own background)
but also undermines the exercise of agency. The very process of deciding
to migrate reflects the powerful sense of agency and control among this
group of women, many of whom moved on their own. The interviews in

---

[18] Interviewee D010 (UK).

[19] It is interesting to note that while the woman in the first interview had
experienced a less macho approach from British men, in the home, she also
suggested that British women were highly critical of working mothers.

Ireland perhaps best exemplify the ways in which women organised their lives (involving decisions about whether or where to marry and how to access contraception or abortion services) in order to maximise their autonomy and negotiate the obstacles that formal policy set in their path. In other cases, where the formal context appears more supportive, women may not take up entitlements, preferring instead to steer their lives in a different direction[20].

The interviews tell us something, not only about how migrant women respond to and shape their citizenship status, but also, on a wider level, about the relevance of the concept of citizenship as a vehicle for the evaluation of women's lives and about the problems of operationalising the concept. Policy evaluation based upon forms of policy description and secondary data no doubt provide us with a more 'objective' measure of the resource framework in each Member State. It was evident from the interviews that women's perceptions of social policy reflected their pre-migration experience and socialisation in another culture, colouring the lenses of comparison. Their analyses thus go beyond the juxtaposition of formal status and legal entitlements to understand the interaction between these and popular culture and the impact on expectations about care and caring responsibilities.

The interviews that formed the basis of this discussion were all undertaken by women with women. As such, they cannot reveal very much about the experience of men who migrate and the motivations that precipitate a move. The focus on women was not, however, intended to give the impression that traditional approaches provided an adequate understanding of male migrations. Indeed, the work referred to in Chapter Five[21] suggests a remarkable similarity in the arguments presented here and the experience of men who migrated to Canada at the turn of the century. The evidence of a genuine shift in parental responsibilities in the Swedish interviews might also suggest that issues of care will become an increasingly important element in the decision about whether and where to migrate on the part of male partners; in that sense, facilitating mobility

---

[20] I am thinking here of some of the women in Sweden who welcomed the existence of state nurseries but preferred to share care with their partners.

[21] I am referring here to the work of Ackers, P.B.H. (1997) 'Exodus: labour emigration from the English Churches of Christ to Canada during 1906 and 1907', *Journal of URC History Society*, vol 6, no 1; and Johnson, S.C. (1913) *Emigration from the United Kingdom to North America, 1763-1912* (1st edn 1966), London, pp 66-7.

may support the call for better arrangements for parental (and paternity) leave and flexible working opportunities for men.

We have seen how the evolution of social entitlement for EU migrants – and Community citizenship – has been primarily motivated by concerns to promote labour mobility and the limitations this narrow objective has placed on the development of the law. Recent cases indicate a shift in thinking, however, suggesting that Article 8a may, indeed, mark a deepening of the relationship between the Community and its citizens. The Opinion of Advocate General Jacobs in *Konstantinidis*[22] suggests a much broader interpretation of the concept of 'citizenship of the Union', at least in relation to the migrant worker:

> **Community law does not regard the migrant worker (or the self-employed migrant) purely as an economic agent and a factor of production entitled to the same salary and working conditions as nationals of the Host State; it regards him as a human being who is entitled to live in that State 'in freedom and dignity' and to be spared any differences in treatment that would render his life less comfortable, physically or psychologically, than the lives of the native population.**[23]

It remains to be seen whether this approach (to the citizenship status of those who qualify as 'workers') can be extended to the partners and families of Community workers. The recent deliberations of the Court in the *Martinez Sala* case[24] open the way for a radically different interpretation of Community citizenship, potentially casting aside previous limitations on personal entitlement and, in particular, established distinctions between economic and non-economic migrants. Should this line of argument be

---

[22] The case itself concerned the inaccurate translation of the applicant's surname (from Greek into German) and the extent to which this constituted an interference with his right of establishment under Article 52 EEC. While the judgment of the Court found in his favour, it did so on the somewhat tenuous 'economic' grounds that the misspelling may "expose him to risk that potential clients may confuse him with other persons".

[23] *Christos Konstantinidis*, Case C–168/91 [1993] ECR I-1191, at para 24.

[24] *Martinez Sala v Freistaat Bayern*, Case C–85/96. One of the key questions raised by the case was whether Article 8a establishes an a priori general right of residence for all Community nationals effectively replacing pre-existing residency directives – and the framework they created for a layering of citizenship entitlement.

pursued in future, many of the concerns expressed in this research over the gender implications of existing systems of entitlement (and in particular the definition of 'worker' and 'spouse' in Community law) may disappear in the face of a more genuinely universal concept of citizenship. It is, however, dangerous to place too much emphasis on one case which may be distinguished on the basis of its facts, particularly given the political implications of this logic and the pressure it might bring to harmonise domestic welfare systems.

Rees, P. 141
refugees 6, 24
regime analysis 50-2, 54, 59
Reina case 103-4
relative poverty 26-7
religion as motive for migration 162
reproductive rights 223, 254-9, 264-9
research
    action-research 23, 24
    EU funding 47, 60, 61
    Training and Mobility of
    Researchers Programme 10, 61
    see also comparative social policy
    analysis
residency *see* right of residency
residential care facilities 301
'resource framework' of women's
    lives 38, 45
retirement migration 96, 98
'reversed discrimination' 110
right of establishment 93, 109, 327
right of residency 92, 95, 96-9, 107,
    115, 127, 131, 133-5, 316, 327
    for ascendant family members
    297, 319
    of jobseekers and unemployed
    121, 122-4
risks: male risks 34
Rose, Damaris 38-9
Rose, R. 54
Ross, M. 111
Rosser, S.V. 277-8
Rubery, Jill 58

S

Sainsbury, Diane 31-2, 35
Sala judgement 90, 99, 111, 114, 138,
    327
Salt, J. 141
same-nationality migrating couples
    159-60, 166, 168, 280, 281
Sandhu case 131-2
Scandinavia 31-2
    see also Denmark; Sweden
Scheiwe, Kirsten 125, 138, 139, 223,
    225

Schunk, Michaela 72
secondary data 77, 130
    limitations of 52-62, 148
    qualitative required 58, 67
    see also European Labour Force
    Survey; official statistics
segregation: inter-generational 240,
    247
self-employment 217-18, 221
separation 128, 131-5, 138, 157, 158,
    318
    of children and mothers 286-8
sexual harassment resolution 2
Shakespeare, Tom 23
Shihadeh, E.S. 165-6
Shuttleworth, I. 172
siblings and caring 38, 294-6, 303
Siim, Birte 245-6
Singh case 134
single mothers 204, 253
    caring for dependants 289, 290,
    291
    dependency 35-6, 40, 235
single women migrants 156, 157-8,
    161, 280, 317-18, 321-2
Singleton, Ann 6, 56-7
sisters/sisters-in-law 38
Smyth, A. 258
social advantages
    'social advantages formula' 103-5,
    106, 118-19, 126, 136, 224, 278,
    316
    see also welfare tourism
social contribution
    caring for dependants as 40, 315
    and citizenship 24, 96, 111, 124,
    311
    marriage as 138
    and social rights 29, 30, 314
    see also employment status; social
    entitlement
social dumping 5
social entitlement
    and caring 35, 116-17, 273-5,
    307-8, 308, 315
    comparability of 300, 308,
    319-20, 323